STRATEGY AND TACTICS
OF THE GREAT
COMMANDERS
OF
WORLD WAR II
AND THEIR BATTLES

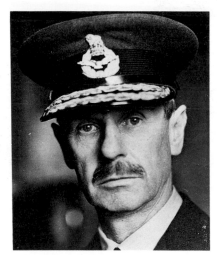

STRATEGY AND TACTICS
OF THE GREAT
COMMANDERS
OF
WORLD WAR II
AND THEIR BATTLES

GALLERY BOOKS
An imprint of W.H. Smith Publishers Inc.
112 Madison Avenue
New York, New York 10016

The Contributors

John Westwood is a highly experienced author and historian. He has held academic positions at Florida State University, the University of Sydney, and the University of Manchester. Among his more than twenty previous books are *The Eastern Front, Atlas of Twentieth Century Warfare* and *History of the Middle East Wars*. Chapters 2, 3, 4, 5, 6, 9, 10, 11, 12, 13 and 15.

Patrick Jennings was born in Chicago in 1937. Educated in both the United States and Great Britain, he is a journalist living in London. Among his works is *A Pictorial History of World War II*, a subject in which he has specialized. Chapters 1 and 17.

Judith Steeh was educated at the University of Michigan and then became a journalist. She contributed to the *Olympiad 1936* and co-authored the *Directors' Guide to the USA*. She has also written *The Rise and Fall of Adolf Hitler*. Chapters 7, 8, 14 and 16.

PAGE 1:(LEFT TO RIGHT) General Chuikov, Air Marshal Dowding and General Eisenhower.
PAGE 2: ABOVE General MacArthur views the ruins of Manila after the recapture of the town from the Japanese.
PAGE 2: BELOW: US troops go ashore during the D-Day landings.
PAGE 3: (LEFT TO RIGHT) General Student, General Patton and General Slim.

Published by Gallery Books
A Division of W H Smith Publishers Inc.
112 Madison Avenue
New York, New York 10016

Produced by
Brompton Books Corp.
15 Sherwood Place
Greenwich, CT 06830

ISBN 0-8317-8040-1

Printed in Hong Kong

10 9 8 7 6 5 4 3 2 1

CONTENTS

CHAPTER ONE

GUDERIAN

AT THE MEUSE

HEINZ GUDERIAN became interested in tanks and armor during World War I and elaborated his own doctrines thereafter. During the invasion of France, in May 1940, he was able to put to the test, at a pivotal point of the battle of France, his basic *Achtung! Panzer!* doctrine which finally made his reputation.

Guderian was a typical descendant of Junker stock from the Warthegau, his father being the first military man of this rather austere and poverty-stricken family. Born on 17 June 1888 to Lieutenant Friedrich and Clara Guderian he was taken all over Germany by his parents who were posted to various obscure garrison towns of the Wilhelmine Reich. While the parents were stationed at St Avold (Lorraine) Heinz went to cadet schools, at first at Baden, and then in Berlin. He liked military life and even enjoyed the rigid obedience and discipline, but he also exhibited intellectual independence in argument, an exceptional quality in a young Junker bent on a military career.

In 1907 he graduated from the war school at Metz (Lorraine), which he had found rather tedious and was posted to serve in his father's regiment. As a serving officer he showed rather catholic cultural tastes: he enjoyed hunting, was keen on shooting and the same time was keenly interested in architecture and the countryside. Once again his intellectual independence was discernible in a healthy criticism of his surroundings. It was noted that he found it difficult to make friends, especially with his elders – this was to mark him for the rest of his life. It would always be easier for him to make friends and inspire his juniors. However, with seniors, be they his brother officers or politicians, he somehow failed to communicate.

In 1912 Guderian became engaged to a young girl, Margarete Coerne, whom he married the following year, just before going to the War Academy in Berlin. The marriage brought him in contact with brother officers Wilhelm Keitel, Erich von Manstein and Colonel Count Rüdiger von der Goltz. Both Keitel and von der Goltz were to exercise a profound influence on his life and career. As it happened Guderian never finished his war

course; it was dissolved when World War I broke out in August 1914, and Guderian went back to his previous posting (shortly before going to the War Academy he had been on a radio course), the Heavy Radio Station No 3, part of the 5th Cavalry Division. He was 26 years of age, specializing in signals, full of patriotism and determined to win the war for Germany. Instead the war proved his *Wanderjahre:* he was to become familiar with tanks and acquire the experience necessary to combat them.

His first combat experience taught him that without good signals, bravery was useless. His I Cavalry Corps under General von Richthofen was given the task of cutting off the French Second Army, but the French had broken the German code and were prepared for this drive. When despite this the corps actually performed the task and found itself north of Soissons in the enemy's rear the army superiors were unaware of this brave achievement and it went to waste as the German cavalry, unprotected against enemy fire, could not press home its advantage. Later Guderian insisted on having radio receivers in each individual tank – the protected cavalry could press home an advantage. While his experience was varied – he fought in initial battles, flew as an observer in aircraft, became a staff officer - he never had to face tanks directly, but heard of the French and British use of the tanks, as a terror weapon at Cambrai, Amiens and elsewhere. When the massed French tanks reversed the German breakthrough on the Marne he was, for the first and last time, involved in the mobile defense of the area of the Marne and Vesle. These experiences marked him for life.

Just before the armistice Guderian was sent to Italy on a liaison mission, and had to escape back to Germany to avoid capture. He witnessed the collapse of the German Reich in Munich, but then made his way up to Berlin where he was appointed to the Eastern Frontiers' Protection Service to keep an eye on the Poles and the Russian Bolsheviks. After a spell with the Iron Division in the Baltic lands, he was finally sent to the Inspectorate of Transport Troops in 1922. This in fact meant that he was back to his hobby-horse, mechanized formations. Furthermore he developed his ideas theoretically by writing articles for the *Militär-Wochenblatt:* he came to advocate the *Stosskraft* (dynamic punch) as the latest combat method. In 1914 the new combat methods had been mobile artillery and infantry machine

LEFT: General Guderian, pioneer of armored warfare.

BELOW: Guderian looks

forward intently from his command vehicle. The framework above his head carries radio aerials.

guns – with technological changes tanks became the new method. In 1927 Guderian was promoted to major and henceforth devoted all his military efforts to the theory and practice of armored warfare.

As early as 1928 Major Guderian founded a tactical center for tanks and their cooperation with other arms. Then he went to Sweden to drive tanks in person – by the Treaty of Versailles Germany was not allowed to manufacture armor – and he also made a technical study of them. Back in Germany and now Colonel Guderian, he insisted on improvements in communications, not only with the tanks but also with field telephones and teleprinters. In fact he was obsessed with the formation of a new command, a sort of army within an army, incorporating elements from each arm. However both the new political leaders – the Nazis had come to power in 1933 – and the pro-Nazi military leaders, Blomberg and Reichenau, did not care for Guderian's ideas for the moment. It is true that so far Guderian had only produced halfbaked ideas and semidigested innovations. For example, at this stage, he saw the future Panzer divisions as weapons of defense. He knew that the Germans had helped the Russians to develop the tank and he intended to use the German armor in defense of the Eastern Frontiers. However all this changed in 1934 when the new Commander in Chief, General von Fritsch, created the *Panzertruppe* and Colonel Guderian became the Chief of Staff of this new branch.

With Guderian's official appointment the theoretical justification of his belief in technological advance and armor finally came. A year earlier he had already had Captain Liddell Hart's articles on deep penetration by armored troops translated into German and the following year he published an article on another favorite subject: tactically, tank commanders needed to ride ahead of their squadrons controlling them by means of individual radios. While Guderian's book, *Achtung! Panzer!*, contained all the tactical innovations gained from long practical experience, the basic strategic ideas were in a sense the military response to Hitler's innovatory ideas on war, and in particular to his concept of the Blitzkrieg, which was the main reason why

this book attracted so much attention in 1935 when it came out.

Learning the lesson of the last war Guderian thought that the remedy for the Allied tank failure lay in the fully mechanized (Panzer) division moving into battle at equal speed: medium 'breakthrough' tanks armed with machine guns and cannon up to 75mm; antitank guns and motorized infantry following closely behind; tactical air forces delaying defenders' reserves and airborne troops capturing important enemy points in the rear. Guderian also spelled out his strategic doctrine, 'concentrated blow applied with surprise on the decisive point of the front, to form the arrow head so deep that we need have no worry about the flank.' As he seriously thought of applying these doctrines Guderian was suddenly replaced as Chief of Staff by Friedrich Paulus, and as a result the Panzers were split up as in all the European armies. Guderian's influence with the upper echelons and Hitler seemed to have vanished.

Guderian was most disconcerted by this development and at one stage lost his nerve, walked up to his old colleague Fritsch and blamed him for ignoring his advice on armored forces. Before Guderian could be punished Fritsch and Blomberg were dismissed by Hitler and Guderian was appointed general officer commanding the XVI Corps and was detailed by Hitler to perform special duties involving the Panzers. Thus on 12 March 1938 Guderian led the Panzers into Austria and subsequently had to remedy the many breakdowns that occurred on that march.

Although an established armor theoretician and practitioner Guderian did not have it all his way. On the contrary top army echelons proved consistently hostile, especially after adverse reports on the armored troops from Spain. Guderian had to counter criticism of himself in print. He praised strategic speed, 'the tanks had to keep moving despite enemy's defensive fire, thus making it harder for the enemy to build up fresh defensive positions.' In 1938, when military exercises had gone disastrously wrong, Hitler forced General Beck's resignation, and at long last showed a personal predilection for Guderian. Their dialogues became very close and personal but this in turn provoked personal hostility from other senior officers. Thus Hitler sent Guderian's XVI Corps to occupy the Sudetenland and subsequently enabled him to visit Britain to do a little more research in British armor progress. Hitler used Guderian to divide top army officers, but though he was thus obviously favored, he made no headway with his obsessive armor warfare because of army obstruction. It took the Polish campaign to vindicate Guderian's theories.

In August 1939 Guderian, who late in 1938 was appointed general in command of Mobile Troops, conducted last-minute exercises with the 3000 tanks at his disposal and came to the conclusion that they could be put to good use in the coming Polish campaign, since the communication systems had been completed and supplies had been improved considerably since the disasters in the previous year. Thus, according to him, six Panzer divisions and four light divisions, aided by massive air intervention, would achieve a complete defeat of Poland in a few days, a feat that would have taken the remaining 45 German Army formations weeks to accomplish. Although his new XIX Corps exhibited certain shortcomings it in fact accomplished its tasks in a few days with perfection so that when Hitler visited the battlefield Guderian proudly showed him round proving to him the effectiveness of armor. As far as Hitler was concerned Guderian was preaching to the converted. Guderian's Corps suffered only four percent casualties in the campaign, accomplished all its tasks and only half of the Panzers needed major

BELOW LEFT: Winston Churchill, General Gamelin and General Gort in France on 8 January 1940. This was during the 'Sitzkrieg' when the Allies and Germans faced each other over the Maginot Line.

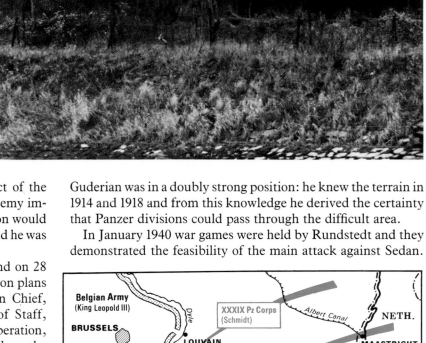

RIGHT: During the *Drôle de Guerre* phase the soldiers indulged in propaganda exercises. They put up slogans on their lines to demoralize the enemy.

BELOW RIGHT: Map of the German advance to the Meuse.

overhaul. Although the generals minimized the effect of the tanks (and Guderian) on the campaign, because of 'enemy impotence,' Hitler became convinced that the new weapon would win him the war. Guderian became his key to victory and he was to be proved right in the near future.

Hitler was already planning the war in the West and on 28 September 1939 the German General Staff set to work on plans for the invasion of France. Both the Commander in Chief, General Walther von Brauchitsch, and the Chief of Staff, General Franz Halder had very little time to plan the operation, and even less confidence in its success. According to them the Maginot Line had to be outflanked and the *Schwerpunkt* of the whole operation was to be north of the difficult terrain of the Ardennes, in the general direction of Namur. On the right wing, Holland was to be subdued and simultaneously on the left wing, a relatively strong force would be sent through the Ardennes to reach the river Meuse between Givet and Sedan. No one seems to have liked this plan of 'improvisation'; its execution was several times postponed and after 10 January 1940, when a staff officer with the details of the plan made a forced landing in Belgium, it was abandoned.

Long before its abandonment the plan was criticized by Hitler, and Generals von Manstein and von Rundstedt. Hitler suggested that the drive through the Ardennes be enlarged and be aimed as the main attack across the Meuse toward Amiens and the Channel coast, thus cutting off the northern enemy wing. Manstein wanted a complete destruction of the northern enemy wing through a strategic encirclement similar to that of the elder Moltke, which the younger Moltke failed to carry out in 1914, and which Manstein and Rundstedt had successfully achieved in Poland only recently. Rundstedt sent the General Staff his suggestions which were remarkably similar to those of Hitler but with military meat in them (Hitler's were based on intuition and dreams).

Inevitably Guderian was brought in as the foremost Panzer expert. Early in November 1939 General Wilhelm Keitel called him in for consultations. He explained that the fear of bad weather which would cause the immobility of the armor was the reason for the delay in the war against France, and he wanted to know if a strong tank force could pass through the Ardennes.

Guderian was in a doubly strong position: he knew the terrain in 1914 and 1918 and from this knowledge he derived the certainty that Panzer divisions could pass through the difficult area.

In January 1940 war games were held by Rundstedt and they demonstrated the feasibility of the main attack against Sedan.

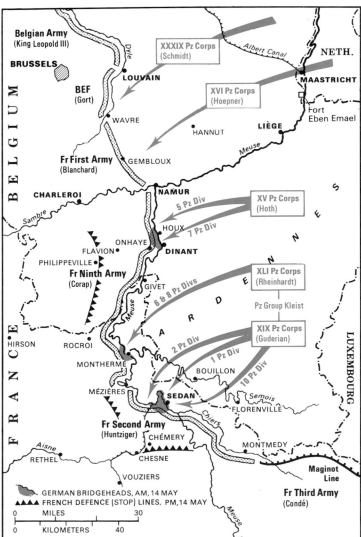

However, Guderian's insistence on the armor spearheading the attack through the Ardennes, executing the crossing of the river Meuse and then advancing deep into France, was treated with scorn. General Halder thought Guderian's ideas senseless and Rundstedt supported him in this opinion. Nonetheless Guderian had the courage to contradict them both and insisted on his suggestions: a surprise drive *en masse* would drive a wedge so deep and wide in the enemy's front that the Germans would not need to worry about their flanks. Some generals were prepared to support Guderian in his stand and among them Manstein tipped the balance in Guderian's favor. On 17 February 1940 Manstein saw Hitler and described to him Guderian's plan, infecting him with his own enthusiasm. Next day Hitler saw Brauchitsch and Halder, told them that Guderian's plan was in fact his: that was the way France would be attacked and destroyed.

Thus on 24 February 1940 *Plan Gelb* was revised and became *Plan Sichelschnitt.* Guderian's concept of the breakthrough in the Ardennes became the *Schwerpunkt;* in addition he personally was going to execute this new plan. Army Groups A, B and C under Generals von Rundstedt, Fedor von Bock and Wilhelm von Leeb remained responsible for their previous sectors, but Army Group B's role was relegated to become, in Captain Liddell Hart's words, a matador's cloak, while Army Group A with its Fourth (General Kluge), Twelfth (General List) and Sixteenth Armies (General Busch) came to occupy the pivotal point of the *Sichelschnitt.* General List created a special Panzer Group under the command of General Ewald von Kleist, who in turn had under him General Reinhardt's XXXXI Corps, Guderian's XIX Corps and General von Wietersheim's XIV Corps. The center of both the strategic blow and the tactical fighting was Guderian with the 1st, 2nd and 10th Panzer Divisions and the crack motorized regiment, *Grossdeutschland.* The Kleist group, with some 1260 tanks (out of the overall 2800) was given priority of air support, while advancing, and massed bombing while actually crossing the Meuse. This arrangement made heavy artillery redundant, as otherwise the operation would have been greatly retarded; the narrow and bad roads in the Ardennes would have made it impossible for the artillery to follow up closely on the tanks – shell supplies would also be delayed. In March 1940 Hitler finally asked Guderian what he proposed to do after the crossing of the Meuse, to which Guder-

ian replied that he would make a dash for Amiens or Paris or, the best option, for the Channel coast.

In the meantime Guderian concentrated on hard training. Tank crews practiced in the Eifel mountains under their general's personal supervision. There were map reading exercises, but the tanks could not fire their guns, because of shortage of ammunition. Infantry and engineers practiced river crossing, ferrying tanks across and then pontoon building. The river Moselle was almost identical with the river Meuse. During these two months of preparation all the ranks came to know their general personally; he inspired confidence and even enthusiasm. Many survivors speak of his fairness, paternal care and the personal share of the bustling general in the hardships of the exercises and combat itself. While his men had complete faith in his plans, Guderian's superiors, and occasionally even himself, were full of doubts. Guderian had no confidence in Brauchitsch and Halder, for although they were belated converts to his plans, they continued to vacillate. List wanted infantry to lead the assault across the Meuse. Rundstedt, like Hitler, refused to consider deep penetration after the Meuse. Kleist had no experience of armor. Busch thought that Guderian would never get across the Meuse, while Bock, whose Army Group was relegated to a secondary role, thought the whole operation was crazy, 'You will be creeping along, 10 miles from the Maginot Line for your breakthrough, hoping that the French will watch

LEFT: A German soldier keeps a careful eye on activities behind the Maginot Line.

BELOW LEFT: German troops take cover as shells burst beside them.

RIGHT: A propaganda picture showing a storm boat being used in an amphibious attack.

inactive. You are massing all those tanks on the narrow roads in the Ardennes as if there was no such thing as air force. You then hope to operate as far as the coast with an open flank, some 200 miles long, with the French army letting you through.' However Guderian, after all the planning and practical exercises, became totally confident. He felt sure that if he were allowed to execute his plans, total victory would be his. Between 8 and 10 May 1940 the tanks of XIV, and XIX Corps, stretching some 100 miles from head to tail, began to move into their border positions. Guderian together with 1st Panzer Division quickly passed through Luxembourg and was ready on the Belgian-French border for the attack through the Ardennes. On the day of assault Kleist suddenly deflected the 10th Panzers from Sedan to Longwy much to Guderian's annoyance. After long arguments the 10th Panzers did not go to Longwy, but changed their axis of advance causing the 1st, 2nd and 6th Panzers to become entangled. Fortunately the French and British air forces made no attack on these confused columns and Guderian was able to sort out the confusion. However, everywhere else the schedules were kept and the advance was smooth. Halder described it as 'a very good marching achievement.'

The first battle on the frontier river Semois was decided before the bulk of XIX Corps arrived in the area. The elements of the 1st Panzers induced the French 5th DLC to retire voluntarily toward the Meuse and at night Guderian took up quarters in the Hotel Panorama at Neufchateau, where he luckily escaped injury after a shell hit the hotel. On the following day Guderian again narrowly escaped injury after an air attack at Bouillon. Although his 2nd Panzers were lagging slightly behind, Guderian took advantage of the French withdrawal and pushed his 1st Panzer toward Sedan, where its forward tanks arrived in the evening of 12 May. By nightfall the 10th Panzers had also reached the Meuse at Bazeilles, but the 2nd Panzers were nowhere and Guderian flew to Kleist's headquarters for further orders. He found out that General Rommel's 7th Panzers had also reached the Meuse at Dinant and that the Kleist Group would attack generally across the Meuse in the afternoon of the following day. On the flight back Guderian's pilot lost his way and almost landed behind French lines.

On 13 May the Meuse was crossed by infantry and motor-cyclists on either side of Sedan. The crossing was preceded by air bombing lasting five hours which demoralized the second-

fusion, despite the fact that General Lafontaine had under his command only reservists. General Grandsard in command of the Meuse sector, at first thought that nothing was lost, but then he heard reports that German tanks were in the La Marfée area. The reports were incorrect, but they panicked two of his colonels into issuing withdrawal orders. General panic spread and Colonel Pourcelet committed suicide. While Lafontaine withdrew his headquarters to Chémery, Grandsard sent two tank battalions and two infantry regiments to counterattack. Behind them General Joseph Georges, who had dismissed Corap and replaced him by General Henri Giraud, was sending up to Sedan the powerful units of the Third Army and 3rd Motorized Division. Lafontaine ordered a two-pronged attack at dawn, but the units were not ready in time for the counterattack, which started at 0700 hours after the German tanks had already crossed the river in force. To plug the hole on the Meuse, between Dinant and Sedan, the French command ordered its 1st, 2nd and 3rd Armored Divisions into counterattack. However, the 1st Division found itself without fuel and was subsequently annihilated and the 2nd entrained and was cut into two at Hirson. Only the 3rd actually went into battle against Guderian, but from the beginning proved rather static, went into battle piecemeal and was chopped up not even by German armor but mainly by the *Sturmpionierbatallion*. Initially the situation looked rather ugly for the Germans, but after they had put out of action about one half of the French tanks, the French turned round and withdrew. During the battle Guderian went back to La Chapelle to prepare orders for the following, decisive day of the battle. After the French counterattack the bulk of the

rate French troops facing the Germans. All through the night the Germans were constructing tank ferries and pontoons under Guderian's personal supervision. After the infantry had established bridgeheads on the other side of the Meuse, Guderian paddled across the river to meet his old friend, Colonel Balck, who greeted him with a joke 'about joyriding in a canoe on the Meuse' and the news that the bridgehead, three miles wide and six miles deep, was secure. The first tanks would begin the crossing at dawn. The French had no idea that the crossing would be attempted only one day after the German arrival and on the whole held their fire to save ammunition until the time when the real assault occurred. They were badly let down by the air forces, which because of the lack of communication between the French and the British commands, failed to support them. The Germans had to do some hard fighting to dislodge the French from their bunkers and defensive lines. However, once they had achieved it the French High Command panicked; General Corap, commanding the Ninth Army ordered general retreat.

However, on the French side it was not all panic and con-

French 55th and 71st Divisions had ceased to exist, fleeing in disorder. The contagion of fear and panic also spread to Grandsard's X Corps boding ill for the French armies still resisting the German assault. By the 14th Guderian's bridgehead was 30 miles wide and 15 miles deep and some 85 Blenheim bombers had been shot down over the German pontoons.

On the 14th Guderian's 1st Panzers moved resolutely against Chémery and the 10th Panzers supported by the *Grossdeutschland* pushed on to the high ground of Bois Mont Dieu, both effectively preventing the French XXI Corps from assembling for a counterattack, though hard fighting went on for the rest of the day at the key village of Stonne. Guderian was presented with a gap of 12 miles through which he could drive his 1st Panzers in order to break toward the west and the Channel thus fulfilling his wildest hopes and executing Plan *Sichelschnitt* to perfection. At noon Guderian reported to Rundstedt on the state of the battle, 'in the very middle of the bridge, while air raids were in progress.' Then he issued new orders to his men: they were to cross the Ardennes canal and head west. This was a risky decision for the Second and Ninth French Armies were

TOP LEFT: German motorcyclists press into France.

CENTER LEFT: The remains of a French column in a wood near Sedan, 14 May 1940.

BELOW, FAR LEFT: A German bicycle squad crosses the Meuse-Scheldt canal in Belgium on 13 May 1940.

BELOW LEFT: Guderian leaves a planning meeting during the invasion of France.

RIGHT: The Blitzkrieg left a trail of destruction in its wake as witnessed from this picture of a Channel town.

BELOW: Czech-manufactured tanks of a German division pause during their rapid advance.

still counterattacking and far from routed. The southern flank at Stonne was only guarded by the battered *Grossdeutschland* and 10th Panzers, while there was a possibility of the Allied air forces succeeding in destroying his pontoon bridges. Guderian therefore moved forward his AA batteries to ring off the bridges: they brought down some 112 aircraft and Guderian's armor went on crossing the Meuse. By nightfall Colonel Balck had reached his objective at Singy and the French Generals Flavigny and Huntziger caused confusion by issuing frequent and contradictory orders. The greatest battle that Guderian had to fight on that day was with his superior, General Kleist: the latter insisted that Guderian consolidate his southern line before pushing westward to Rethel. Guderian was both furious and bitter, as he saw himself deprived of the fruit of his tactical victories. In the end Guderian won the argument, for the generals on his flank, Hoth

and Reinhardt, were also on the point of breaking through.

Some French historians speak of 15 May as the day France lost the war, but for Guderian it was a day of miracles: considering the nature of the terrain it seemed miraculous that his Panzers succeeded in breaking through. French counterattacks were constantly delayed for technical reasons and the Germans were able to deploy antitank guns and rush up reinforcements. However, the progress of 1st and 2nd Panzers on that day was not impressive as they had to smash through tough French defense not yet confused and demoralized by superiors' orders. General Brocard was dismissed, but the French armor was nevertheless routed by all three German generals, Guderian, Hoth and Reinhardt. Nonetheless Guderian once again had a verbal battle with Kleist who ordered him in the evening to stop advancing. Some lively shouting on the telephone won Guder-

ABOVE: Another French town is engulfed by flames.

LEFT: German soldiers on the watch for snipers in a small French town.

BELOW LEFT: French forces surrender to the Germans in Lille, 29 May 1940.

ABOVE RIGHT: A Czech-made PzKw 35(t) seems to be stopped and abandoned in the foreground as infantry and Pz IVs of Guderian's corps advance behind.

RIGHT: The destruction of the Maginot Line.

BELOW RIGHT: Guderian plans the advance of his Panzer Group at Langres, June 1940.

ian 24 hours of freedom to advance: at dawn he arrived at Bouvellemont where the 14th French Division, after fighting hard all day under the future Maréchal de France de Lattre de Tassigny, had just withdrawn from the combat. There and then Guderian personally briefed the commanders for the operation ahead and instead of resting the troops set out immediately.

On 16 May Guderian thrust forward only with his 1st and 2nd Panzers, leaving the 10th Panzers and *Grossdeutschland* on his southern flank as insurance, and in deference to Kleist. By the end of the day they were 40 miles west, at Dercy on the Serre, while other forces reached Guise on the Oise. Guderian then issued orders by radio for the following day: the advance was to continue. However, he did not reckon with Kleist whose orders he was disobeying. Kleist's HQ monitored Guderian's orders and issued counterorders. Kleist also asked Guderian to report to him the following morning. When they met, on 17 May 1940, the exchanges were acrimonious as both men were on edge and their nerves were rapidly giving up from excitement. Kleist accused Guderian of deliberately disobeying his orders and Guderian offered his resignation on the spot. When Rundstedt heard of it he immediately ordered Guderian to remain in charge and sent General List to act as mediator. Once again Guderian won the day: his HQ remained on the spot, but his troops were permitted a 'reconnaissance in force.' Guderian just laid his

communication wires and dashed away from his HQ to join his advancing tanks. At the end of that day his vanguard passed Montcornet and Laon. However, on that very day Hitler joined Brauchitsch and Halder and the rest of the generals in their fear of French counterattacks from the south: thus the disputes continued, while the Panzers rolled on gathering speed as they went. The very speed of their advance made it impossible for the French armies to react

Guderian's 2nd Panzers reached St Quentin on the 19th and Abbeville on the following day. At long last the French command ordered counterattacks, but because of the changes in the personnel the offensive was disrupted and never materialized.

On 21 May, near Amiens, British 4th and 7th Tank Regiments and the French 3rd Mechanized Division unexpectedly turned on General Rommel's 7th Panzers and caused a lot of anxiety, but Guderian would have dealt with the threat as efficiently as he did at Montcornet, when de Gaulle's 4th Armored Division counterattacked. Though Guderian was ultimately halted for four days (24-27 May) which saved Dunkirk for the British Expeditionary Force, his tanks took Boulogne and Calais thus cutting Allied armies into two. On 28 May Hitler put him in command of a special Panzer group which then transferred to the east and which during the first three weeks of June 1940 cut across eastern France from Châlons sur Marne to Pontarlier and Belfort. France was defeated and on 22 June signed an armistice.

Even with hindsight it is thought by military experts that the battle of France, had it been fought along the lines of Plan *Gelb*, would have ended in a deadlock. It can be said without exaggeration that Guderian's tactical and strategic ideas embodied in Plan *Sichelschnitt* virtually decided the issue. The factors of surprise and the psychological blow that the French command and armies suffered after the Germans emerged from an impenetrable area and effected their main breakthrough were decisive for this battle of France. In the execution of his ideas Guderian acted resolutely, having absolute faith in them, while his political and military superiors and masters dithered.

At this stage of World War II he was years ahead scientifically and technologically of his friends and foes and his achievements on the battlefield fully vindicated his theories and doctrines. Thus for Guderian the battle of the Meuse, which really meant the battle of France, was a perfect victory, never to be repeated again so clearly by any other warlord.

CHAPTER TWO

DOWDING

AND THE BATTLE OF BRITAIN

'THANK GOD we're alone now!' These words of Air Chief Marshal Hugh Dowding at the fall of France in 1940 echoed the thoughts of many British commanders, but had a special significance coming from him, for throughout his career he was regarded as something of a loner. Indeed, in the days before he joined the air force, his army colleagues nicknamed him 'Stuffy' Dowding.

This preference for the serious over the convivial had several consequences. Allied with his keen intelligence, it meant that when he became Commander in Chief of Fighter Command in 1936 Britain's air defenses were in the hands of one who would not only exploit the technical advances of the period but would also hold fast to his convictions irrespective of how that might spoil relations with his colleagues. But it also meant that, although he was the virtual architect of victory in the Battle of Britain, he never became celebrated, and in fact was quietly shunted into a professional backwater as soon as the battle was won.

On the eve of World War I Dowding had transferred from the artillery to the flying corps, and by 1915 was commanding a squadron in France. In the war he had various clashes with Hugh Trenchard, the future Chief of the Air Staff, but in the 1920s, after performing well as an RAF staff officer in Iraq, he regained Trenchard's favor. In 1935, he was the member of the Air Council responsible for research, and was one of that group of six men who tried out the first attempt at radio direction finding (radar), and discovered that it worked.

He was put in charge of Fighter Command just as Britain's defenses, and especially the air force, were entering a period of transformation. Churchill's 'Ten-Year Rule' (introduced in the 1920s, and enjoining the service ministries to plan on the assumption that there would be a ten-year warning of the next war) had helped to cut defense expenditure but with the rise of Hitler and the rearmament of Germany was increasingly seen to be perilous.

The first expansion scheme for the RAF had been approved in 1934 but, like its successors, was never completed. However, in the late 1930s there was certainly some growth, even though it was too small to achieve the object of deterring Germany. In

1936 came the reorganization of the RAF command system; the service had become too large and complex for a single Commander in Chief. Instead, semi-independent entities were created: Bomber Command, Fighter Command, Coastal Command, and Training Command. These were each headed by an air marshal answerable to the Chief of the Air Staff. Dowding was the first head of Fighter Command.

He took command at a time when radar needed development into a practical device, and at a time when it was clear that the existing fighter aircraft, biplanes of partly wooden construction, and with only two guns, were on the verge of obsolescence. The last of this breed, the Gladiator, would enter service in 1937 but already the shape of things to come was clear. Building their aircraft around the new and powerful Rolls Royce Merlin engine, two designers, Sydney Camm and R. J. Mitchell, had created metal single-seat monoplanes that promised top speeds of well over 300mph. Prototypes had shown that in battle at such speeds the time available for firing at an enemy plane would be much reduced, so the concept of the 8-gun fighter had been accepted. The results were the Hurricane and Spitfire fighters. However, although production of these aircraft accelerated in 1939 they were outnumbered by the corresponding German design, the Me109. It would not be until 1940 that British military aircraft production outpaced German. Moreover, it seemed doubtful whether the training of pilots could keep up with increasing fighter production, even though the new Royal Air Force Volunteer Reserve was expected to provide an additional 6500 pilots by 1939.

Dowding's task, which he saw clearly, was somehow to take all these changes and integrate them into an organization that would defend Britain from enemy bombing attack. Although this may seem a commonsense deduction, there was at the time a revolutionary tone to this conclusion. The RAF, like most air forces, had always insisted on the primacy of the bomber. The concept of the rain of high explosive, delivered at will by fleets of bombers, had been fostered so as to reinforce the air force claim to parity with the two older services. At a time when defense budgets were small, this was vital. Trenchard, the so-called

LEFT: Air Chief Marshal Sir Hugh C. T. Dowding, GCVO, KCB, CMG.

RIGHT: Hurricanes of 85 Squadron during a January 1940 inspection. Note that at this stage the Hurricanes are still fitted with the less-efficient 2-blade propeller.

ABOVE LEFT: Before the advent of the radar-directed night fighter, anti-aircraft guns were the main defensive weapon after dark.

ABOVE: A British fighter pilot, Pilot Officer Lewis of 85 Squadron, climbs down from his Hurricane fighter.

LEFT: Dornier bombers, a mainstay of the German bombing offensive.

TOP RIGHT: German 'Stuka' dive-bombers, whose short range and vulnerability limited their participation in the Battle of Britain.

'Father of the RAF,' had always insisted on the invincibility of the bomber, and British ministers had been infected with the dogma of 'the bomber will always get through.' They believed that there was no sure defense against the bomber. Therefore a nation's air power had to consist of a bomber force stronger than those of its potential enemies. This reasoning, with its forecasts of terrible and inevitable devastation of cities, not only distorted the pattern of defense expenditure but also was a large factor in persuading the British government to carry appeasement of Hitler too far.

This dogma was still believed by most RAF officers and their political masters when Dowding took charge. Many resented expenditure on fighters, because money spent on fighters could have been spent instead on bombers. The only point of fighters, many said quietly, was to make ordinary people feel that something was being done to defend them. All the same, the creation of Fighter Command was itself an indication that opinion might be changing. The political master of the RAF, the Secretary of State for Air (Kingsley Wood), who was appointed in 1938, was another who favored change. It was he who planned to increase Fighter Command to 50 squadrons, and it was also he who decided in 1939 that Dowding, 57 years old and due to retire, should have his term of service extended into 1940.

What Dowding was trying to do was to supplant the dogma of the invincible bomber with that of the fearsome fighter, and thereby divert some of the resources spent on bombers to his own arm. In this endeavor he was indirectly aided by a new Commander in Chief of Bomber Command who, immediately on taking office and looking around, admitted that Bomber Command would be unable to reach, find, or hit targets in Germany. Dowding believed that his Command was special, equivalent to the Royal Navy in that its task, defense of the home base, was special; if it failed, all else would fail. In this belief he was not prepared to compromise. If decisions went against him he would not react like a gentleman and smilingly accept the verdict, but continue arguing. The story that at a meeting summoned by Churchill in 1940 he lay down his pencil as a sign of threatened resignation is probably apocryphal, but nevertheless expresses the essence of the man. He often did not get what he wanted but, once having decided on a minimum requirement, he did not pretend he could change it simply to fit in with other people's priorities. Given the narrow margin by which the Battle of Britain was eventually won, he was evidently the right man in the right place.

The existing plan for the air defense of Britain seemed to him unreal. It specified 46 fighter squadrons (the squadrons each consisted of 16 fighters plus two in reserve), which was more than he actually had. More important, it assumed that bombing raids would be prolonged, so that if one or other of the four fighter zones was hard pressed there would be time to send reinforcements from one of the other zones. Just before the war started he replaced this plan with another, which became an integral part of the so-called 'Dowding System.' In this, Britain was divided into just three zones, each entrusted to a fighter group. No 11 Group, in the south, was the strongest, as Dowding realized that for political and military reasons, as well as questions of aircraft ranges, the southern part of England was likely to bear the brunt of an air attack. The next strongest, with its HQ at Nottingham, was No 12 Group, while No 13 in the North was the weakest of the three. Each group was to defend its own area, while also acting as a reserve for the other two. This grouping, a constructive use of radar, and a sophisticated command and communication network, were the constituents of Dowding's system.

But while developing his strategy he had to ensure that his basic building blocks, the men and machines, would be enough and of the right quality. He never could quite solve the pilot problem; the RAF training establishment was not producing enough, and too many of its products were taken by Bomber Command. This would mean that in 1940 freshly-trained pilots had to be plunged into battle before they had enough experience to cope with their situation. As for machines, in 1939, when fighter production really got going, the archaic Gladiators were still being produced as well as the modern Hurricanes and Spitfires. The 46 prescribed squadrons were still not there, and not all the squadrons that were available had modern aircraft.

Moreover, and this was Dowding's most worrying struggle, if not nightmare, there were repeated threats to remove some of the squadrons which he already had. After the Munich Crisis the need for a British expeditionary force to help the French in case of war with Germany became accepted, and such a force would obviously need air support. Dowding was asked to earmark four squadrons of fighters for possible transfer. A lesser man might have allocated four squadrons of biplanes, but he was honest enough to admit that only Hurricanes would be good enough. In July 1939, against his protests, an additional six squadrons were earmarked. He at once called for the formation of more fighter squadrons, but the Air Staff at this stage were unwilling to divert resources from bombers to fighters.

Dowding continued to argue that Fighter Command simply did not have enough fighters to defend the country. Meanwhile, the 46 squadrons that were still the accepted minimum for this purpose were far from available, and it was beginning to be realized that the original calculation which produced that number had been based on optimistic assumptions. It had not been foreseen, for example, that the Royal Navy's Scapa Flow base and Northern Ireland would require fighter protection, but obviously they did. So did the coastal shipping of the east coast. Moreover, the original calculation had not considered the possibility of a German conquest of the Low Countries. If this should happen, the Germans would have airfields close enough to Britain to allow employment of their dive-bombers and also permit a more intensive use of their conventional bombers. These new requirements, plus the commitment to France, meant that Dowding really needed a minimum of 74 squadrons, and all he had in early 1939 was 39.

In the eight months between the outbreak of war and the defeat of France, some of Fighter Command's deficiencies were made up. But Dowding still had deep misgivings about the commitment to operations in France. He described this as a tap, which once opened might drain away his fighter squadrons. The ten earmarked Hurricane squadrons did leave for France, and to Dowding's horror the equivalent of two more squadrons were soon despatched to make up losses. Then came the German onslaught in the west, and French appeals for more British

fighters. The tactical air support of the German armies was overwhelming, and could only be countered by strong fighter forces. Dowding had long feared that this situation might arise, with his Fighter Command drawn into a wearing battle in France that it could not win, and then emerging too weak to win the far more important battle in the skies over Britain. In a cabinet meeting he appears to have spoken solemnly but clearly of the danger of despatching more fighters and Churchill, probably already of the same opinion, did refuse the French request.

But then came Dunkirk. Most of the remaining Hurricanes in France were lost, and there were further losses (but with some victories) in Fighter Command's battles over Dunkirk. All in all, the French campaign had cost Fighter Command almost 400 Hurricanes and about 70 Spitfires, and the Germans could now build airfields close to Britain. The only cheering news was that the Spitfires had proved to be a match for the famed German Me109s.

Hitler began to plan a seaborne invasion of Britain. Because of the British naval strength, such an invasion could not be safely begun until German air power could command the sea passages.

RIGHT: Defiants, an interesting but disappointing design of gun-turret fighter, ready for take-off in 1940.

BELOW: Inside an operations room, with the Womens' Auxiliary Air Force hard at work.

Although Göring, head of the Luftwaffe, believed that bombing could subdue Britain without the need for an invasion, any strategy demanded the destruction of British air defenses. To achieve this, the German command envisaged repeated bombing attacks designed to draw the British fighter strength into battles that would eventually wear it down.

Signals intelligence kept the British well informed of German intentions, and Dowding, even without this, realized that the decisive air battle which he had always expected was only a few weeks away. In fact, because the Germans had no ready plans for the attack on Britain, and because in any case the Luftwaffe needed to rest and re-equip after the French campaign, it was not until July that the air assault began. It was also in July that Dowding was due to take his delayed retirement, but the Chief of the Air Staff persuaded him to extend his service until October. Dowding's grumble at this change was presumably for form's sake, since he was almost indispensable at that time. The air defense system was virtually his own creation, had been provided with its final essential (a protected operations room) only that March, and he was certainly the person best qualified to understand it.

The assumption of the 'Dowding System' was that Fighter Command with its scant resources could not maintain continuous patrols over and around Britain. There had to be a procedure in which advance information about enemy attacks was quickly gathered and processed, decisions made, and then fighter aircraft despatched directly to meet the bombers. The place where the decisions were made was the central operations room, which shared its protective concrete with an adjoining information center. The main feature of the room, at Stanmore, near London, was its table, on which all of Britain as well as its neighboring seas was depicted. Positions of enemy and friendly formations were marked on this map by plotters with long rakes moving arrows. In action, not only Dowding but the commander of the army's AA Command, and the commander of the Observer Corps, would be overlooking the table, as well as representatives from other commands and services.

Incoming information was analysed in the information center, and then plotted on the table. However, Dowding played a strategical rather than a tactical role. The information would be relayed to the operations rooms of the three Fighter Command groups, and it was the commander of the group who made the basic tactical decisions. Each group was divided into sectors, and the operations rooms of the latter unleashed the squadrons, directed them, and then brought them back to base. When there was contact with the enemy, the squadrons were free to act according to circumstance. At all other times they were under control. It was a highly disciplined system, and needed to be if the best use was to be made of the resources available. There was no room for air heroes of the World War I type, acting alone and impetuously.

Good radio and telephone communications, good intelligence, and above all radar were the technical foundations of this system. In summer 1940 there were already 21 long-range radar arrays in service, supplemented by short-range for use against low-flying aircraft. The former, in particular, were highly visible – one could be seen from the French coast – but for some reason the German planners paid little attention to them. These stations could spot an incoming attack while it was still over France and give increasingly accurate appreciations of its course, height and strength.

This advance warning was supplemented by more detailed information sent in by ground observers, organized as the Observer Corps. These sent their information direct to the appropriate group operations room, which used it for its own purposes but also sent it on to other groups and to the central operating room. Finally, there was an increasing contribution made by signals intelligence. While Enigma decrypts sometimes revealed a change of tactics, the main contribution came from the interception and decryption of short-range German radio communications. Sometimes these were in plain language, like the conversations between pilots in the air. With experience,

ABOVE: The nose of a German bomber, designed for the wide angle of vision so essential for both attack and early warning.

LEFT: A Spitfire is stalked by an Me109 in a faked German propaganda photo.

RIGHT: A low-level flight of Me109s, not usually recommended because of its vulnerability and high fuel consumption. The English coast is in the background.

such interceptions could provide very detailed foreknowledge of German tactics, plans, personalities, home airfields, and types of aircraft being used.

Neither the start nor the finishing date of the Battle of Britain can be stated precisely, but 10 July, when German incursions into British airspace became more intensive, is usually considered to mark the beginning, and 31 October, when the trend toward substituting night bombing for day raids became marked, is regarded as the date by which the Germans abandoned the attempt to destroy Fighter Command, an abandonment which led automatically to postponement of the plan to invade Britain ('Operation Sealion').

In the first phase both sides discovered their enemy's and their own capabilities and weaknesses. For the British, this meant a realization that only the Spitfire and Hurricane were up to the requirements of the battle, although other types might be used for night fighting, when and if it developed. They also, slowly, realized that their tight tactical formations might look smart, but provided enemy fighters with easy targets. For the Germans, it became clear that their twin-engined Me110 fighter was not fit for combat against single-seater fighters, so that the battle devolved upon the Me109, whose effective range meant that the battle would be fought over south-east England. They also discovered that their bombers needed far more fighters in their escort than had been the case in France, ideally two or three fighters per bomber, a ratio they could rarely sustain. The geographical limitation of the battle, determined by the lack of supplementary fuel tanks for the Me109, meant that Fighter Command's No 11 Group bore the brunt of the German onslaught. Its commander, Air Marshal Keith Park, saw eye-to-eye with Dowding and was a calm and flexible tactician; it was these two who, in effect, won the Battle of Britain.

On August 8 the battle entered a new phase, with Göring issuing an order for 'Operation *Adler*,' designed, as he put it, to 'wipe the British air force out of the sky.' British signals intelligence was sufficiently well developed at this stage to ensure that Göring's order was on Dowding's desk only an hour after the commanders of the three *Luftflotten* involved received it. On 15 August the Germans achieved almost 1500 sorties, mainly directed at Fighter Command's airfields, in the hope of destroying aircraft on the ground or, failing that, attracting them into the air to be destroyed by Me109s. A feint attack by bombers was made on the north-east coast of England, with the aim of drawing away Dowding's reserves, but thanks to radar and intelligence forewarning this was repelled with heavy loss. On 16 August even more sorties, about 1700, were made. Some airfields were damaged and one radar station in the Isle of Wight put out of action. An even tougher battle was fought on 18 August, before a break in the weather gave Fighter Command a chance to recover.

Dowding's strategy had been for fighters to concentrate on attacking the German bombers, whereas the German aim was to engage in fighter versus fighter actions in the expectation that the British fighter strength would be worn down faster, or at least first. In practice, neither strategy could prevail, although a typical action would have the somewhat slower Hurricanes attacking German bombers while the Spitfires occupied the escorting Me109 fighters. German losses were on most days

more than double those of the British in terms of precious air-crew, and in terms of aircraft almost double. Fighting over its own territory enabled Fighter Command to recover many downed pilots and to land its damaged aircraft. Both sides claimed more successes than they in fact achieved, which was unsurprising in the confused and very short encounters. Even now, the precise number of aircraft shot down by each side is disputed.

What is certain is that by 18 August Fighter Command was still undefeated, although reeling. From the beginning of that month it had lost 106 pilots through death and others through injury, and a little over 200 aircraft. Its pilots were beginning to feel the effect of strain and its losses were beginning to drain its reserves of stored aircraft even though, from April, there had been a surge in aircraft production, with over 400 fighters being produced monthly. A very high proportion of fighters was under repair, due to battle damage and a shortage of repair personnel. Pilots were becoming increasingly scarce, although two Czech-piloted squadrons, two Polish and one Canadian, together with pilots from other Commonwealth and occupied countries, as well as a few from neutral countries, notably the USA, went some way to filling the gap, as did transfers from Bomber and Coastal Commands.

The struggle continued in late August, and a number of airfields, lacking fighter cover at the vital moment, were badly hit. Manston airfield, on the exposed tip of Kent, had to be abandoned. Meanwhile Dowding found he had another battle to fight, this time against his own side. Air Vice Marshal Trafford Leigh-Mallory, commanding No 12 Group in the Midlands, disliked Dowding and Dowding's system. He was also aware that many of his pilots did not relish their role of first reserve for No 11 Group. They were aware that a desperate battle was being fought and that No 11 Group was hard-pressed. Some of them were painfully aware that it was pilots of No 11 Group who were winning the glory while they themselves, tied to their task of defending the Midlands, had little to do except when called upon to provide cover for 11 Group's more northerly airfields.

ABOVE: Air Marshal Trafford Leigh-Mallory, a portrait taken in 1944.

LEFT: At a makeshift airfield, German crews lunch beside their Heinkel 111 bomber.

RIGHT: Map of the 1940 campaign. The crucial importance of British radar is evident.

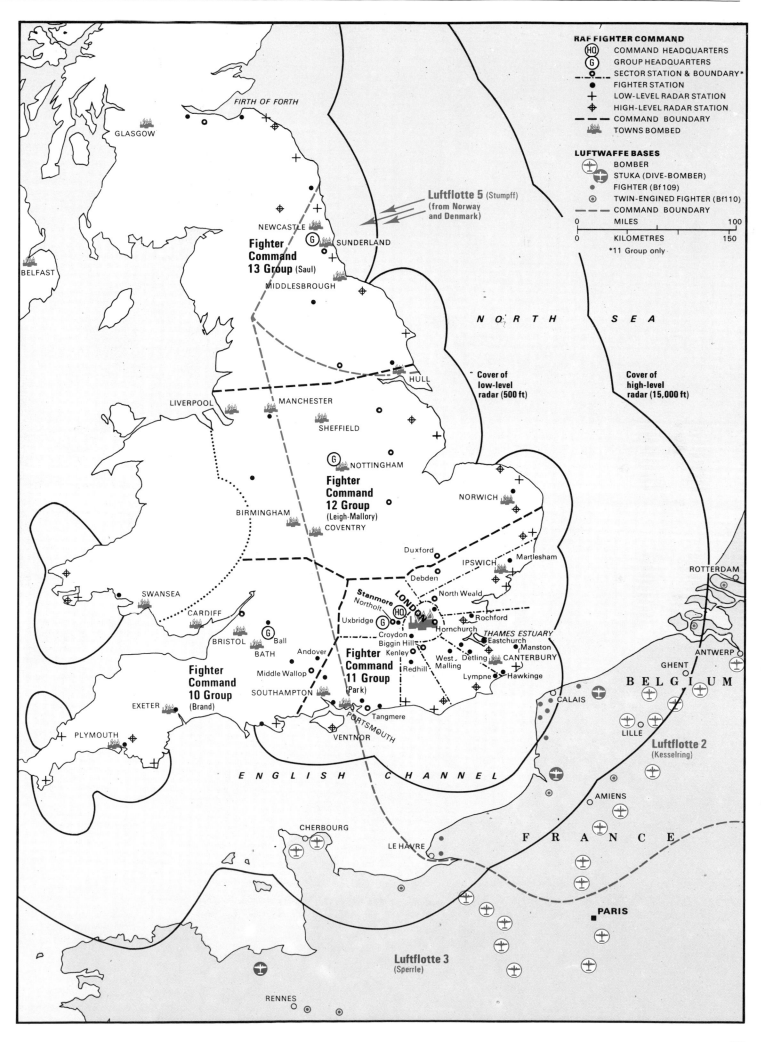

RAF FIGHTER COMMAND
- (HQ) COMMAND HEADQUARTERS
- (G) GROUP HEADQUARTERS
- ○ SECTOR STATION & BOUNDARY*
- ● FIGHTER STATION
- + LOW-LEVEL RADAR STATION
- ⊕ HIGH-LEVEL RADAR STATION
- COMMAND BOUNDARY
- TOWNS BOMBED

LUFTWAFFE BASES
- BOMBER
- STUKA (DIVE-BOMBER)
- FIGHTER (Bf109)
- TWIN-ENGINED FIGHTER (Bf110)
- COMMAND BOUNDARY

| 0 | MILES | 100 |
| 0 | KILOMETRES | 150 |

*11 Group only

FIRTH OF FORTH

GLASGOW

BELFAST

Luftflotte 5 (Stumpff)
(from Norway and Denmark)

NEWCASTLE
Fighter Command 13 Group (Saul)
SUNDERLAND
MIDDLESBROUGH

NORTH SEA

Cover of low-level radar (500 ft)

Cover of high-level radar (15,000 ft)

HULL

LIVERPOOL
MANCHESTER
SHEFFIELD

NOTTINGHAM
Fighter Command 12 Group (Leigh-Mallory)
BIRMINGHAM
COVENTRY

NORWICH

Duxford
Debden
IPSWICH • Martlesham

ROTTERDAM

SWANSEA
CARDIFF
BRISTOL • Ball
BATH
Andover
Middle Wallop
SOUTHAMPTON

Fighter Command 10 Group (Brand)

EXETER

PLYMOUTH

Stanmore
Northolt
Uxbridge (G)
LONDON
(HQ)
North Weald
Hornchurch
Rochford
Croydon
Biggin Hill
Kenley
Redhill
West Malling
Lympne
Fighter Command 11 Group (Park)
THAMES ESTUARY
Eastchurch
Manston
Detling
CANTERBURY
Hawkinge
Tangmere
VENTNOR
PORTSMOUTH

CALAIS

GHENT
ANTWERP
B E L G I U M

LILLE

Luftflotte 2 (Kesselring)

E N G L I S H   C H A N N E L

AMIENS

F R A N C E

CHERBOURG
LE HAVRE

PARIS

Luftflotte 3 (Sperrle)

RENNES

25

Leigh-Mallory, with the backing of some of his officers, accordingly began to lobby for a change of strategy, proposing that No 12 Group should be thrown into battle over southeast England as a supplement to 11 Group.

Superficially, this strategy was attractive, but Dowding could argue that there was little fundamental wisdom in committing the reserve to action even before a battle had begun. Moreover, changing strategy in the middle of a campaign was likewise unwise, especially when the existing strategy seemed to be working well. There was a critical situation, it was true, but it was not at all hopeless. In the end, it was Park who bore the brunt of Leigh-Mallory's dissidence. There was considerable acrimony between the two, especially when it became evident that Leigh-Mallory implicitly approved the actions of some of his squadron leaders, who disobeyed control instructions in the belief that they knew better. All the same, Dowding's failure at least to visit the most dissident of the 12 Group squadrons, and to acknowledge that there was a critical problem here that might be smoothed out by personal contact, must count as one of his mistakes.

Meanwhile, the Battle of Britain was in its most critical month. In that month, from mid-August to 15 September, Fighter Command lost almost 500 aircraft and 201 aircrew while the Luftwaffe lost almost 900 machines but over 1100 aircrew. By this stage British fighter production was not enough to replace losses, and experienced and fresh pilots were in increas-

TOP LEFT: A bomber crew makes final preparations before taking off to attack Britain.

LEFT: A formation of Spitfires. They seem to be flying in 3-aircraft sections, a tactical formation that had become outdated by the Battle of Britain but was still widely used by British squadrons.

ABOVE RIGHT: Adolf Galland, one of the German fighter aces of 1940, who survived to write a book about it all.

LEFT: Robert Stanford-Tuck, a high-scoring RAF fighter pilot.

RIGHT: Göring welcomes German airmen returning from the Spanish Civil War in 1939. Taking the salute with Göring is General von Richthofen, commander of *Fliegerkorps VIII* during the Battle of Britain.

ingly short supply. All the same, the German command realized that it had not won command of the air and 'Operation Sealion' remained impracticable. Attacks on British airfields accordingly intensified, and at last a real effort was made to destroy radar stations; the vital role of these had at last been realized. Aircraft factories were also attacked with more determination.

The exposure of British fighter strength to really decisive encounters remained the aim of the German command, and it was decided that attacks on London might, if only through political repercussion, force Fighter Command to put all its strength into the air against a superior force of German fighters. This change of policy also satisfied Hitler's wish to hit London in retaliation for an RAF night raid on Berlin on 25 August.

On 7 September, therefore, about 300 German bombers with no fewer than 600 escorting fighters attacked London docks. No 11 Group, preoccupied with several damaging attacks on its airfields, could only put four squadrons in the air to meet this force, which meant that almost all the bombers reached their target. The attack was repeated that night, and the result was that thousands of Londoners were killed in what was the first mass attack on the capital.

Luckily, the Germans at this point decided that their major effort should be directed against cities, and this relieved Fighter Command from a situation in which things were not going well, for the intensive attacks on its airfields had been very damaging. It was also finding it difficult to cope with a new German tactic, numerous random attacks by single or small groups of Me109s, which could be countered only by the flying of continuous patrols, very costly in terms of flying hours. But it soon found it could cope with mass daylight bombing attacks on London. On 15 September the last of such raids was made. Almost all the German formations were intercepted before they reached their targets, and their bombs were dropped randomly. Moreover, more than 60 German aircraft were shot down for the loss of 29 British. After this, Hitler postponed 'Operation Sealion.'

There is probably some justice, then, in the choice of 15 September as 'Battle of Britain Day.' The battle was still not quite over, but by the end of October daylight raids were petering out, and German air activity was shifting to night bombing. Against this, Fighter Command had initially little success, but that would be another chapter of the war. The fact was that Fighter Command still existed and that Hitler's succession of great victories had been checked by a great defeat.

This was not just a victory of 'The Few,' so effectively dramatized by Churchill. A share of the credit was deserved by the creators of the Spitfire and Hurricane, and of radar. And there were The Many, those who operated the radar, those who exemplified the higher amateurism by serving in the Observer Corps, those who put their linguistic and analytical talents at the service of signals intelligence. Above all, The Few depended on The Two. Dowding and Park were the creators of this historic victory.

In November both lost their jobs. The anti-Dowding faction in the Air Ministry secured his transfer and subsequent retirement at the same time as they engineered Park's replacement by Leigh-Mallory. The lack of public appreciation shown to these two at the time was almost as astounding as the victory they had won. Dowding was an awkward character, not good at personal relationships, but abnormal personalities were common enough at the higher levels of the RAF organization. Indeed, there were several air marshals who reached their eminence not because of extraordinary competence but thanks to extraordinary ambition and extraordinary self-assertion. Dowding was certainly not one of those.

CHAPTER THREE

CUNNINGHAM

AND THE BATTLE OF MATAPAN

WITH THE entry of Italy into the war in June 1940, the Mediterranean inevitably became a center of conflict. For Britain, it gave access to the troops in Egypt, to the Suez Canal, to Malta, and to interests in the Middle East. For Italy, it provided opportunities for damaging Britain but at the same time gave the British a chance to attack major coastal cities and also the supply ships on which the Italian forces in North Africa depended. The struggle for dominance in the Mediterranean was not clear-cut because air power sometimes meant that navies could exert command of the sea only during darkness.

In 1940, before German bombers were transferred to the Mediterranean, the Royal Navy could cope with bombing, which took the form of high-level and not very accurate attacks. Running convoys to Malta and Egypt involved risks in the narrow waters south of Sicily, but good management avoided disaster. However, so long as the Italian fleet was capable of large-scale operations it presented a threat to the convoys, and the neutralization of that fleet was the first priority of the British.

Two operations, Taranto in November 1940 and Matapan in March 1941, achieved the British objective of crippling and demoralizing the Italian Navy, thereby removing one threat to the British position in the Mediterranean at a very critical period. Both these battles, and many smaller encounters, were directed by Vice Admiral Andrew B. Cunningham, familiarly known as 'ABC,' who won a reputation as the greatest British admiral since Nelson.

Cunningham's early naval career had, by choice, been spent mainly in torpedo craft, and he was a destroyer captain in World War I. He served with distinction at the Dardanelles and in the Dover Patrol, as well as in the post-war Baltic campaign that helped to preserve Estonia and Latvia from German and Bolshevik designs. His promotion was fast, for he was a marked man throughout. This was partly because he was lucky enough to serve under men who were destined for high appointments and could help him onward, but largely because of his capabilities. He had intelligence, a capacity for hard work, and an aggressive, if not pugnacious, nature uneasily combined with a caring attitude toward his subordinates. As a destroyer captain he was notorious for his rapid dismissal of successive lieutenants; this was because they did not meet his exacting standards, and he believed that prompt rejection was kinder than uncomfortable tolerance.

Even during World War II, at the height of his success, he was not universally popular. While sailors had every confidence in his leadership, officers who worked with him sometimes found his fussiness about dress and his reluctance to spend government money on worthwhile objectives something of a trial. Nor was he very understanding in technical matters. For some, his acidity and occasional bad temper were disturbing, although they invariably found that he was a man quick to forgive. Really he was in the British sea-dog tradition, demanding high standards of seamanship and expecting everyone, most of all himself, to give of their best in all circumstances. Sometimes he seemed to take pride in his prejudices, but he was more ready than most of his colleagues to change his mind on fundamentals;

his quite sudden acceptance of the importance of naval aviation was remarkable, and had a significant outcome in World War II.

In the interwar period, apart from destroyer appointments, he commanded the battleship *Rodney* for a time, and also the Battlecruiser Squadron. A year at the Admiralty as Deputy Chief of Naval Staff gave him some much-needed insight into administrative problems. A disproportionate part of his career had been spent in the Mediterranean and he was a good choice as commander of the Mediterranean Fleet in June 1939, at a time when war seemed inevitable.

His fleet consisted of the flagship, the modernized battleship *Warspite*, and three unmodernized old battleships, with an aircraft carrier and two cruiser squadrons. But after a few months of war, and with Italy's neutrality, this was soon reduced to three cruisers and a few destroyers, with Cunningham making his headquarters at Malta. He kept his large and mainly self-chosen staff, however, because it was expected that a Mediterranean war would not be long in coming. Indeed, by the time Mussolini decided to take Italy into the war as an ally of Hitler, Cunningham's fleet had been restored to its former strength, and additional submarines transferred from the China station.

Even with the French navy covering the Western Mediterranean, Cunningham had a difficult task. That task was to maintain sufficient control of the sea to enable British shipping to use it, to deter Italy from attacking Malta, and to interrupt Italian communications with Libya. This was in the face of an Italian fleet that comprised four modernized and two new battleships, numerous heavily-gunned fast cruisers, scores of torpedo craft and a very large submarine fleet. In addition, Italy had command of the air in much of the central Mediterranean, thanks to airbases on its mainland, Sicily, and Sardinia. Although the Italian Navy did not have its own air arm, relying on the unreliable cooperation of the air force, Cunningham's possession of one old aircraft carrier, *Eagle*, was far from enough to give his ships secure air cover.

LEFT: Cunningham finished his career as Admiral of the Fleet Viscount Cunningham of Hyndhope, KT, DSO and Bar.

RIGHT: HMS *Illustrious* at sea in 1941 during flying operations.

ABOVE: HMS *Illustrious,* whose advanced design was betrayed by the provision of obsolete aircraft, like the Gladiators seen in this photograph.

LEFT: HMS *Illustrious,* bombed off Malta, survives to fight another day.

RIGHT: The battleship HMS *Barham* off Gibraltar in 1940, on her way to join the Mediterranean Fleet.

With the surrender of France the situation worsened. Cunningham had good relations with the French admiral commanding a cruiser squadron at Alexandria, and secured the demilitarization of the French ships without violence, but the loss of French naval power in the Western Mediterranean was serious. A British squadron, Force 'H' under Vice Admiral Sir James Somerville, was soon stationed at Gibraltar for work in both the Atlantic and Western Mediterranean and this eased the situation, because Gibraltar was only a thousand miles west of Malta. But Cunningham was still outnumbered, and although much of the Italian armed services were unenthusiastic about Mussolini, it could be expected that Italian naval officers as a matter of pride would do their best to defeat the Royal Navy.

The Admiralty in June 1940 did envisage abandonment of the Eastern Mediterranean, with Cunningham's ships moving to the safer waters of Gibraltar and thereby abandoning Egypt and the Suez Canal to the Italian army poised in Libya. However, Cunningham reported that he had the strength to hold his position, and pointed out that to surrender the Eastern Mediterranean would probably mean the loss of Malta, Cyprus and Palestine, and the entry of Turkey into the war against Britain. In the end, the British Chiefs of Staff concurred, and he stayed. Later, he wrote that a withdrawal would have been a disaster, and he was surely right.

Cunningham's readiness to answer back, and sometimes to actually ignore orders, is in retrospect one of his most endearing features and one in which he followed the Nelsonian tradition.

In his Mediterranean campaign he was not only fighting the Axis powers, but also coping with Churchill, who rarely seemed able to distinguish between guidance and interference. Ever ready to dismiss a commander whom he thought lukewarm, Churchill was a menace to any admiral or general who thought it wiser to husband resources than engage in offensive projects. Usually acting through the Chiefs of Staff, Churchill secured the removal of many capable officers but Cunningham escaped, probably because his aggressive instincts were so obvious. But Somerville, his colleague in the Western Mediterranean, who at this period gave protection of a vital convoy priority over a possible engagement with the Italian fleet, had to face the humiliation of a board of inquiry.

Even Cunningham roused Churchill's wrath when in an official report he wrote that an Italian destroyer commander had fought bravely. In the intricate negotiations with the French admiral at Alexandria he was pestered by instructions to hurry up. At a critical phase of the Greek campaign his order to a transport to return to port was actually countermanded by London, but he responded by ignoring the intervention.

In the summer of 1940 he faced a daunting situation. Malta, so close to Sicilian airfields, was no place to base a fleet, and he used Alexandria. The latter was outside effective bombing range but also 800 miles from the most likely scene of operations in the Central Mediterranean. Its approaches could be mined by Italian submarines; minesweepers, like destroyers, were scarce, and only one rather long channel was kept open. The shortage of

aircraft was critical. The RAF could offer only occasional fighter protection – Malta was provided with just twelve Hurricane fighters at this period – and RAF reconaissance was hampered by aircraft shortage and the inexperience in naval matters of RAF aircrews. The one aircraft carrier had to be reserved for the most urgent needs, and in any case normally carried only Swordfish torpedo/reconnaissance aircraft. Battleships and cruisers carried their own reconnaissance seaplanes, but picking these up out of the water took time, and bad weather could prevent their use.

The submarines, and from time to time destroyers, were based at Malta and attacked Italian convoys to Libya. Cunningham despatched his cruisers on periodic sweeps that occasionally found a prey, but his big ships remained at Alexandria except when called out to provide distant cover for a convoy, to seek the Italian fleet, or, occasionally, carry out coastal bombardments.

The first encounter between battleships occurred in July, when both fleets were engaged in covering convoys. Four Gladiator biplane fighters had been found, and these were added to *Eagle*'s 17 Swordfish, subsequently shooting down a couple of Italian bombers. Warned initially by one of his submarines, Cunningham arranged air reconnaissance that located the Italian force of two battleships and 16 cruisers. An air strike by Swordfish was unsuccessful but, in an exchange of fire later, *Warspite* hit the battleship *Cesare* at 13 miles. The Italians thereupon broke off the action, pursued by Cunningham to within 25 miles of the Italian coast. Very heavy bombing followed, and Cunningham later described it as frightening, but there were no direct hits. Although at first this seemed an indecisive action it was very important in establishing a British moral superiority,

with Cunningham's ships displaying an ability to operate really close to the Italian coast and an offensive spirit that the Italian Navy was not allowed to match.

In August the new aircraft carrier *Illustrious* and the modernized battleship *Valiant* joined Cunningham's fleet. But he could still be outnumbered by the Italians. In September, while covering a troop convoy with his two modernized battleships and *Illustrious*, his reconnaissance aircraft reported Italian battleships 120 miles distant. He decided not to get entangled with them, but to concentrate on getting the transports safely to Malta; presumably this difficult decision was aided by his relatively weak strength at the time. But though wise, it was also a courageous decision to avoid combat. Not even an air strike could be launched, because *Illustrious* had only nine serviceable Swordfish that would have had little chance in the face of local Italian air superiority. A few weeks earlier, an Italian force, consisting of five battleships, 13 cruisers and 39 destroyers, had been despatched to destroy Cunningham when he was covering another convoy but, because of poor air cooperation, it was unable to locate him. If he had been found, he would have been lucky to survive.

The Italian naval threat became even greater after Italy invaded Greece, for Cunningham anticipated that he would be required to protect a stream of transports taking British troops and supplies to that country. He was faced with an enemy that was stronger than he was, and a battle area that was hundreds of miles from his own base.

His solution was revealed in November 1940, and took the form of a naval air attack on the Italian base at Taranto. This operation was timed to fit in with an excursion that was necessary in any case, to cover British convoys. On 11 November, the

ABOVE LEFT: Another view of HMS *Barham.* Old unmodernized battleships like this were vulnerable, and after her hour of glory at Matapan this vessel succumbed to a submarine later in 1941.

ABOVE: The cruiser HMS *Orion,* Pridham-Wippell's flagship at Matapan.

RIGHT: Captain D. W. Boyd, who commanded the aircraft carrier HMS *Illustrious* in 1940.

moon and weather being favorable, and RAF reconnaissance having reported six battleships in harbor (Italy's full strength at that time), Cunningham detached *Illustrious* and eight smaller ships to make the attack. He had hoped to use *Eagle* also, but that carrier was not fit for service; however, some of its aircraft were flown on to *Illustrious*.

Soon after nightfall, about 170 miles south-east of Taranto, the first flight of 12 Swordfish took off, followed an hour later by another nine. Evading barrage balloons and launching their torpedoes at short range so as to avoid the protective nets, they scored three hits on the modern battleship *Littorio*, and one each on the modernized *Duilio* and *Cavour*. All three were badly damaged, and *Cavour* was never repaired. Cuningham would have liked to have repeated the operation the following night, for he had lost only two aircraft, but an unfavorable weather forecast, and perhaps a realization that the Italians would be better prepared next time, deterred him.

As it was, he had scored a notable victory. He had halved the Italian battleship strength and, as it turned out, forced the Italians to relocate their surviving battleships much further north, at Naples. He had also been the first to conduct a fleet action entirely carried out by carrier-borne aircraft, and at night too. The victory was not only strategic, but moral as well. Not only did it discourage the Italian fleet, but it also provided much-needed cheer for the British, who had faced a series of disasters in 1940 and were to experience more in the following months.

Taranto also enabled Cunningham to rid himself of his two oldest battleships, which with their obsolete gun mountings and slow speed could well have been a hindrance in a fleet action. 1940 ended well for him. He had thoroughly beaten the Italian navy; he had successfully protected the east-west convoys; his interruptions of Italian north-south supply routes and his coastal bombardments had contributed to the Italian defeat in North Africa; Italian bombers and submarines had proved less effective than feared; and Malta was surviving. But in January the first German air squadrons took up station in Sicily, and Germany was preparing to intervene in North Africa and Greece.

German dive-bombers made themselves felt in January when, in a series of complex moves to cover a Malta convoy, Cunningham came under heavy attack. *Warspite* was hit once but *Illustrious* sustained six heavy bomb hits and it was only thanks to her armored flight deck that she survived to reach Malta, where she suffered further attacks before being sent to Alexandria and thence to the USA for major repairs. In the preceding weeks this

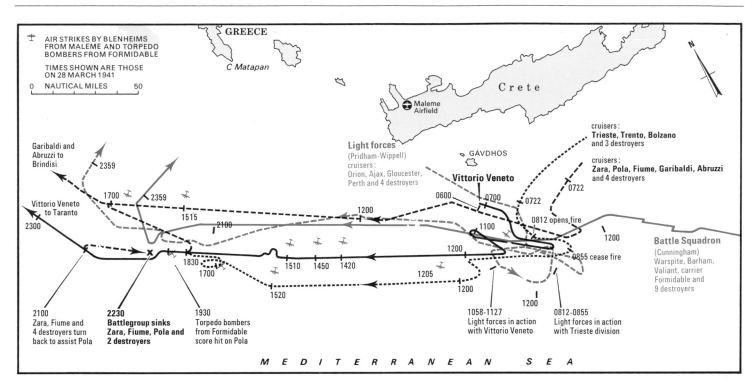

AIR STRIKES BY BLENHEIMS
FROM MALEME AND TORPEDO
BOMBERS FROM FORMIDABLE

TIMES SHOWN ARE THOSE
ON 28 MARCH 1941

0   NAUTICAL MILES   50

GREECE

C Matapan

Crete

Maleme
Airfield

Garibaldi and
Abruzzi to
Brindisi

2359

Vittorio Veneto
to Taranto

2300

1700

2359

1515

2100

1830

1700

X

1520

2100
Zara, Fiume and
4 destroyers turn
back to assist Pola

**2230
Battlegroup sinks
Zara, Fiume, Pola and
2 destroyers**

1930
Torpedo bombers
from Formidable
score hit on Pola

Light forces
(Pridham-Wippell)
cruisers:
Orion, Ajax, Gloucester,
Perth and 4 destroyers

GÁVDHOS

Vittorio Veneto

1200

1510   1450   1420

1205

1520

0600

1200

0700

1100

1200

0722

0812 opens fire

0722

0855 cease fire

1200

1200

1058-1127
Light forces in action
with Vittorio Veneto

0812-0855
Light forces in action
with Trieste division

cruisers:
Trieste, Trento, Bolzano
and 3 destroyers

cruisers:
Zara, Pola, Fiume, Garibaldi, Abruzzi
and 4 destroyers

1200

Battle Squadron
(Cunningham)
Warspite, Barham,
Valiant, carrier
Formidable and
9 destroyers

M E D I T E R R A N E A N   S E A

LEFT: Cunningham's flagship HMS *Warspite,* sister of HMS *Barham* but thanks to reconstruction a much more formidable battleship.

ABOVE: A plot of the opposing fleets' movements at Matapan.

aircraft carrier had led a busy life, with aircraft attacking shore targets and also Italian shipping. Its withdrawal was partly responsible for the failure to damage southbound convoys taking the German Afrika Korps to Libya. On the other hand corresponding British convoys taking troops northward from Egypt to Greece were well-protected. It was not until March that *Formidable,* sister of *Illustrious,* arrived via the Suez Canal to join Cunningham's Mediterranean Fleet.

One of Cunningham's handicaps was the dearth of good intelligence. The RAF allocated a few Sunderland and Maryland aircraft to ocean patrol work, but their crews were not good at identifying ships, and in any case they were too few to provide anything except spasmodic glimpses. Submarines provided accurate reports, but had a very limited field of view. Signals intelligence had yet to get into its stride. The Italian navy had somewhat similar handicaps; air reconnaissance was not limited so much by shortage of aircraft or airfields, as by the uncooperative relationship between the navy and air force. On the other hand, the Italians had several good sources reporting the movements of the British ships. One of these sources was reputed to be the Japanese consul in Alexandria (Japan, of course, was not yet at war).

However, the arrival of the Germans in the Mediterranean resulted in much more signals traffic as the incoming units' movements were arranged. At the same time, the British ability to decipher high-level messages coded through the Enigma machine began to yield useful information, and the Battle of Cape Matapan was the first Mediterranean operation to be initiated on the basis of signals intelligence.

On 25 March 1941 a Luftwaffe signal revealed that all twin-engined (that is, long-range) fighters were to be temporarily transferred to Sicily. Soon afterward Italian Navy signals revealed that an operation was being prepared, that preliminary

attacks were being planned on Aegean airfields, and that information was being sought about British convoys between Alexandria and Greece. Cunningham could not decide whether it was a sea or an air attack that was being planned on his convoys. Late on 26 March he cancelled a southbound convoy and instructed a northbound convoy to reverse course, but only after nightfall so as not to indicate to the enemy that he knew that something was in the wind. He also ordered his cruiser squadron, four six-inch gun cruisers under Rear Admiral Pridham-Wippell, to be ready south of Crete at dawn on 28 March. Meanwhile he prepared to move out with his three battleships and *Formidable,* although in order to conceal his departure for as long as possible he intended to leave only after nightfall on 27 March. In the course of that day an RAF flying boat glimpsed three Italian cruisers off Sicily steaming toward Crete, which suggested that the enemy was planning a surface attack. That afternoon Cunningham presented himself at the local golf club, complete with overnight bag, in the expectation of misleading the Japanese consul. Signals intelligence subsequently decrypted an Italian report that the battlefleet was still at Alexandria in the evening of 27 March.

The situation on the Italian side was that in late 1940 there had been a shake-up in the higher levels of the navy. A new navy minister and a new Commander in Chief afloat had been pressed to attack British convoys in the Eastern Mediterranean and on 15 March such an operation had been agreed. Pressure from the local German naval representatives appears to have been a strong motivation for this. Iachino was probably not greatly enthusiastic, and when on 16 March two German torpedo aircraft reported scoring hits on two large British ships, probably battleships, he was scornfully sceptical. However, he made his plans, and with a little more luck he might have won a notable victory.

Iachino was short of serviceable battleships, and took only one, his new fast *Vittorio Veneto,* when he left Naples on 26 March. He was soon joined by three eight-inch-gun cruisers with destroyers, and later by his 1st and 8th cruiser divisions, the 1st also being composed of three eight-inch-gun ships *Zara, Fiume,* and *Pola).* Their aim was to destroy British convoys, entering into action with British warships only in favorable circumstances. Air support, and especially reconnaissance, had

been promised by the Italian and German air forces. However, this air support failed to materialize, and it was the *Veneto*'s own plane that spotted Pridham-Wippell's cruisers at dawn on 28 March. Iachino thereupon increased speed in the hope of forcing the British into an unequal battle.

At about the same time Cunningham with his main force received the first concrete intelligence since leaving Alexandria, when two of *Formidable*'s aircraft sighted two separate Italian cruiser squadrons. Soon after 08.00 Pridham-Wippell found himself under fire from Italian cruisers at about 13 miles distance. Outranged, and slower than his opponents, he retired at full speed in the hope of drawing the Italians toward Cunningham's battlefleet. However, Iachino soon became suspicious and ordered his cruisers to break off the action. Pridham-Wippell then altered course in order to shadow them, and at 11.00 found his ships under the guns of the *Veneto*. The latter opened fire at about 15 miles and for half an hour the British cruisers' retirement was encouraged by a threatening but luckily harmless bombardment. Iachino's aim, however, was to drive the British into his own eight-inch gun cruisers, and he would have succeeded had Cunningham not despatched six Albacore torpedo planes from *Formidable* to the rescue. They attacked the Italian battleship but all the torpedoes missed, and Iachino was now alerted to the presence of a British aircraft carrier and could assume that Cunningham and his battleships were also there. Accordingly Iachino decided to break off the chase and retired westward.

Having been forced to reveal his presence earlier than he had wished, Cunningham's best hope was to launch air attacks that might delay the Italians long enough for him to catch up with them. It was still not clear how many Italian groups were in the vicinity, but in the meantime he sent five torpedo aircraft after the *Veneto*. This time they scored one hit, which slowed her down, but not enough to enable Cunningham to catch up before nightfall. In the late afternoon he was still about 60 miles south of the Italian battleship, and ordered a third air strike of eight torpedo aircraft. They discovered the *Veneto* still proceeding northward but well covered by columns of cruisers and destroyers. Despite intense gunfire they were able to make a low-level attack at sunset and scored one hit on the cruiser *Pola*, putting its electrical power out of action and thereby rendering it helpless.

Still hoping to destroy the Italian battleship, Cunningham had to decide whether to seek a night battle or to wait for daylight. The latter course would place his ships within range of German dive-bombers by dawn. On the other hand, night actions were regarded as risky ventures, presenting many opportunities for small craft to slip in and torpedo the big ships. However, the British crews had long been trained for night fighting and, no doubt remembering the 1916 Battle of Jutland, when the German fleet had escaped while the British were waiting for daylight, Cunningham decided on a night action. He ordered his destroyers to go ahead and seek out the enemy, believed to be 30 miles away, while he followed at his best speed.

In making this decision Cunningham was aware that he would have the advantage of advanced technology which, normally, he distrusted. Two of Pridham-Wippell's cruisers, and also his battleship *Valiant*, had radar, which the Italians lacked. Shortly after nightfall the two cruisers detected a stationary vessel about six miles to the west. Uncertain whether this was *Veneto*, Pridham-Wippell did not stop, but reported the position of the stopped ship to Cunningham.

Cunningham changed course to investigate. His force consisted of his flagship *Warspite*, the similarly modernized *Valiant*, followed by *Formidable*, with the old battleship *Barham* at the end of the line. There were two destroyers in attendance. At about 22.00 *Valiant*'s radar picked up the stationary ship, and Cunningham closed. Visibility was about two miles, there being no moon, and the sea was smooth. The target was on the port bow, the radar ranges transmitted by *Valiant* grew steadily smaller, and the gun crews awaited orders to fire. At this tense moment Cunningham and his officers were surprised to see, on the starboard bow about two miles distant, dark shapes that appeared to be two large and one or more smaller vessels.

Cunningham reacted promptly. He turned his ships toward the new targets, forming a line ahead and presenting the targets on the port bow. *Formidable*, redundant and vulnerable, was despatched to starboard. *Warspite* opened fire at the same moment as one of the destroyers illuminated the enemy by searchlight. Confronted at such close range by three 15-inch gun battleships, the two Italian cruisers and the leading destroyer had no chance at all. Cunningham later wrote of seeing huge pieces of debris, including gun turrets, being toppled into the air and water.

It was all over in four minutes, The two Italian cruisers, *Zara* and *Fiume*, crippled and ablaze, were left to be finished off by destroyers, as was *Pola*. Cunningham, having observed other Italian destroyers following the cruisers, turned away in case of torpedo attack.

This turn away was less remarkable than his turn toward possible torpedo attack which opened this engagement. Ever since the development of the torpedo, the standard tactic for battle-ship formations was to turn away when threatened by hostile torpedo craft, the reason being that the big ships would then present only their sterns to the oncoming torpedoes which, additionally, would catch up with them more slowly. Thus Cunningham's decision to turn toward the unknown enemy was a tactical novelty that earned its due reward. How far his decision was due to memories of Jutland, when the British turn-away from German destroyers resulted in contact with the enemy being lost, and how far it was influenced by his background in destroyers, where turning toward the enemy was a natural reaction, is hard to decide. Quite possibly he was simply following the logic of the given situation, untroubled by theoretical considerations.

Theoretical considerations, on the other hand, had played a large part in the disaster that overtook the Italian cruisers. Italian naval doctrine propounded that fleet actions would not take place at night, the opposing heavy ships being kept out of trouble by screens of destroyers. On cruisers and battleships, whose crews were not trained for night actions, the main guns were not even manned at night, yet Admiral Iachino had seen no danger in allowing *Zara* and *Fiume* to turn back under darkness to rescue their stricken consort *Pola*.

Cunningham's ships were unscathed. Whereas the Italians lost three heavy cruisers and two destroyers, the British loss was just one aircraft. However, Cunningham had failed to sink the *Veneto*. Admiral Iachino had changed course during the night and thereby evaded the British cruisers and destroyers. He returned to port an angry man, having been let down by the air force. Mussolini comforted him by promising to convert a liner into an aircraft carrier. Hitherto, it had been Italian doctrine (proposed by the air force and approved by Mussolini) that the Italian navy did not need aircraft carriers because the air force would look after its needs.

Cunningham radioed the position of the sunken Italian ships,

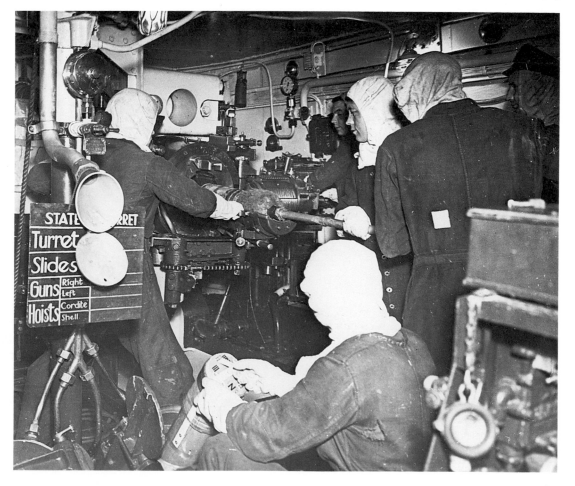

ABOVE LEFT: Alexandria naval base at the beginning of the war. British and French battleships can be seen in the distance, with French cruisers and destroyers in the foreground.

RIGHT: Inside a 6-inch gun turret of the cruiser HMS *Orion*.

and eventually an Italian hospital ship arrived to pick up those survivors that had not been found by British destroyers. Cunningham defended this breach of radio security by pointing out that the position of his ships was already known to the enemy. When the expected air attack did come in the norning, it gave Cunningham some anxious moments, but did not score any hits.

In the end, the Battle of Cape Matapan was more important than the list of losses suggested. The destruction of those three cruisers was an inportant success in any case, because the Italian possession of eight-inch-gun cruisers that were both considerably faster and heavier-gunned than Cunningham's had always presented a threat, and now their number had been halved. But the deeper significance of Matapan is that it finally deterred the Italians from seeking a fleet action and, most important, it removed the threat of seaborne attacks on the Greek convoys.

In due course, as Cunningham and most local British leaders expected, the northward move of British troops to Greece was followed by their evacuation south back to Egypt, with a stand at Crete as a final challenge to the Germans. These Greek and Crete operations were a severe trial for Cunningham's crews. Lacking air cover almost always, they were subjected to repeated daylight dive-bomber attacks. Losses of cruisers and destroyers were heavy, and at the end Cunningham decided to curtail the evacuation of the final units from Crete; he had viewed the messdeck of a cruiser, crowded with troops, that had been shattered by a German bomb. He had been against the Greek campaign from the first, although he had accepted it on political grounds. The navy had done all it could, he felt, to back up the army in its difficulties, but with ships running short of ammunition and their crews dog-tired, further heroism would have been useless. At this point he told the First Sea Lord that he was willing to give up his appointment, but in the end he stayed on.

May was the month of greatest loss, but April had been stressful, with criticisms by Churchill of the navy's performance against Axis convoys to Libya. At one point Churchill hinted that the fact that the British ships had not received a scratch at Matapan suggested that the Navy preferred not to risk its ships.

Cunningham did in due course obtain a rest from his responsibilities when he was sent to Washington in 1942 as British naval representative. When he returned to the Mediterranean it was as C in C of all the Allied naval forces, answerable to General Eisenhower and charged among other things with the North African landings. In summer 1943, after the Italian surrender, he was able to send to the Admiralty his classic signal: 'Be pleased to inform Their Lordships that the Italian battle fleet now lies at anchor beneath the guns of the fortress of Malta.'

Later in 1943 he became First Sea Lord, an appointment that Churchill was reluctant to approve, but the two men got on reasonably well. Cunningham's lack of deference was compensated by his sensitivity and tact, and he retained his position until retirement in 1945.

During the war he became something of a hero to the British people, yet his full achievement was not quite appreciated because it was official policy to portray the Italian Navy as incompetent and cowardly, even though it was neither of those two. What Cunningham had done was maintain command of the Mediterranean at a critical time and against superior forces. The qualities which enabled him to do this were not always obvious. His offensive spirit was certainly appreciated, and was exemplified among many other things by his unorthodox turn toward the Italians at Matapan. What was less noticed was that he was also strong enough to take the unheroic course. More than once, in reach of superior enemy forces, he preferred not to fight. He seemed to know when to fight and when not to fight, and his robust attitude toward others allowed him to listen to their opinions without necessarily doing what they wanted him to do.

ABOVE: The Australian cruiser *Perth,* part of Cunningham's cruiser squadron at Matapan.

RIGHT: Two Italian battleships resting on the shallow bottom of Taranto harbor after the British attack in November 1940.

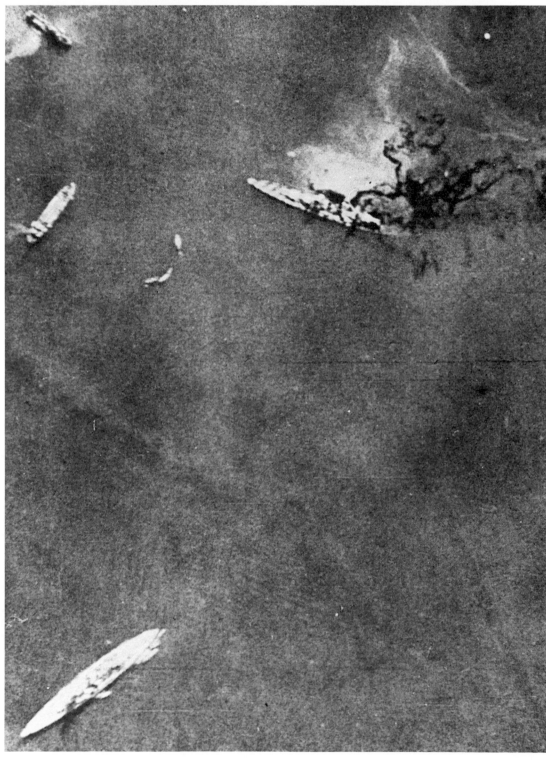

LEFT: A planning session aboard HMS *Illustrious* shortly after she entered service. Efficient management of aircraft movements on a carrier's decks was not a simple matter but could greatly enhance the speed of operations.

CHAPTER FOUR

STUDENT

AND THE CAPTURE OF CRETE

AT THE beginning of 1941 Hitler was interested above all in his forthcoming invasion of Russia, but the misfortunes of Mussolini induced him to divert his attention, and some of his forces, to the Balkans and Mediterranean. Mussolini had unwisely embarked on two major campaigns, in North Africa and in Greece, and was doing badly in both. Luftwaffe squadrons were therefore sent to Sicily, to challenge British naval dominance of the Mediterranean, the Afrika Korps was set up, and armies sent to conquer Yugoslavia and Greece.

If these new campaigns taxed German resources, the same was even more true of the British, who were already stretched thin in East Africa and North Africa, and who at this precise moment were compelled to intervene against pro-Nazi movements in Iraq and Syria. British commanders were repeatedly goaded by Churchill to take offensive actions which they thought ill-advised, and some lost their jobs because of their quite justified caution. The British decision to intervene when the Germans invaded Greece was militarily indefensible, although General Archibald Wavell, British Commander in Chief in the theater, accepted it. Probably he had been worn down by previous arguments, but he saw that the British cabinet's arguments were not entirely sentimental; it would look bad if Britain did not come to the aid of a small country attacked by the Nazis.

The campaign in Greece was short, with the British and Greek forces being pushed south and finally compelled to evacuate by sea. British losses of military equipment were considerable, and the Royal Navy suffered heavily from German dive-bombers. Of the 62,000 men sent to Greece, about 50,000 got away, and many of those were landed on the island of Crete. For the British, Crete was not simply the tail-end of Greece, but because of its location was a valued air and naval base whose loss would jeopardize their ability to pass supplies through the Eastern Mediterranean. On the German side, there were many who regarded the island as not just a base from which air control over the sea might be exercised, but also as a stepping stone to that other island, Cyprus, and from there into the Middle East.

Hitler, confident that he could finish this campaign without further delaying his invasion of Russia, ordered Operation *Merkur*, the capture of Crete, as soon as the last Greek troops surrendered on the mainland. It was to be a notable campaign, the first such assault to be carried out purely by an airborne corps. Naturally enough, its commander was to be General Kurt Student, the specialist in large-scale airborne tactics. Student was to find his place in the annals of military history firstly as the virtual creator of airborne techniques, and secondly as a victor in the Low Countries campaign of 1940 and the Crete operation of 1941. He would also be interesting as one of those rare men who

LEFT: Kurt Student had been a fighter pilot during World War I and joined the Luftwaffe on its formation in 1934.

RIGHT: Two views of German paratroops going into action during the invasion of Holland in May 1940.

LEFT: German troops attempt to retrieve a supply canister entangled in the structure of a Dutch bridge.

RIGHT: Hitler congratulates junior paratroop officers after the capture of the Eben Emael fortress complex in Belgium.

LEFT: A paratrooper jumps from his Ju52 transport. Short intervals between jumps were essential, so that all men of a drop would land close together.

developed a technique, showed that it worked, but then saw it abandoned at the very moment of its triumph.

In 1935, impressed by the mass parachute drops staged by the Red Army, the German High Command had begun to train its first paratroopers, and within months the first parachute battalion was formed. Kurt Student, a Luftwaffe general, was appointed to command the airborne forces in 1938, and quickly showed his drive and enthusiasm. He rejected the idea of using paratroops simply as behind-the-lines saboteurs and diversionists, and favored what became known as 'three-dimensional' warfare, in which large formations of troops dropped from the sky behind the enemy's front. Since the enemy would never know when and where these troops would land, they would always have the value of surprise, and hence their vulnerability to small-arms fire during their descent would be insignificant so long as they did not land in zones already occupied by alert hostile forces.

In the next couple of years Student produced what Hitler regarded for a time as a new and powerful secret weapon; under Student, the Germans pursued the concept of airborne troops with far more zest and inventiveness than the Russians. The new commander saw that his volunteer personnel required a new style of military life; these were officers and men for whom mutual reliability and resourcefulness were essential. Traditional authoritarianism was therefore relaxed, being regarded as inferior to the self-respect and comradeship to be gained by responsible performance of dangerous and skilled tasks. Among the technical innovations were better parachutes and, above all, the concept of landing troops not only by parachute or by troop-carrying aircraft at airfields, but also by glider. Troop-carrying gliders, it was realized, offered the same advantage of surprise

and mobility as parachutes, but had the advantage of keeping men together, ready to fight as a unit the moment they landed. There was also a realization that specialized, easily-transportable, fighting equipment was desirable. In 1938 the first airborne artillery battery appeared, using 75mm guns designed to be hauled by dog teams if horses were unavailable.

German airborne forces were known, for security reasons, as the 7th Air Division of the Wehrmacht. The paratroop battalion, however, was controlled by the Luftwaffe so far as operations were concerned. The division of responsibility between Luftwaffe and Wehrmacht, and the necessity of their close cooperation, does not seem to have been a weakness, possibly thanks to Student's air background.

In the Czechoslovakia crisis of 1938, Hitler ordered the 7th Air Division to prepare an operation to capture part of the Czech defenses. However, the Munich Agreement made this superfluous and only part of the plan, the transportation of troops by 250 Ju52 aircraft, was carried out, an exercise which, apparently, much impressed Göring and led to an expansion of the airborne forces. The 7th Air Division was to be joined by a new 22nd Airborne Division. Göring's enthusiasm was presumably why, at this point, the Luftwaffe took operational control of all airborne forces, not just the parachute units.

The anti-climax of the Czechoslovak events was repeated in the war against Poland. The airborne formations were entrusted with the advance capture of certain key bridges and airfields, and many units actually waited in their aircraft, but in each case the planned operation was cancelled. Hitler told Student that this was because the regular armored troops had moved faster than expected. The airborne forces were not really required, therefore, and it would have been foolish to reveal their true capacity to the world for no valid tactical reason. That surprise, continued Hitler, would be reserved for the forthcoming offensive in the west.

However, the airborne forces were first used not in the west, but in Norway. Hitler demanded a parachute battalion, whose separate companies would capture vital airfields in Norway and Denmark. Student at first protested that this operation would disrupt his training program, in which his troops were preparing for the assault on Belgium and the Netherlands, but was overruled. The airfields were successfully seized, and in addition paratroops were used to block a road badly needed by the British forces. In the end, the company carrying out the last operation had to surrender, having lost most of its men and run short of ammunition, but its holding operation had been of great value. All in all, the Norwegian campaign showed that Student's confidence in his new technique was fully justified and persuaded some officers that airborne troops would be just as revolutionary a battlefield concept as armored divisions.

In the 1940 blitzkrieg in the west the reputation of Student's divisions was further enhanced. They were entrusted with several tasks that at first seemed near-impossible, but were vital

to the success of the whole operation. Student was personally briefed by Hitler a few days before the start. His job was to secure vital points needed for the advance of the regular armored formations. Glider troops were to be used for the first time, and it was hoped that the surprise factor involved in their use would help to achieve the most difficult of the four objectives. The first three requirements in Belgium were for the capture intact of three bridges over the Albert Canal. One of these bridges, at Canne, was under the guns of Belgium's strongest fort, the Eben Emael complex, a steel and concrete mass harboring field artillery weapons as well as AA and anti-tank guns. The fourth task of Student's men was the capture of this fort.

Again, Student was completely successful. The bridges were captured intact and the great fort surrendered after its defenders' morale had been shattered by the knowledge that some parts had been captured by the attackers. Most of the gliders landed, as planned, adjacent to parts of the complex, and demolition charges made the first breaches.

For the assault on the Netherlands, the airborne forces were given two main tasks: the capture of the Waalhaven airfield, and of river bridges in advance of the oncoming armored divisions;

ABOVE: General Sir Archibald Wavell (in breeches) and his staff land in Greece to inspect defensive preparations.

RIGHT: Off-duty tourism for German troops in 1941 Athens.

LEFT: A British howitzer is towed along the main street of a Greek village during the short-lived and unsuccessful campaign of 1941.

LEFT: German troops in action during the Crete campaign.

RIGHT: Interest and incomprehension; Greeks and Germans meet in 1941.

BELOW: General Freyberg, the New Zealand commander who made the best of a bad job in Crete. The top left of his medal ribbons is that of the Victoria Cross, won in an earlier war.

and an operation in the capital, The Hague, designed to destroy the Dutch political and military leadership. These objectives were only partially achieved. Unexpectedly fierce Dutch resistance, and the dropping of some parachutists in the wrong places, led to quite heavy losses, and the The Hague operation was called off. But the bridges were captured, and the taking of Waalhaven airfield meant that more airborne troops could be flown in by Ju52 transport aircraft. Many of the latter were lost, however, either to Dutch gunfire or in chance encounters with RAF fighters.

Student claimed that his 1940 operations had been a complete success. This was an exaggeration, but nevertheless was essentially true. In two ways, however, it had been a Pyrrhic victory. Firstly, the reality and potential of airborne forces, and especially the novel use of gliders, was now apparent to the enemy, who could think up countermeasures. Secondly, unknown to the Germans, the British picked up a copy of the parachutists' training manual, and this helped them, in the subsequent Crete operation, to anticipate many German tactics that otherwise would have taken them by surprise.

Like many other enthusiastic commanders of technically-advanced forces, Student was apt to exaggerate the potentialities of his men. Certainly the 1940 campaign in Holland and Belgium gave him plenty to talk about, but it also contained the lesson that airborne forces had their own limitations. The importance of everything going to plan, and especially the fact that success depended so much on surprise, were two of these lessons. Student's claim that his men could have changed the course of the war if Hitler had let them loose against Britain at the time of Dunkirk seems sweeping. It is true that if they had been used to capture southern ports just as the British army was preparing to escape across the Channel, and at a time when British home forces were negligible, they might have transformed the situation, but to undertake such an operation at a time when air and naval command of the English Channel could not be guaranteed would have been a gamble that even Hitler could not accept.

However, Hitler's plan for Operation Sealion did give a prominent place to Student's command, which was to seize Folkstone. But even this might not have been achieved. Forewarned and forearmed, the British were already erecting obstacles in potential glider landing places. In another reaction to Student's achievement, Churchill had demanded that the British army form its own paratroop arm.

Student was not himself available to discuss these plans. He was in hospital. After the notorious bombing of Rotterdam at a time when the Dutch commandant was negotiating with him (a bombing which he tried to avert), he had continued to discuss surrender terms inside the city. Hearing shots outside the building, he committed the elementary error of looking out of the window, and was immediately shot in the head. Only the expert attention of a Dutch surgeon saved his life. However, he recovered in time to take command of the reorganized airborne troops in January 1941. These, expanded, were now organized as Fliegerkorps XI. This comprised the existing two divisions, the 7th and 22nd, together with a parachute assault regiment, and its own attached air contingent, two wings of Ju52s and a glider wing. Meanwhile, it had been provided with new equipment; the development of a quintuple parachute made it possible to drop quite heavy items, including light artillery guns.

In conversation with Hitler, Student discovered an interest in attacking British power in the Mediterranean, and went away to develop plans for airborne assaults on Crete, Cyprus, Malta and even the Suez Canal. There was no limit to his confidence, it seemed, but Hitler's enthusiasm had also to be developed if sufficient resources were to be granted for these possible operations. His chance came as the battle for Greece approached its victorious conclusion in April 1941. Hitler did not need much persuading, realizing that not only would the capture of Crete be a logical conclusion to the Greek campaign, but that its geographical location was such that whichever side possessed it would hold a great strategic prize.

Having obtained Hitler's sanction, Student went ahead to plan his operation which, apart from its strategic significance, would make military history, being designed to capture an island without the conventionally accepted prerequisite of command of the surrounding sea. Although having no doubts about the ultimate success of his operation, he found that the preparations were not easy. The various units had to be moved from Germany to Greece over an enfeebled rail system. Usable airfields had to be obtained. Above all, scarce supplies of aviation fuel had to be claimed and then delivered to the air bases. And over everything hung an air of urgency. Student himself, obsessed with the importance of surprise, was in a hurry. He also feared that the longer he waited the more firmly would the British and Greek forces entrench themselves in Crete. Moreover, Hitler wanted to wind down this theater of activities in order to concentrate on the imminent invasion of Russia. A successful venture by the parachute regiment, which dropped to capture the bridge over the Corinth Canal by which the British hoped to withdraw their last troops from Greece, had been encouraging for morale but did nothing to ease the preparations for the Crete battle.

Student also feared that this Corinth operation would alert the British to the threat of German paratrooper invasion. As it happened, though, the British were already well aware of this threat. Not only did they remember the Netherlands, but from various intelligence sources they had a good idea of what was being planned.

Although the importance of the British ability to decipher German higher command messages coded by the 'Enigma' machine cannot be doubted, conventional intelligence alone revealed something of the German intentions. The 'Enigma' messages, obtained both from military and railway transport communications, were important because they eventually revealed to the British the date and place of the attack (the preparations on the mainland could equally well have been directed against Malta or Cyprus). They also confirmed British expectations that the main German effort would initially be devoted to the capture of the Crete airstrips. Because German preparations were hurried, and because several delays persuaded German com-

LEFT: German paratroops drop on Crete. The clustered parachutes are for landing equipment canisters.

BELOW: One of the many stricken Ju52 transports littering the Maleme airfield.

LEFT: German paratroops make one of their final drops in the battle for Crete.

RIGHT: Many German paratroop units lost more than half their strength in the descent. This is one of the unlucky parachutists.

manders to avail themselves of ordinary signal communications more than they should have done, British signals intelligence was presented with additional information. In the end, the German plan was known fairly completely to the British, and was supplemented by knowledge of the paratroops' training manual and of the drop patterns used in the Netherlands. Surprise, on which Student counted so much, was utterly compromised. Moreover, he had no reason to know that this advantage had been lost. Nor did he know the strength of the opposition; again because of haste, German air reconnaissance failed to indicate that the island was much better defended than was thought.

On the other hand, everything else was against the British. Although they had more men (about 40,000) in the island than the Germans expected, those men were of very mixed fighting value. Some were Greek, demoralized by their retreat and evacuation from the mainland. The 'British' forces (largely New Zealanders and Australians) were in somewhat better spirits, but in no sense enthusiastic. Moreover, although most of those who had been evacuated from Greece still had small arms, they were lacking in heavy weapons and equipment. The troops who made up the original garrison did have some artillery and light tanks, but the latter were few and no match for anti-tank weapons. Because of the shortage of resources the garrison had been kept small.

Major General Bernard Freyberg, the New Zealander who was appointed local commander at short notice, did his best to prepare the island for defense. Crete is a mountainous island, about 260km (162 miles) from west to east and never more than 65km (40 miles) wide. It had one main road along the north coast, and few others. It is less mountainous in the north, which contained most of the settlements and all the ports. The latter, even the main ports of Suda Bay and Heraklion (Iraklion) could take only small vesels, and not many at one time. The three airfields were also in the north, with Maleme in the west, Retimo (Rethimnon) in the center, and Heraklion toward the east.

The obvious defense strategy of holding a few key points and maintaining a strong reserve to support hard-pressed areas would not have worked in Crete, because that reserve would lack mobility; there were very few motor trucks and the single east-west road could easily be cut by the enemy. Freyberg therefore divided his strength between what he correctly forecast would be the enemy's main objectives, the three airfields. A fourth defensive sector was placed to protect Suda Bay and the nearby capital, Canea (Khania). Likely landing beaches were kept under observation. Having only 68 AA guns, Freyberg decided to keep most of them in the Suda Bay area. He also decided that since artillery was so scarce, consisting of a few light guns, the Retimo sector would have to do without. In the two weeks at his disposal before the onslaught, he received enough small arms to equip those troops who had arrived without any, and he also shipped to Egypt about 7,000 men from unwanted, non-fighting, units.

The main problem for Freyberg was that Crete was virtually beleaguered. To the north, on the mainland, there was a semicircle of airfields at the Germans' disposal, and the island was under daily air attack. The RAF strength was pitifully small, and by 19 May, the eve of the German invasion, had been worn down to just four Hurricanes and three archaic Gladiators. Since these would have been overwhelmed, probably without causing any loss to the enemy, Freyberg agreed that they should be sent

back to Egypt. RAF bombers from Egypt made sporadic attacks on the Greek airfields, but these had little effect. Fighters from Egypt had too short a range to operate effectively over the island, which was 300 miles distant. Lacking command of the air, the British had only a theoretical command of the sea. The Royal Navy could operate at night but, as had already been shown, would suffer heavy losses if caught by German dive-bombers in daylight. This was one reason why British intelli-

gence successes could not be properly exploited. Having belatedly realized that it would be possible to give the Germans an unpleasant surprise, Churchill urged that the Crete defenses should be strengthened, but shipping in supplies and reinforcements could only be done in small amounts and at great risk.

Meanwhile, back at Berlin, Student with his small group of staff officers planned the assault. His first plan involved drops at seven points, saturating the defenders and permitting the island

RIGHT: Maps of the Crete campaign and (lower) the fighting around Maleme and Suda.

LEFT: The cruiser HMS *York* lying on the bottom of Suda Bay after an attack by Italian explosive boats.

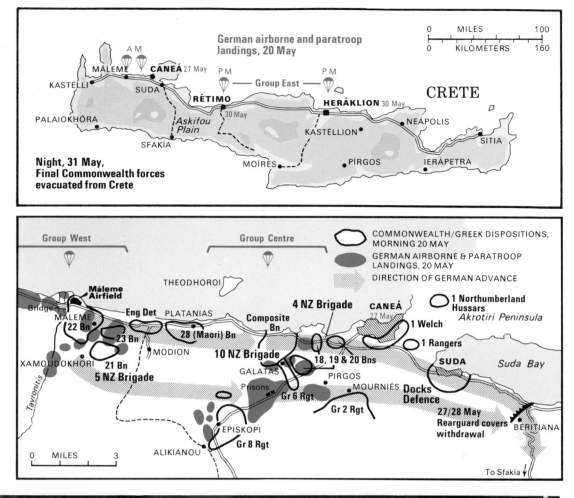

BELOW LEFT: The British destroyer HMS *Kelly,* Louis Mountbatten's flotilla leader, which was sunk by air attack in the Crete campaign.

BELOW: General Archibald Wavell, one of the best British generals of World War II.

ABOVE: In Crete after the German victory; Iron Crosses are distributed.

RIGHT: The German intention of a benign occupation soon fell victim to harsh reality.

to be overrun in a day or so. But the staff of the air corps charged with supporting the airborne troops thought that the attackers' strength should be concentrated in just the western part. In the end it was decided to compromise, with four drops. In the morning of the assault Maleme and Canea, both in the west, would be assaulted. The transport aircraft, expected still to number more than 500, would return to pick up a second wave of troops who would be dropped in the afternoon to take Retimo and Heraklion. The key Maleme and Heraklion airfields would each be captured by a parachute regiment; as soon as they were taken, transport aircraft could land to bring in additional troops. More troops, and heavy equipment, would be taken by sea using small vessels to be commandeered from local Greek ports.

Student's corps, Fliegerkorps XI, was ready in the middle of May. However, it was without its 22nd Division, which was on other duties in Rumania. To compensate for this, the 5th Mountain Division, another elite formation, was put under his command. Student, however, was not granted his request to have operational control of Fliegerkorps VIII, which was responsible for reconnaissance and ground support. Whether this lack of control made a difference became a controversial subject afterwards, because these air support operations were carried out imperfectly, it was said. Air reconnaissance did not reveal that the defenders numbered about five times more than had been estimated. Also, it was fooled by dummy gun installations and failed to pick out many of the genuine guns, so that the regular daily bombings did not, as had been hoped, destroy the British artillery. As for the assumption that the Cretans would

be friendly, this seems to have been pure wishful thinking; in the event the locals proved to be savagely hostile.

The British were well aware that 20 May was the date of the invasion, and were not surprised when the regular dawn air attack proved more intense than usual, lasting about two hours. These attacks raised a great deal of dust, which made navigation difficult both for the paratroop carriers and the gliders. Many sticks of paratroops and some gliders failed to land in the places allotted, but this was not necessarily a disadvantage. Stray unplanned landings made it difficult for the defenders to gauge where the centers of attack actually were. Moreover, since the allotted landing zones were so often precisely where the defenders were waiting for action, those who landed outside the planned zones tended to survive better.

At Maleme the invaders landed among the New Zealanders and suffered heavy casualties. Many parachutists were shot in the air, and others as they hurried to their weapon containers. However, the defenders also took heavy losses and made some withdrawals in the evening, being unaware of how badly their opponents had suffered. Defending officers in the next couple of days often made withdrawals in circumstances that were later found to be not as bad as believed. A major handicap was bad communications, which progressively became non-existent.

Absence of radios and consequent reliance on the telephone system led to defending units being completely cut off from information held by other units or by HQ, for it was not long before the telephone wires were cut.

The second morning attack was directed against Canea, the Germans landing in nearby Prison Valley and Galatas. Here German losses were especially heavy, and many experienced officers were hit. Some companies finished the day under the command of their medical officers (who proved just as steadfast and competent as their stricken predecessors). Again, many landings were made in the defenders' own zones, and the New Zealanders picked off many parachutists as they descended. Although one company of the assault battallion captured and held a key highpoint, the battalion was virtually wiped out; one company parachuted into a reservoir and was drowned.

Student and his staff, who had transferred from Berlin to Athens in time for the operation, waited tense hours for news.

Even the traditional expedient of listening to enemy radio transmissions to find out how the battle was progressing failed in this operation, simply because the British troops had virtually no radios. Waiting to despatch the second wave, but anxious to receive news before he did so, Student ordered a Ju52 to land at Maleme and find out how the battle was progressing. The pilot discovered the hard way that the airfield was still in British hands, but managed to take off again with only a few bullet holes in his aircraft.

Receiving this news, Student decided to make the first move of the afternoon attack. This consisted of the preliminary bombing, but for several reasons, including the resultant dust cloud, the troops were dropped some time after the bombing ceased, enabling the defenders to re-establish themselves in the meantime. At Retimo the events of the morning repeated themselves. There were heavy losses and at nightfall the attackers had established themselves in only part of the airfield.

At Heraklion the schedules were even more disorganized. Many of the transport aircraft took off hours late, because of refueling delays and because telephone communications between Student's HQ and the airfields were interrupted. The troops landed piecemeal, and were shot up piecemeal. Several transports were shot down before unloading their paratroopers.

By nightfall Student was receiving radio messages from his men. They were all reporting only limited success and they were all asking for help. Facing total failure, he decided to take the only course which might possibly bring success. Everything depended on capturing a usable airfield, so he decided to concentrate all further effort on gaining Maleme, hoping that once captured its primitive airstrip would accept a flow of Ju52s with fresh troops and supplies. Luckily the confused situation at Heraklion had prevented all the Ju52s dropping their parachutists. They had returned to base and now represented a valuable reserve that could be thrown into the battle for Maleme.

However, these paratroops when dropped on the morning of 21 May were no luckier than their predecessors, and suffered heavy losses. By afternoon the situation at Maleme was that the defenders had been slowly driven from the airfield, but were fighting hard and were still within gunfire range. In a last desperate bid, Ju52 pilots carrying part of the 5th Mountain Division were ordered to land on the airstrip and disgorge their troops regardless of risk. This they did, at great cost. Some aircraft landed unscathed but others were hit by shells. By nightfall the airfield was littered with the ruins of Ju52s, and also with corpses of mountain troops. However, enough of the latter had survived to make the airfield safe. This capture of an usable airfield made a German victory inevitable. A counterattack by Australians and New Zealanders that night failed.

In retrospect, the British loss of Maleme was judged to be unnecessary. One of the several withdrawals was not justified, the defending officer being unaware that the attackers were themselves in great difficulty. If the airfield had been held for a few more hours, the disaster that was about to befall Student's operation might well have forced him to give up his attempt to capture the island.

This disaster was at sea. Thanks to signals intelligence, the British became aware of the two convoys of motor fishing vessels that the Germans planned to despatch with reinforcements to the island. This knowledge made it worthwhile to risk sending a scarce reconnaissance aircraft to take a look. This spotted the first convoy, and that night the Royal Navy intercepted and sank it, drowning hundreds of mountain troops. The second convoy escaped more lightly, but was forced back into port. Student was thereby deprived of his seaborne reinforcement, and was additionally burdened with the knowledge that hundreds of elite troops had been lost for no gain whatever. For him, it was small comfort to know that the British squadron was overtaken by dive-bombers in the morning and lost two cruisers.

These naval losses meant that reinforcement of the British forces in Crete became even more unlikely. Some slight air support was given from Egypt, but it was only a question of time

BELOW LEFT: A German paratrooper in battle kit.

RIGHT: German paratroopers, one wounded, on Crete in 1941.

LEFT: The wreck of an RAF aircraft on a Greek airfield, 1941.

before the Germans with their powerful air support captured the entire island. British resistance continued, taking the form of scattered fighting retreats. The defending units' performance was variable. Given that these were ordinary troops faced with elite and better-equipped German units, they did quite well. There were some premature surrenders, and the Greek units were apt to surrender at the drop of a paratrooper. On the other hand there were some very heroic last stands. In the end, most of the defending troops were evacuated, and Crete was finally in Student's hands on 1 June.

It was a victory, of sorts. Hitler congratulated Student both on the capture and on the fighting qualities of the men. But the cost had been heavy, both in lives and aircraft: of about 22,000 invading troops, 6000 became casualties, and 220 aircraft had been lost. Hitler was not prepared to repeat the experiment. Student found that, although resources were still made available, his 7th Division, shattered on Crete, was never to be reconstituted. Instead, in future campaigns the airborne forces were given limited roles. Some of these were spectacular and vital, like the 1943 drop which helped to secure Rome for the Germans when Italy surrendered, or the rescue of Mussolini from his mountain prison soon after, but Student's concept of airborne troops as a fundamental war-winning technique had been rejected. For him at least, Crete had been a pyrrhic victory.

CHAPTER FIVE

YAMAMOTO
AND PEARL HARBOR

'THE FATE of the Empire rests on this undertaking,' was Admiral Yamamoto's signal to the task force about to descend on the unsuspecting US Pacific Fleet at Pearl Harbor. Unlike many other such signals, it was literally true, for the Pearl Harbor venture really was a decision that settled once and for all the controversy about whether Japan's development should proceed in cooperation with other world powers, or whether it should use its military prowess to dominate the East.

The 1905 victory over Russia had inflamed many imaginations. If Japan could beat an enormous power like Russia, it was said, she could beat anybody so long as the gods smiled on her. For a time, more level-headed views prevailed. Japan joined the allied cause in World War I but took little part in it, and the militant faction claimed that her share of the spoils (mandates over certain ex-German Pacific islands) was insultingly small.

In the interwar years Japan's population rose fast, but her economic growth depended on imports of raw materials. Exports to pay for these imports were limited by written and unwritten trade barriers placed by Britain and other industrial nations. The USA was alarmed by increasing Japanese influence in China. Naval treaties fixed Japan's navy at a size six-tenths those of Britain and the USA. The Japanese militants had little difficulty, quoting these facts, in producing convincing arguments that Japan's rightful and glorious place in the world was being denied it by the western powers. Increasing numbers of Japanese were drawn to the concept of an expansion based on two ancient traditions, *bushido* (the way of the warrior, of ruthlessness, toughness, and will to win), and *hakko ichiu* (bringing the world under one roof). Pearl Harbor marked the end of a long and often savage debate and Yamamoto Isoroku participated in all of it, from a junior role in the 1905 Battle of Tsushima to an initiating role in the December 1941 attack.

Because of this role in the Pearl Harbor attack, and because in Japan the militarized regime imposed a peacetime censorship that amounted to a complete news blackout, Yamamoto was completely misunderstood in the West. In Japan, his life had been in danger after the mid-1930s with the pro-war elements regarding him as not only anti-war but also pro-British and pro-American. Pearl Harbor, and the crudities of wartime propaganda, meant that he was regarded, especially in the USA, as treacherous, war-mongering and anti-American. In fact, the attack on Pearl Harbor was his gamble, the only way he knew to avoid disaster in a war he had always opposed.

Somewhat of a buccaneer in his private life, Yamamoto loved the navy almost as much as he loved games of chance, women, and good food. But, unlike some officers, he did not regard the navy as a weapon to be used against Britain or America. He had been to both countries, respected them, and realized that Japan was economically too weak to make war against either of them. But in Japan the lower and middle ranks of the army officer corps, by intrigue and assassination, slowly took control of political life and sought expansion by military means. Yamamoto once said that seeing an army officer's face was enough to make him want to vomit, and most naval officers despised, while sometimes fearing, the army. On the other hand the navy was split between those who wanted a big navy, big enough to fight the USA if need be, and those like Yamamoto who thought Japan would benefit by staying within the limits proposed by the Washington and London naval agreements.

Most contemporaries found Yamamoto rather taciturn, but agreed that there was something special about him, an obvious intelligence combined with a childlike curiosity and wish to examine things for himself. He had a keen interest in the supernatural, but was not easily hoaxed. He wrote poetry, of a sort, and his calligraphy was much admired. He was an avid gambler, and because of his keen intelligence and powerful intuition, regularly won large sums from his colleagues. His tactic was to attack right from the start, even when his hand was weak, and this usually threw his opponents off balance.

Although Yamamoto was of samurai ancestry his childhood had been poverty-stricken. He was adopted by a wealthy patron, whose name, Yamamoto, he took. Before that, he had entered the naval academy. A gunnery specialist, he lost two fingers in the Russo-Japanese war when a gun exploded during the Battle of Tsushima.

Like many other young officers, he was sent to America to improve his English and to see how things were done in the outside world. He spent two years at Harvard, attending courses that interested him. In 1923, after a spell as a naval instructor, he made another foreign tour, visiting the USA and Europe, and on his return was posted to a naval aviation corps, of which he soon became second-in-command. He took flying lessons and became an advocate of naval air power, a conversion which in due course brought him into conflict with the 'battleship interest.' In 1928, after two years spent as naval attaché in Washington, he took command of the aircraft carrier *Akagi*, but in 1930 he

LEFT: Admiral Yamamoto studies a chart during a planning meeting.

RIGHT: Admiral Nagano Osami, a senior member of the Imperial Japanese Navy's planning staff.

was in London as an assistant at the Naval Disarmament Conference, and on his return he spent three years heading the technical section of the naval air department. By now a rear admiral, he did his best to encourage a Japanese school of aircraft design, that would no longer need to imitate foreign planes. He also specified the navy's requirement for a long-range attack aircraft that would enable Japan to attack a hostile fleet hundreds of miles from its shores.

In 1933 he was back aboard *Akagi*, but this time as commander of the 1st Aircraft Carrier Division. In late 1934 he was again in London, heading the Japanese delegation preparing for the second London Naval Disarmament Conference. The Japanese government, unlike Yamamoto, wanted the right to have a fleet as strong as Britain's or America's, rather than the six-tenths level accepted at previous conferences. The Conference could reach no agreement, and the western press blamed Yamamoto.

Henceforth, Japan would build up to the limit of its resources, and the Japanese navy was immediately convulsed by an intense but secret argument about whether to build two battleships, *Yamato* and *Masashi*, that would be almost double the size of any battleships then being planned by Britain and the USA. Yamamoto, believing that the future of the Japanese navy lay with aircraft carriers, opposed this proposal strongly, but the new ships were begun in 1936. By then, the army, following its murder of leading government figures, was well on the way to dominance.

After a period as head of naval aviation, Yamamoto in late 1936 became vice-minister of the navy, a non-political post under the minister, who was invariably an admiral. For over two years he opposed the aggressive militarism advocated by the increasingly powerful army. In 1937 the army engineered what it soon called the 'China Incident,' an excuse for attacking China in a steadily extending war. Yamamoto joined with like-minded naval officers to discuss the situation, but no inkling of the navy's dissidence was revealed to the public.

From 1938 the navy ministry was preoccupied with thwarting the army's intention to bring Japan into a tripartite pact with Germany and Italy. It realized that this would be interpreted as a hostile act by Britain, France and the USA, countries that it had no wish to fight. Possibly this opposition helped the government to resist the army's demand, but it was Hitler's decision to sign a pact with Russia in 1939 that finally caused the signature to be postponed. By then Yamamoto was receiving death threats almost daily, and it may have been in order to save him from assassination that he was appointed Commander in Chief of the Combined Fleet. The world's third largest navy was now at his command.

His appointment coincided with the outbreak of World War II in Europe, and in the two years before Japan entered the conflict Yamamoto carried out a gruelling training program. Although the navy was not as severe as the army, men were driven to the limits of their endurance, and fatal accidents were accepted as a necessary evil. As much as possible of the training was carried out at anchor because the specter of an oil shortage seemed likely to become a reality. Yamamoto had himself been obsessed by the oil question, and in the 1920s had studied the Texan and Mexican oil industries on the spot. Japan had invested considerable effort in stockpiling oil, and it was reckoned that the navy had a 30-month supply on shore, but current consumption had to be limited if only for reasons of foreign exchange.

In summer 1940 a new government finally signed an alliance with Germany. Germany was then at the height of its military success and reports from the Japanese naval attaché in London, to the effect that the British were far from beaten, were brushed aside. Yamamoto, however, was probably expressing the view of most senior naval officers when he wrote that Japan should at all costs avoid a conflict with the USA, because such a war would leave the two nations exhausted and then either Germany or Russia would dominate the world. He regarded the alliance with Germany as a long step closer to war with America. However, when he was officially asked his views on the Tripartite Pact, after the navy minister had given it his blessing, he asked simply how the Japanese forces, that derived four fifths of their materials from America and the British Empire, would cope if these supplies were cut off as a result of joining the Pact. He received no reply, probably because in the political circumstances of that time no thought had been given to this rather essential question. Awkward questions were usually rejected by references to the will of the gods.

Soon afterward Yamamoto was called to the prime minister and asked how the navy would fare in a war against America. He said he could make things very difficult for the Americans in the first six months but had absolutely no confidence in winning a war that lasted more than two years. He urged the prime minister to avoid war with the USA, but saw that such a war was almost inevitable. He returned to his flagship, the battleship *Nagato*, realizing that although he did not like what was happening he had to do the best he could for the navy and the country. It was now that his thoughts began to turn to a surprise attack on the US Pacific Fleet at its base in Hawaii.

Both his own staff officers and the Naval General Staff were against this idea. Operational plans were composed each year for possible hostilities against China, the USSR, or the USA. For tackling a threat from America the staffs composed highly detailed plans that, as the years passed, tended to become unrealistic. Essentially, the Japanese plan was to repeat the success of the last war but one. In that war, the Russian fleet had been lured from Europe to fight far from its bases, and was annihilated at Tsushima. The plan for war against America visualized a naval attack against the Philippines that would force the US Navy to counterattack. As the Americans steamed westward, they would be attacked by aircraft from the Japanese-held Pacific islands so that when they eventually made contact with the Japanese fleet they would be denuded, worn out, and an easy prey for annihilation, at which point the war would end.

Yamamoto realized that this plan was based on wishful thinking. Quite apart from the fact that the air bases on the islands were far from ready, there was the assumption that the Americans would react in just the way the Japanese wanted. At one planning conference, an officer who suggested that the American fleet might head straight for Japan, and not the Philippines, was reprimanded for making difficulties.

Yamamoto's wish for a preemptive strike had its antecedents in the Russo-Japanese War too, because Japan had begun that war with a surprise torpedo attack on the Russian squadron at Port Arthur before any declaration of war. But his reasoning was more complex than that. He did not want war, but he wanted even less to lose a war. He realized that Japan could only survive if the war was short, and he hoped that the USA, after taking some hard blows, would be willing to negotiate a peace satisfactory to Japan. Here, too, there was an element of wishful thinking, of which he was probably aware. His conduct in the war would often be inconsistent, and this was probably because he was unable to resolve his inner conflict, his professional need to defeat the Americans and his deeper, political, insight that Japan could not and should not be at war with the USA. He

must have realized that to repeat Port Arthur would so antagonize the Americans that they would not want a negotiated peace, in which case Japan would have to follow Pearl Harbor with further heavy blows aimed at actually driving the USA out of the war. Like other staff officers, he was also beginning to dread the possibility of war not against one power but against three, the USA, Britain and China. During 1941 the possibility arose of war actually against five, with the USSR and Holland involved. And so, while developing his plans against Pearl Harbor, he did what he could to put backbone into the navy ministry, which thought like him but could not find the strength to oppose the militants.

In 1940, during fleet exercises, he was very impressed by the way carrier aircraft located the opposing battleships and pressed home their attack. He must also have been impressed by the British victory at Taranto. If less than two dozen torpedo aircraft from one carrier could inflict so much damage on a navy at war, the effect of six carriers launching hundreds of aircraft against a navy at peace could only be devastating. The main problem would be getting the aircraft carriers close to distant Hawaii without being spotted, and ensuring that their attack would find the US Pacific Fleet in harbor.

The first circulation of a written proposal by Yamamoto appears to have been in November 1940, with a limited number of staff officers being invited to comment. A first draft plan was worked out by the staff of one of the aircraft carrier divisions, and proposed that both the navy's carrier divisions should take part. This draft was then submitted to the Naval General Staff, but at the same time Yamamoto's own staff was developing its plan. His senior staff officer, Captain Kuroshima, a glutton for work and for fine detail, wrote most of it. One of the many eccentrics in the Japanese navy, Kuroshima was a man who preferred to work stark naked in the darkness of his cabin, cured by a dense atmosphere of incense and cigarette smoke. He disappeared for days, and when his plan was presented it not only encompassed the raid on Pearl Harbor, but the other fronts as well.

In July 1941 Japanese troops entered French Indo China, the weak Vichy French government having been more or less forced to agree. Just as opponents of the move had predicted, this inflamed American antagonism. President Roosevelt froze Japanese assets and embargoed the export of a wide range of commodities to Japan. Chief among these was oil, difficult to obtain elsewhere, and militant proponents of a Japanese economic zone in the Pacific could claim that only a swift capture of the oilfields of the Dutch East Indies would now save Japan from strangulation.

The navy, above all, was dependent on oil, and this new situation caused many officers to accept the inevitability of war. As for Yamamoto, he continued with his fleet training. This time, activity was concentrated around Kagoshima, whose harbor and topography was quite similar to that of Pearl Harbor. His crews were not told why, and those pilots strongly attracted by the *bushido* ideal resented the requirement to practice against easy

JAPANESE EMPIRE, 1933
OCCUPIED BY JAPAN, JULY 1937/DECEMBER 1941
MILITARY BASES ESTABLISHED BY JAPAN, SEPTEMBER 1940
ABDA (American, British, Dutch, and Australian) COMMAND
MERCATOR'S PROJECTION

targets like battleships at anchor. Most officers who knew what was being planned remained against the idea. They included officers of the Naval General Staff as well as the chiefs of staff of the carrier divisions. Some of them submitted a written request that the Pearl Harbor venture be abandoned but gradually, with a combination of charm and keen argument, Yamamoto brought a majority around to his point of view. In October 1941

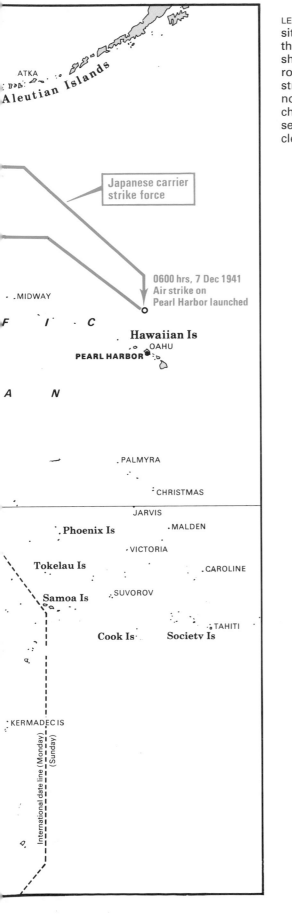

LEFT; The strategic situation at the start of the Pacific war, showing also the route of the Japanese strike force. The northerly routing, chosen mainly for security reasons, is clearly shown.

the Naval General Staff formally approved the operation, and at the beginning of November the Chief of the Naval General Staff, in the name of the Emperor, informed Yamamoto that Japan intended to go to war against the USA, Britain and Holland in the first ten days of December.

Yamamoto immediately distributed to his units the thick document embodying the secret operational order. On 18 November the ships of the striking force slipped, separately, from their respective harbors and made for Hitokappu Bay, in the Kuriles far to the north. Yamamoto, to avoid detection, had decided to route the force well north of the shipping lanes. To ensure radio silence in a situation when the shortest, weakest transmission might reveal the position of the fleet, all transmitters were sealed. The commander of the force, Admiral Nagumo, could receive signals, but not send them.

Nagumo flew his flag in *Akagi* and there were five other aircraft carriers. In effect, all Japan's first-line aircraft carriers were engaged for this operation and Nagumo disposed of more than 400 aircraft. Evidently the use of naval aviation in the Pacific war was going to be on a massive scale compared to that of Britain's Mediterranean theater.

8 December (Tokyo time) had been chosen for the attack, because in Hawaii (where it would be 7 December) that would be a Sunday, a day when the US Pacific Fleet was habitually in port. Espionage at Pearl Harbor was well-developed, a former naval officer masquerading as a Filipino sending in especially well-informed news. Nagumo's fleet set sail on 26 November, presenting a front of almost 50 miles. In the Naval General Staff it was believed that chances of approaching unobserved were about even. Yamamoto, in port with his flagship, expected to lose half his ships if surprise was not achieved.

On 6 December, Hawaii time, after an eastward passage in cold, stormy and foggy seas, the strike force was descending southward and took fuel from its remaining supply tankers, which were then released to the west. A message relayed from Tokyo informed Nagumo that eight battleships were anchored in Pearl Harbor, but the aircraft carriers had gone. This disappearance of the aircraft carriers was a setback, but in all other respects luck favored the Japanese, and they reached their launching position unobserved. Nagumo hoisted the signal that Admiral Togo had used at Tsushima, and for which Togo had drawn inspiration from Admiral Nelson 'The Empire's fate depends on this battle. Let every man do his utmost duty.'

In Washington the US government, which for long had been able to read the Japanese diplomatic code, knew that war was imminent, and on 6 December knew that the Japanese ambassador had been instructed to hand over a declaration of war on 7 December. Earlier, US military and naval units had been instructed to remain on the alert, but a later warning stating that war was imminent does not appear to have been sent to Hawaii. An attack on this island, so distant from Japan, does not appear to have been considered as a possibility. President Roosevelt knew that some attack was imminent, and indeed wished for such an attack. He saw that war was necessary but wanted Japan to be the clear aggressor, and to strike hard enough to persuade the majority of Americans that war could no longer be refused. It seems unlikely, however, that Roosevelt knew about Pearl Harbor and let it happen, as was alleged after the war. The failure to send the final urgent warning to Pearl Harbor was most likely simple negligence. That the USA had received several reports of an impending attack on Pearl Harbor, including one from its ambassador in Tokyo just as the operation entered its planning stage, has to be set against the fact that warnings of attacks against many other conceivable and incon-

ceivable points were also coming in. Moreover, an essential element of the Japanese war plan was a simultaneous attack toward the East Indies, beginning with an invasion of Malaya. Preparations for this attack, and notably the putting to sea of troop transports from Indo China, were obvious and served to convince British and American staffs that the initial attack would come in that area. Finally, US signals intelligence had been misled into reporting that the Japanese aircraft carriers were in home waters at the beginning of December.

The Japanese operational plan for the attack specified launching the aircraft when the fleet was within 200 miles of Pearl Harbor. A reconnaissance flight by a seaplane launched from a cruiser was to precede the main attack, and would report local conditions. The attack was to be in two waves. The first would be of 189 aircraft (in fact six of these failed to take off) and the second of 170. At the last moment, after the seaplane's data had been digested, a choice would be made between a surprise attack, in which the torpedo aircraft would attack first in ideal conditions, or an orthodox attack against an alert enemy, in which dive-bombers would attack first to put fighter airfields and anti-aircraft guns out of action. The leader of the first wave would signal his choice of attack by firing a Very flare pistol once for a surprise attack, or twice for an orthodox assault. This arrangement is symptomatic of much that was wrong with the Japanese armed forces in 1941; along with carefully detailed planning and rigorous training, wishful thinking led to tolerance of unreliable techniques.

A vital element of the plan was timing. The raid was not to start before 03.30 Tokyo time, half an hour after the declaration of war was to be delivered in Washington. This was to avoid accusations of attacking before a declaration of war, but in the event the declaration was presented almost an hour after the first bomb dropped. There were two reasons for this. The Japanese embassy staff in Washington was charged with translating the declaration but, because it was a Sunday, it had no typists on hand and the translated document had to be typed out by diplomats using the two-finger method. Secondly, the attacking aircraft confused their signals and went in a few minutes too early.

The six aircraft carriers turned into the wind at 01.30 Tokyo time and the aircraft were away within fifteen minutes. On the way in, the radio operator of the command plane, which had a distinctive red and yellow tail and led the attacking wave, received a signal from the reconnaissance seaplane to the effect that the Americans were showing no signs of activity and that there was cloud cover at 5500 feet above the harbor. The commander thereupon fired one shot from his Very pistol, signifying that the surprise attack sequence would be followed. But the commander of the fighter force, which had great difficulty in maintaining formation at the slow (150 mph) approach speed, missed the signal and drifted away from the other aircraft. The leader thereupon fired one shot again from his pistol. This was seen by the fighters, but the dive-bombers decided that this was the second shot signifying an orthodox attack. As a result, control was lost and while the dive-bombers went in to bomb the airfields the torpedo and conventional bomber aircraft adhered to the surprise attack plan. The torpedo pilots, unwilling that the dive-bombers and not themselves should lead the attack, decided to go in immediately, five minutes ahead of schedule.

But in the conditions of absolute surprise, and with the sitting targets that the attackers encountered, this chaotic beginning was no great disadvantage. While the dive-bombers dealt with the airfields, the 40 torpedo bombers swooped low and released their torpedoes at the US battleships, anchored in a line close to the shore. These ships lay in pairs, moored side by side, and those closest to the coast were thereby sheltered. The exposed battleships suffered severely from torpedoes, while bombs later

ABOVE LEFT: The crew of a Japanese aircraft carrier cheer a departing 'Kate' torpedo bomber.

ABOVE: One of the most modern Japanese aircraft carriers, the *Shokaku*, which was completed only in 1941.

RIGHT: USS *Pennsylvania*, one of the US battleships damaged at Pearl Harbor but returned to service in time to take part in other, more victorious, engagements.

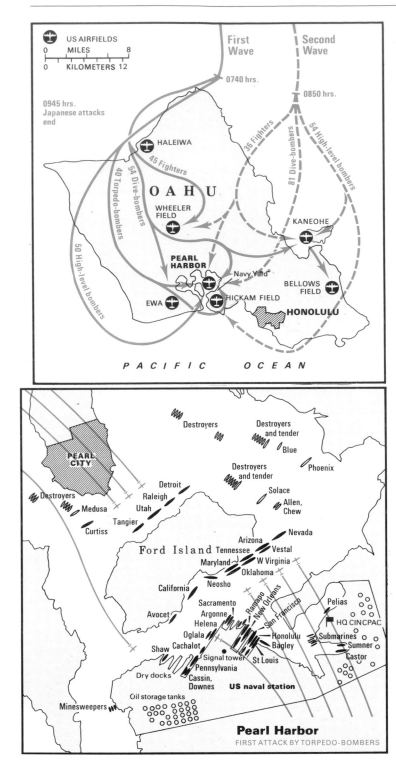

damaged the others. An hour after the first wave, the second wave of aircraft was sent in; this did not include torpedo planes but was preponderantly dive-bombers (81 units) and high-level bombers (54).

The final result represented a crushing defeat of the US battlefleet. Of the battleships, the *California, Nevada, Oklahoma, West Virginia,* and *Arizona* were sunk (although the first four were subsequently salvaged), and three others heavily damaged. Smaller ships also suffered, but did not bear the brunt of the attack. Nearly 200 US aircraft were also destroyed against a loss of 29 Japanese aircraft. Despite some pressure from his staff, Nagumo decided against another assault. Yamamoto did not dissent, and as a result repair facilities and fuel oil stocks, which were vital to the subsequent renaissance of the US Pacific Fleet, were virtually untouched. Japanese reluctance, born of the *bushido* tradition, to attack unexciting, undefended, targets, was probably a factor in this mistaken decision. Far more

ABOVE LEFT: Maps of the Japanese air strikes against Pearl Harbor.

ABOVE: Japanese naval aircrew later in the war. The photo shows 'kamikaze' pilots about to set off on their one-way trips.

ABOVE RIGHT: Japanese fighters about to leave their carrier for the Pearl Harbor strike.

RIGHT: The old destroyer USS *Ward,* which in sinking a Japanese midget submarine at the entrance to Pearl Harbor fired the first shot by US forces in the Pacific war.

ABOVE: The debris of war comes to the Pacific.

LEFT: Hickam Field, the US airbase, after the attack.

UPPER RIGHT: The end of the battleship USS *Arizona*, damaged beyond repair, and of over 1100 of her crew.

RIGHT: Defenders of Hickam Field, at the ready after the attack, but the low standard of the defenses remains obvious.

serious, however, was the failure to hit the two US aircraft carriers. Both of them, *Lexington* and *Enterprise,* together with most of the Pacific Fleet's cruisers, had been delivering aircraft to Midway and Wake islands.

Yamamoto, long aware that the aircraft carrier had replaced the battleship as the key element in naval warfare, felt acutely that the failure to destroy the US carriers would have grave consequences. But in the meantime he had become a national hero. Quite apart from the victory at Pearl Harbor, he was credited with the destruction of the British *Prince of Wales* and *Repulse* off Malaya that occurred three days after Pearl Harbor. Certainly this second victory was a fruit of his past labors. The 61 naval long-range torpedo aircraft that achieved it were of a design he had sponsored, and their crews had been trained under his guidance and according to his tactical principles.

But he was well aware that his victories were incomplete, and that so long as the US Pacific Fleet retained its aircraft carriers the USA would certainly not consider a negotiated peace. On the other hand, he must also have realized that so long as the Japanese forces continued their victorious progress the Japanese government would not consider a negotiated peace either. From the point of view of world history, whatever he did would be wrong, and this inescapable contradiction rather than his gambler's instincts may explain his inconsistent and listless attitude toward his responsibilities throughout the remainder of his life.

Early in 1942 he shifted his flag to the new giant battleship *Yamato,* whose construction he had so fiercely and vainly opposed six years earlier. His staff were engaged in planning the next stage of the war. Whereas the Naval General Staff was recommending that the main effort should be directed at cutting Australia off from the USA, Yamamoto's staff recommended carrying the war into the Indian Ocean, landing at Ceylon and eventually joining up with Germans coming south from the Cau-

ABOVE: The battleship USS *Nevada* struggles for survival at Pearl Harbor. After heavy repair, she was returned to service.

LEFT: Two wrecked US destroyers, USS *Downes* and USS *Cassin.* Behind them in the drydock is the damaged battleship *Pennsylvania*.

ABOVE RIGHT: A close-up of the forward 5-inch gun turrets of the destroyer USS *Downes,* damaged beyond repair.

RIGHT: Newspapers printed special editions on December 7. This picture was taken in California on that day.

casus. But the army was opposed to this, preferring an advance against Russia from Manchuria. This opposition caused Yamamoto and his staff to study a second alternative, another advance into the Central Pacific with the aim of luring out the remains of the US fleet, and especially its aircraft carriers.

The new plan, which envisaged an attack on US-held Midway Island as a bait to draw the US fleet, was vehemently opposed by the Naval General Staff, and some of Yamamoto's staff officers were also against it. Midway was two thousand miles away, and no fleet likes to fight far from its bases. The idea of capturing Midway and using it as a forward air base was also criticized on the grounds that it would be hard to keep supplied. However, Yamamoto insisted on his plan, and his standing was now so powerful that the Naval General Staff decided to let him do as he wanted. The attack in mid-April on Japanese cities by bombers flying from US aircraft carriers was militarily ineffective, but psychologically had an enormous effect on both the Japanese planners and the population as a whole. After this attack, Yamamoto's plan to destroy the US carriers off Midway seemed more appetizing.

But nonetheless it could only be described as a gamble. Also, it was to be carried out by a fleet that, although gloriously victorious, had had little rest for the previous six months. Tiredness and over-confidence resulted in several oversights and acts of carelessness, the most important of which was laxity in the use of radio communications. The Americans had already had some success in decoding Japanese naval signals, and by mid-May the US Pacific Fleet's staff knew that something was planned in the Midway area.

Yamamoto's plan was to stage a real but diversionary attack on the Aleutian Islands while sending his main forces to Midway

LEFT: Bombs falling around the US battleships.

BELOW RIGHT: A Japanese ocean-going submarine. This particular unit later sank the aircraft carrier USS *Yorktown*.

Island. Here on 7 June, after two days of air attack, he would land troops to capture the island and this would lure out the US fleet stationed at Pearl Harbor. With the advantage of surprise and preponderant numbers, the Japanese carriers would then destroy the US ships. But right from the beginning things went badly. The incoming aircraft were spotted by a US reconnaissance aircraft and were met by US fighters. The airfield that was bombed held no aircraft, because they had been removed in time. A second attack was therefore necessary, so the aircraft waiting on the Japanese decks, armed with torpedoes for attacking the US fleet as soon as it was sighted, were taken below for rearming with bombs. Then a Japanese reconnaisance aircraft reported sighting US ships, and the aircraft had again to be taken below for torpedoes to replace the bombs. Just as they were about to fly off, attack aircraft from the US carriers appeared, and in the resultant carnage three of Nagumo's four carriers were set ablaze by dive-bombers. The fourth carrier, too, was soon hit.

Yamamoto, suffering from worms, had looked ill for some days, and to all appearances he received the news calmly. He ordered his *Yamato* and its consorts to steam to the aid of

Nagumo, but next day he abandoned the operation. He had lost four aircraft carriers and a cruiser, while the Americans had lost only one aircraft carrier, *Yorktown*, that had fallen victim to a final sortie from the last surviving Japanese carrier. With this battle, the Japanese aircraft carrier fleet had been more than halved, especially as so many experienced aircrew had been lost.

Yamamoto took full responsibility for the defeat and, although he sometimes longed for retirement, was kept on as Commander of the Combined Fleet. Ironically, he was now stronger in battleships than the Americans, but considerably weaker in what he had always considered to be the decisive arm, aircraft carriers. His public reputation was still high (not least because Midway was portrayed to the Japanese public as a great victory). The headquarters of the Combined Fleet was soon shifted to the southern Pacific, and his flagship was based at Truk. He insisted, however, on visiting bases in the front line and it was on one of these visits (undertaken, characteristically enough, against the advice of his staff) that his aircraft was set upon by US fighters and he was killed. In fact he had been ambushed, because careless radio signals had informed the US command of his precise route and timings.

CHAPTER SIX

YAMASHITA
AND THE FALL OF SINGAPORE

THE JAPANESE invasion of Manchuria in 1931 had alerted London to the possibility of further aggression, and in the following year the British began to strengthen the defenses of the island of Singapore, their major naval base in the far East. But it was some years before it was realized that the safety of Singapore depended on the security of the Malayan Peninsula, of which it was the southern appendage. In 1937 the army officer commanding in Malaya reported, very perceptively as it turned out, that a future Japanese invasion would probably take place between October and March (when the monsoon would hamper British air reconnaissance), and that there were three likely landing places. Two of these were at Singora and Patani, in south-eastern Thailand just north of the frontier with Malaya, and the third was Kota Bharu, just south of the frontier. It was clear, therefore, that northern Malaya needed to be strengthened.

But before an unwilling government could be persuaded to meet this need, Britain was at war with Germany, and resources became scarce. The local commanders in Malaya thereupon submitted to London their opinion that the Royal Air Force would be the main means of defending Malaya, given that a sizable army and navy were unlikely to be sent there. It would be aircraft that would locate and destroy enemy landing forces, leaving the army the job of mopping up any Japanese troops that happened to find their way ashore. However, although it was an air marshal who was appointed as British Commander in Chief, Far East, not many aircraft were allocated to Malaya and the chiefs of staff in London decided to strengthen the army there, sending a second infantry division.

Lieutenant General A E Percival, who commanded the army in Malaya, reported that six divisions, together with tank, anti-tank and anti-aircraft units, were needed, as well as four bomber and two fighter squadrons. He based this appreciation on his belief (well-founded, because Percival was a fine staff officer, even if he had shortcomings as a commander) that the Japanese would only use three divisions for an invasion, given the difficulty of supplying troops over so great a distance from their home bases.

The local British commanders were handicapped by their inability to take things into their own hands, even if they had

LEFT: General Tomoyuki Yamashita (1885-1946), the 'Tiger of Malaya.'

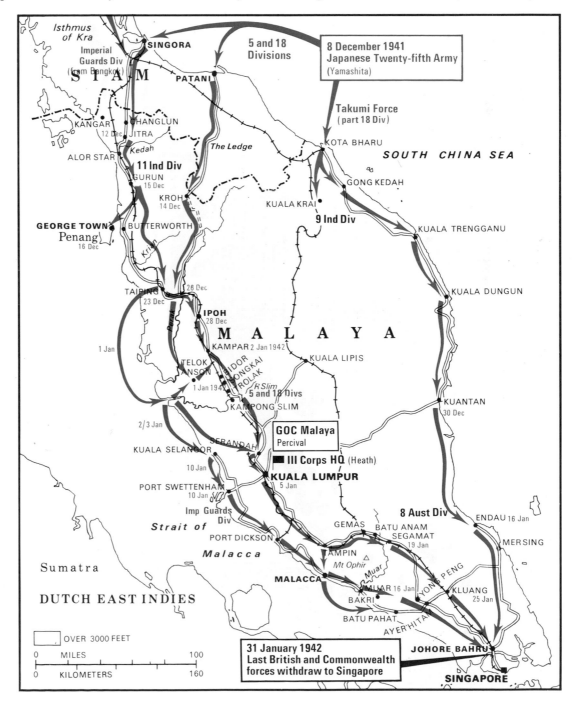

RIGHT: The invasion of Malaya and the fall of Singapore.

wished. Only the smallest sums could be spent on new defense works without London's permission, and such permission took months to obtain. Moreover, any defense works to provide fall-back positions would be bitterly resisted by the local British civilians, who demanded that any enemy should be held at the frontiers. The civilian administration, from the governor and top civil servants downward, was reluctant to cooperate with the military whenever the disturbance of peacetime routines might result, and this attitude would even persist when Singapore was under fire. In London the defense ministries and the colonial office repeatedly interfered without knowing the true situation. Churchill, in his wishful thinking and his belief that Singapore was a formidable fortress, was no worse and probably better than most British politicians, but was not really qualified to give directions.

The British Commonwealth troops had no experience of jungle training, and were not given any. In fact, the power of the rubber planters was so great that it was hard to find suitable training areas, because the entry of troops into plantations was not welcomed.

In 1941 the local commanders were well aware that any Japanese invaders would probably land first in southern Thailand, where they could establish air and supply bases. A plan, 'Matador,' was in fact worked out for just such an eventuality, but dithering, first by London and then by the local Commander in Chief, meant that the plan was never put into effect. Even when the Japanese troop transports had been sighted it was considered unwise to do anything that might be regarded as provocative.

In London, up to a few weeks before war started, it was believed that Japan would not attack in a southward direction. It was thought that her objective for further expansion would be Russia, and she was unlikely to start that kind of campaign before the Germans captured Moscow. But the faction of the Japanese command that favored an attack on Russia had lost its impetus during the summer of 1941 and plans had already been made for the southward thrust.

This thrust, ultimately, would spell the end of the British Empire in the Far East, and although superficially the British failure resulted from lack of power, the Empire ended not because it lacked strength, but because it lacked intellect. For two decades preceding the Japanese attack British policy had been a series of half-measures, half understood. Rigorous thought and objective appreciation of facts took second place to wishful thinking. Neither in the political nor the military field did power go to those best fitted to use it. It was quite typical that when, in September 1941, just as the Japanese were preparing their December onslaught, a conference of high British and Australian military and diplomatic leaders, chaired by a cabinet minister, was held in Singapore, it came to the collective conclusion that the Japanese would most likely attack Russia, not Malaya, and even if they did come south it would not be until the monsoon was over. What is so interesting about this double misjudgement is that there was absolutely no evidence, only prejudice, that could support it.

In Tokyo, it was decided to entrust the conquest of Malaya to the 25th Army, and Yamashita Tomoyuki was appointed its commander. Yamashita, known as the 'Lion of Manchuria' and soon to be transmogrified into the 'Tiger of Malaya' was a strange character, and his prompt execution at the close of the war prevented any calm study of his personality. Certainly he was regarded both by the Japanese public and by most of the

RIGHT: Japanese infantrymen in action in 1942.

BELOW LEFT: A destroyer takes off survivors from the battleship HMS *Prince of Wales.*

BELOW: HMS *Prince of Wales* at Singapore, just before her last voyage. The loss of the only two British capital ships in the area cleared the way for Japanese seaborne landings.

Japanese military as the country's most gifted commander, and this was true even before the start of the war. In 1941 he was in semi-disgrace, so his appointment signified a real respect for his capabilities.

In 1908 he had passed out from the Military Academy in fifth place, and eight years later won sixth place at the Staff College. Posted to the General Staff, he proved to be a highly competent planner and organizer before he went abroad as military attaché to Switzerland and, later, to Germany and Austria. In the 1930s he became deeply involved in the intrigues and violence that accompanied the officers' step-by-step takeover of the political system, but in 1936 he found himself on the losing side in an unsuccessful coup that was aimed at the civil government but also involved a struggle between two military factions. Yamashita's faction lost, and some of the younger officers whose actions he had supported were executed or committed suicide. But while he approved, even advised, these suicides, he himself chose to live, and was rusticated to command a brigade in Korea. That the Emperor Hirohito had shown his displeasure appears to have been the hardest blow of all, and from this time, according to some witnesses, Yamashita's character changed. Gradually, while still believing in the sacred mission of Japan and its army, he moderated his behavior, became more kindly to individuals and to his men, refrained from involvement in further plots, and strove for professional perfection. Meanwhile, he grew fatter, and began to snore so loudly at night that fellow-officers did what they could to avoid sleeping in the same building.

By 1937 he was a lieutenant general commanding a division in China but in 1940, as Japan became more aligned with the Axis Powers, he was sent to view military establishments in Italy and Germany. From this tour he returned convinced that the Japanese Army had a long way to go before it could match the best Europeans. Tojo, the War Minister, did not like this report, and Yamashita was immediately posted out of Tokyo again, to Manchuria. Tojo was a member of the faction that Yamashita had opposed in 1936, and still opposed, and his belief that Tojo hated him was probably justified.

In September, preparatory steps for beginning the war in

FAR LEFT: Japanese troops advance in south-east Asia.

LEFT: Captain Leach, the commander of HMS *Prince of Wales* who was lost with his ship.

BELOW LEFT: General Percival, commander of the Allied ground forces in Malaya.

RIGHT: Admiral Tom Phillips (right), commander of the ill-fated British naval squadron.

December were taken. Japanese troops had entered southern Indo China in July, and now this occupation was extended, again with the enforced consent of the local French administration, to northern Indo China. The Tripartite Pact was at last signed with Italy and Germany, and those countries promised help for Japan's mission in the Far East.

Thus when Yamashita arrived to take over the 25th Army in November, much of the planning for the Malayan operation had already been done. Since the beginning of the year some serious research into the problems of tropical warfare had been accomplished, and Malaya had been thoroughly examined as a future battlefield. Thanks to its highly-developed intelligence sources, the Japanese command knew more about the real state of the Malayan defenses than did the British government. It knew, for example, that although fresh Commonwealth troops had been arriving they were far from battleworthy, having been neither acclimatized nor trained for jungle warfare.

Yamashita's main contribution at this stage was to request that each division be provided with its own well-supplied engineer unit, in view of the large number of bridges along the roads linking north and south Malaya. He also made sure that, in the few weeks left, these units were thoroughly trained in bridge-building. He also chose to use only three divisions (plus one in reserve) for his campaign, not the five that were offered. Knowledge of the campaigns fought in China had convinced him that the Japanese always tried to throw too many men into battle, only to find themselves running short of supplies. The divisions he received were the 5th, experienced and well-mechanized, the 18th, not so well known but with a commander who was a friend of Yamashita, and the allegedly elite Imperial Guards. The latter division apart from being commanded by a general, Nishimura, with whom, for factional reasons, Yamashita was in a state of barely-contained enmity, was also in great need of battle-training, although its commander was reluctant to admit this. Nishimura was a protege of Count Terauchi, who as commander of the Southern Army was Yamashita's superior and who, according to Yamashita's diary, was also hostile, being a member of the same faction as Tojo. Tojo, who had become

prime minister in October, also sent a young officer to join or, rather, observe, Yamashita, so the latter came to feel hemmed in by his service enemies. How far Yamashita was paranoid, and how far his suspicions were genuine, is impossible to judge, but for him the war was certainly a war on two fronts and at times he seems to have feared the Japanese more than the British.

To his staff officers, however, this dark side of Yamashita's mind was secret. These officers, who had been brought together hastily and for the most part had never worked together before, soon became an integrated and smooth-working group, united in their respect for Yamashita's competence and their appreciation of his various small kindnesses. The operational plan, as finally approved by Yamashita, was to land the 5th, and part of the 18th, divisions at Singora and Patani, with another part of the 18th landing at Kota Bharu. The Imperial Guards would deal with Thailand and then come south by rail. Singora and Patani were at the head of roads leading down the west coast of Malaya toward Singapore, and Yamashita anticipated that he would be able to land and get his troops on the move before the British overcame their scruples and crossed the frontier to meet him. The Kota Bharu landing, however, would probably be opposed. Operations were to begin on 8 December, and he allowed himself one hundred days to capture Singapore.

On 6 December the invasion fleet, which had set out from Hainan two days previously, was sighted by a British reconnaissance aircraft. Permission for the local British forces to begin the 'Matador' plan was so long delayed that the landings in Thailand were unopposed. However, the force that was to land at Kota Bharu met rough weather, landed a mile from its planned destination, and found itself under the guns of an Indian defense work. Only after some delay, and with serious casualties, was it able to establish itself on shore and capture the nearby airfield. By that time Yamashita was safely in Singora, preparing the next moves.

After disarming the local police Yamashita secured an agreement whereby the Thai government allowed his troops to pass through its country. Truckloads of troops, some masquerading as local refugees, began to hurry south to seize bridges on the other side of the frontier. The news of Pearl Harbor relieved Yamashita of one of his anxieties, that his seaborne supply lines would be cut, and everything pointed to local air superiority as well. He anticipated that the first major action would be at Jitra, where intelligence reports spoke of a British defensive position covering, among other things, the road to Alor Star and its vital airbase.

Putting his faith in the expectation that British units would stay close to the road, and thereby lay themselves open to flanking movements by the Japanese troops, who had been trained for jungle operations, Yamashita sent his main force toward Jitra. He found that the position was held by an Indian division, but did not learn until later that it had been disorganized by preparations for the aborted operation 'Matador.' Having assumed an offensive posture for this offensive, it was in course of taking up a defensive stance, but was handicapped by heavy rainfall that filled trenches and prevented all but a few rudimentery communication links being established. Its morale, once high, was rapidly falling.

Action began when a Japanese scouting force with ten tanks in support came across a battery of unattended anti-tank guns and captured them, their crews having gone off to seek shelter from the rain. But there were some heavy losses when British and Gurkha troops were encountered. Abandoning any hope that a frontal attack would succeed, the Japanese resorted to flanking and night movements which led to confused reactions by the British Empire forces, who soon had to retreat. There was a collapse of organization and morale, following which the Indian troops (many of whom had never seen a tank before) surrendered in large numbers while the others struggled to create new positions in the rear. Yamashita had defeated a division, using only his advance scouting force.

By the standards of World War II, the Jitra battle was small-scale, but it determined the course of the campaign, for after it the British never recovered their balance and retreated, sometimes in confusion and sometimes impeccably, from one position to another, the several east-west rivers providing natural barriers that, in better circumstances, might have been held. The British need to stick to the open road, and Japanese domination in the air, meant that the retreating formations got little rest.

Yamashita ascribed his success to the low morale and low competence of the Indian troops, but he was only partly right in this. The British collapse followed almost automatically from the failure to hold the Japanese in the first two days, from the Japanese air and naval superiority, and from the British commanders' repeated inability to make the right decisions. Although the Japanese infantry was better trained, the invading divisions were far from being the finely-tuned instruments of war portrayed in the Japanese press. Coordination between units was very poor, often because of rigid attitudes on the part of commanding officers, their communication and other ancillary arms were sub-standard, their map-reading was unreliable, and they were continually taking the wrong turning; in many ways the Japanese army had become complacent after its victorious campaigns against the Chinese. Yamashita's part in the early victories was manifested in his logistic talent and his readiness to try mobile tactics that gave no hint of the weaknesses of his forces, which often operated with dangerously small reserves of supplies and ammunition.

But, in general, if Malaya had been defended by the better units of the British army under determined political and military leadership, Yamashita would have had a far harder task, and might well have needed to call for his reserve division. As

things were, even the not entirely battleworthy Imperial Guards Division could win encounter after encounter using simplistic frontal assaults, and Yamashita was half-way down the Peninsula before the last units of his 18th Division needed to be landed. On 11 January, little more than a month after the first landings, his troops were in Kuala Lumpur, and the southernmost state of Johore seemed within reach.

Foreseeing that the British would make a stand at the Muar River, Yamashita ordered the Guards Division to force a crossing. But this line was defended by Australians, who had developed considerable skill in fighting over this terrain. It was only by making landings down the coast that the Guards could finally force the Australians to withdraw. After this, the Commonwealth forces withdrew over the causeway to Singapore and prepared for the siege of that island. Yamashita celebrated this victory by inviting his divisional commanders for a ceremonial drink, and appears to have given no hint of the dark thoughts that had latterly been passing through his mind. To his men, too, he presented a face of tranquil and honorable confidence. His choice of a new headquarters, the Sultan's prominent palace overlooking the Johore Strait (and at which the British artillery was forbidden to fire) seemed to emphasize his cool, unfearing, confidence.

In Japan he had become a national hero, and this was one of the causes of his worry. He knew the power of jealousy, he knew that Tojo, master of the secret police, had always disliked him, and he knew that assassination was a tried and tested technique in Japan. In his blackest moments he believed that he would be assassinated as soon as he could be dispensed with. Even on normal days, moreover, his dark thoughts did not leave him, and his diary testifies to his distrust of his immediate superior Terauchi, and of the men in power in Tokyo. As for his subordinates, he had a lively dislike for Nishimura, whom he believed sought every opportunity to disobey his instructions. In January, when staff officers from Tokyo visited him, and again when Terauchi sent him an officer loaded with instructions on how to capture Singapore, his own staff officers became anxious about his mental health.

LEFT: Japanese aircrew record their plan fulfilment.

RIGHT: A meeting in Java of Allied commanders to discuss the Japanese threat. The British General Wavell (at left) talks to Admiral Hart, commanding the US Asiatic Fleet, and US General Brett.

BELOW RIGHT: The light battle-kit of Japanese infantry shows clearly in this picture taken at a Buddhist shrine in Burma.

Despite all this mental stress, and having torn up Terauchi's instructions, Yamashita supervised the reconnaissance and the planning needed for crossing the Johore Strait into Singapore. The attack would begin on 7 February, and Yamashita hoped that Singapore would be in his hands within a week. This target date was not simply a matter of creating an impression, but was necessitated by the supply problems that he could foresee. Either he would win a quick victory or he would have to halt for regrouping and re-supplying.

Knowing that the British had put much of their strength at the eastern end of the Strait, Yamashita decided that the Imperial Guards should make a feint attack there on 7 February in the evening. There would then be an interval to allow the defenders to rush extra troops to that area and then, in the evening of 8 February, the main forces of the two other divisions would cross near the western end. These could be expected to meet some resistance, but would break through and capture their first objective, Tengah airfield. There could also be a subsidiary attack near the causeway, and the Imperial Guards would move to prevent the British retreating to defensive positions at Changi.

Although the British had not done much to strengthen their defenses along the Strait, and although the crossing was preceded by heavy artillery and air bombardment, Yamashita did lose many men in the crossing. Partly this was because the surviving British machine guns had excellent targets as the Japanese infantry, by no means adept at this kind of operation, struggled across the water. It was only after enough troops had got ashore to conduct outflanking moves against the machine guns that the bulk of the infantry could cross.

But on 9 February, under a ceiling of smoke from burning oil tanks, enough infantry were ashore to justify the despatch of the artillery across the Strait to support their further advance Yamashita, too, moved himself and his staff to a new HQ across the Strait near Tengah airfield. His sharp nose for imminent logistical problems meant that he was well aware that his guns had enough ammunition for only five more days. Moreover, Terauchi's staff was failing to send the supplies he needed, and

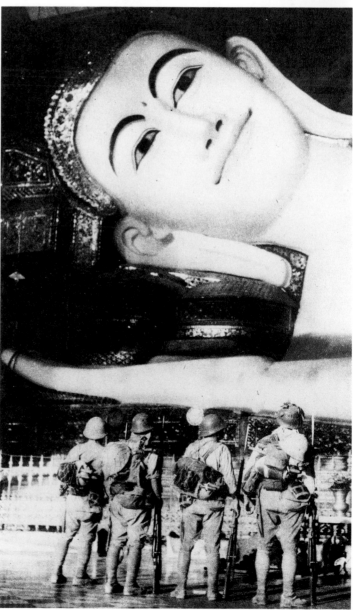

LEFT: A temporary prisoner-of-war camp for Allied captives. Yamashita did his best for prisoners at this stage.

BELOW LEFT: Yamashita confronts Percival at the surrender of the Allied forces.

RIGHT: Australian prisoners after transfer to work-camps in Thailand. The camps in Burma, Thailand and Malaya were notorious for the dreadful ill-treatment of the prisoners.

Yamashita believed that this would not improve, partly because the staff was incompetent and partly because it was filled with officers who disliked him.

It was in this situation, where the 25th Army was poised between triumph and stagnation, that Yamashita's careful confidence won the day. Instead of conserving his resources, he decided to spend them as though he had limitless reserves on which to draw. In this way he would conceal his true situation from the enemy, for he realized that once the British command discovered the true state of his ammunition supply it would take heart and recover its poise and spirits.

So he continued to push his troops forward as fast as they could go. At Tengah airfield his advance had been so rapid that the British troops retired from their barracks leaving their half-finished meal on the tables. At Bukit Timah, a fairly defensible hill a few miles outside the city, the British failed to make a stand, for their morale was low and the chain of command disrupted. Only their artillery continued to take its toll as it retreated from one position to the next.

However, on 15 February the British were still resisting on a line around the northern border of the city, even though Yamashita had sent an aircraft to drop a letter suggesting that they surrender. He could see the city, and reckoned that at the current rate of progress his troops would be at the northern outskirts by evening, although heavy losses would be inevitable. He ordered the advance to continue and stipulated that the artillery should maintain its rate of fire until no more rounds were left.

Percival had been instructed to fight to the end, moving to street-fighting when necessary. But his logistic problems were even greater than Yamashita's. Singapore had about a million civilian inhabitants and they were dependent on a water-supply system fed by reservoirs that were in Japanese hands, and by pipes that were increasingly broken by shells and bombs. Percival decided that the civil disorder and the civil deaths that thirst would bring were sufficient reason for bringing the battle to a close, and on 15 February an anxious Yamashita was relieved by reports that the British had raised a white flag in one sector.

A British delegation was admitted to the Japanese lines and it was agreed that Percival should come in person. Yamashita had intended to observe all the civilized conventions that the situation demanded, but he was so anxious to obtain the British surrender before his ammunition ran out that he became angry when Percival asked to delay signature until the next morning. Evidently, he subsequently regretted this loss of nerve, and explained it away by saying that he had become irritated by his interpreter, who seemed unable to convey that he was demanding a Yes or No answer to his request for an immediate surrender. In the end, Percival conformed, after Yamashita had guaranteed the safety of the Allied prisoners, and to Yamashita's great relief it was agreed that hostilities should end that very evening.

Yamashita's victorious campaign had lasted just 73 days, and it was Japan's greatest military triumph since the Russo-Japanese War. About 130,000 prisoners were captured, but the moral effect of capturing Britain's prized bastion in the Far East was of far greater importance. British prestige in the Far East had suffered, deservedly, a blow from which it would never recover even though, in various subtle ways, London tried to put the blame not on its own ineptitude but on the shoulders of Percival. Percival had, it is true, failed badly in this campaign. In particular, he had paid too much attention to defending airfields, even though there were no longer aircraft available to use them. He had also, largely for reasons of public relations, failed to build defenses along the British line of retreat, defenses which, if sited at river crossings, might well have delayed Yamashita for several precious weeks. But Percival's efforts to improve things in the months preceding the war, and his decision to surrender at the end, stand to his credit.

The fall of Singapore, opening the way for further advances to the East Indies and perhaps Australia, cemented Yamashita's reputation as Japan's greatest general. But he refused to make a triumphal entry to the city; he would hold a funeral ceremony but not a victory parade. Probably this decision had less to do with modesty or the realization that the administration of the captured city demanded all his time, than with a wish to keep the mass of his soldiers out of the city. Although he was prob-

ably unaware that there had already been a massacre at a hospital outside the city, he knew enough about the atrocities committed by Japanese infantry in China to realize what might happen in Singapore. In fact, the Japanese takeover proceeded smoothly, with British technicians assisting in restoring the water and other supplies.

Despite his gloomy intimations, there was no attempt to assassinate him, even when Terauchi's arrival to set up headquarters in Singapore made him dispensable. Yet the treatment he did receive suggests that his belief that powerful enemies were working against him was not entirely explicable by paranoia. A victorious general of his status could have expected a triumphant return home, an audience with the Emperor, and then a posting to another key operational area. What happened to Yamashita was different. He was posted to Manchuria, where his command could only be important should Russia, already hard-pressed by Germany, decide to invade. Tojo made sure that there would be no public celebration in Tokyo by specifying that he would proceed to his new appointment by the shortest route, and he was told that the Emperor was unwilling to forgive his part in the events of 1936 and would never condescend to meet him.

It was only when Japan faced obvious defeat that he was brought back to the war. He was sent to take command in the Philippines just as the Americans prepared to recapture those strategically vital islands. Here he did the best he could, and the fact that he was still active with 50,000 men when the war ended testifies to his ability. As soon as he surrendered he was tried for war crimes by a US military court. The hearing was a travesty. Japanese war crimes were undeniable, but nothing said before the court connected Yamashita with any atrocity. In fact, much of the accusation revolved around the savage events in Manila when it was held by Japanese naval troops at a time when Yamashita's orders to evacuate the city had been spurned by the local commander. Considering his life in its entirety, it is quite possible that Yamashita deserved to hang. But his condemnation to be hung for crimes he did not commit only discredited his victorious opponents, as some US and British newspapers pointed out at the time.

CHAPTER SEVEN

ROMMEL

AND THE CAPTURE OF TOBRUK

EVEN BEFORE the beginning of World War II the great desert wastes of North Africa captured imaginations in Europe and America, and once the Desert War began in earnest, much of the romance formerly engendered by the French Foreign Legion became attached to the new desert warriors. The Afrika Korps, the Long Range Desert Group, the spies sipping gin in the clubs of Cairo and the British Tommies sweltering in their tanks – all have won a place in modern mythology.

The campaign in North Africa fascinated the British, especially Churchill, to the extent that soon its strategic considerations became almost overshadowed by the psychological need to win a great victory over the Afrika Korps and its legendary leader, General Erwin Rommel, the Desert Fox.

Churchill described Rommel as a master of war. Troops on both sides called him, half-affectionately, 'that bastard Rommel.' During the desert campaign he was to become the best-known and – even in Britain and America – practically the most popular figure in the Middle East owing to his brilliance, his courage, his skill at tactical maneuver (often when gravely outnumbered), and his old-school, chivalrous attitude toward his opponents. To the British soldier he came to be the personification of the bold feint, the surprise attack, the wild chase. 'Rommel is coming!' would race through the troops with the speed and destructive force of a forest fire. In fact, General Sir Claude Auchinleck, Commander in Chief of the British forces in the Middle East, even found it necessary at one point to issue an extraordinary Order of the Day, begging his senior officers to 'make every effort to destroy the concept that Rommel is anything more than an ordinary German general,' adding that, 'this matter is of great psychological significance.'

Tobruk, a Libyan port not far from the Egyptian frontier, soon assumed an importance far beyond its already vital strategic position. The British captured it from the Italians early in the desert campaign in January 1941. In the middle months of 1941 the stubborn Australians who held out for some nine months against Rommel's siege became the heroes of the Empire. When the fortress fell to the Afrika Korps in 1942 it was a crushing blow to the British public and Rommel's reputation was not so much made, as confirmed.

Erwin Johannes Eugen Rommel was born in Heidenheim, near Wurtemburg, on 15 November 1891. He was one of five children, and his sister describes him as a gentle, amiable, dreamy child. He was small for his age, and had little interest in books or sports. In his teens, however, he suddenly woke up and developed a keen interest in physical fitness, spending every spare minute on his bicycle or on skis in winter. The dreamer became a hard-headed, practical youth who did well in school and studied aircraft design as a hobby.

In June 1910 Rommel joined the army. Since the family had no military connections (his father and grandfather were both schoolteachers and mathematicians), he joined the 124th Infantry Regiment at Weingarten as an 'officer cadet' – which meant he had to serve in the ranks before going on to a *Kriegsschule* (War Academy). He was promoted to corporal in October, made sergeant by the end of December, and was posted to the *Kriegsschule* at Danzig in March 1911.

As a young officer he was good at drill and was found to be especially effective in training recruits. Like the young Montgomery he showed an unusual interest in the smallest details of military organization – but unlike Monty, he was never argumentative, usually preferring to listen rather than talk.

During World War I Rommel showed the boldness, independence, and understanding of the value of surprise that he would use to such advantage almost 30 years later. He stood out almost

immediately as a perfect fighter. He was cold, cunning, ruthless and untiring – quick to make decisions and incredibly brave. Before the first year of war was out he was transferred to a mountain battalion where his remarkable eye for country and his ability to ignore physical discomfort were invaluable. By the end of the war he had been wounded twice and had been awarded not only the Iron Cross Classes I and II, but also Germany's highest decoration, the *Pour le Mérite* (corresponding to Britain's Victoria Cross or the United States' Medal of Honor).

His comrades from this period invariably describe him as having *Fingerspitzengefühl* – a sixth sense, or intuition in his fingertips. To a man they credit his tactical genius – but remark that he was often disliked by his fellow officers, from whom he expected as much as he did from himself.

At the end of the war Captain Rommel turned to peacetime soldiering, ending up in November 1938 a colonel in command of the *Kriegsschule* at Wiener Neustadt. He lived a quiet life with his wife and son. He did not smoke, drank little and did not care much about food or parties. He was good with his hands, and could make or fix almost anything.

Like the majority of his fellow countrymen, Rommel considered the Nazis upstarts but saw Hitler as an idealistic patriot who had a chance to pull the country together and oust the Communists. This attitude may have come more easily since he was not part of the snobbish Prussian clique that included so many regular army officers. He was never close to Hitler, which perhaps is one reason why his admiration took so long to wear off, but through their brief encounters in the early days of the war the Führer developed a liking for him. Rommel, for his part, admired Hitler's magnetic personality, his amazing memory for technical detail and his physical courage.

At the outbreak of World War II he was commander of the Nazi headquarters in Poland, but by June 1940 Hitler had given him a fighting command, at the head of the 7th Panzer Division of the XV Armored Corps (the 'Ghost Division' that took part in the stunning German advance through France).

On 15 February 1941 Rommel – now a newly appointed lieutenant general – was given command of 'the German troops in Libya.' His mission was to assist the Italians and help prevent a British breakthrough to Tripoli. In two months General Sir Archibald Wavell's small force of three British divisions – 31,000 men, 120 guns and 275 tanks – had chased 10 Italian divisions totalling over 200,000 men across 650 miles. Though Hitler still could not bring himself to take North Africa all that seriously, he had finally realized that if something were not done quickly Britain would gain control of the entire southern shore of the Mediterranean, leaving Europe's 'soft underbelly' dangerously exposed.

Rommel built up his army and eventually had at his disposal two Panzer divisions (the 15th and the 21st), an Italian armored division (the Ariete), a German infantry division (the 90th Light), a 'frontier group,' two Italian motorized divisions and four Italian infantry divisions. They formed Panzer Army Africa but the German section called itself the Afrika Korps.

For the next two years they would be fighting over a featureless wasteland of gravel and scrub, dotted with ancient wells and the tombs of sheiks. The battlefield stretched almost 400 miles, from Derna in the east to El Alamein in the west. The only road followed the coast and the only dominant physical feature was a 500-foot escarpment that faced north to the coastal plain, descending from the limestone plateau where the armies maneuvered. With no natural obstacles and few civilians or settled areas except along the coast, the campaign over the vast spaces of the desert bore more resemblance to a naval war than to a tra-

ditional European land conflict. Rommel was the first really to appreciate the fact and fully exploit the freedom of movement it gave him.

In addition to their human adversaries, the soldiers fought the desert. Temperatures rose to 120 degrees in summer, with the stones and sand remaining burning hot until late at night. The sand got everywhere, in hair, underclothes and machinery. In-

sects and sand fleas viciously bit everyone, general and enlisted man alike, and dysentery was rife. The men grew lean and tanned, with skins like leather. The infantry prepared their positions, the sappers laid their mines and the tank crews sweated in their tanks, all in a climate which many would have considered impossible for Europeans to work in at all.

The existence of a common enemy – the desert – may have

ABOVE: Rommel and other German officers relax in the far-from luxurious surroundings of their mess tent.

ABOVE LEFT: General Rommel and General Cavallero inspect Italian troops in Tripoli.

FAR LEFT: A German tank passes through a Libyan town.

LEFT: Rommel and his Chief of Staff, Fritz Bayerlein, walking through the Libyan Desert.

RIGHT: Rommel and General Gariboldi on a tour of inspection in Tripoli.

been one reason why the North African campaign was, by and large, a 'gentleman's war.' Neither the Afrika Korps nor the British abused prisoners. In fact the former, according to Rommel's biographer Desmond Young, treated enemy prisoners of war with, 'almost old-world courtesy.' Compliments were traded sincerely: Rommel often described General Wavell as a 'military genius' and commander of the highest order, while for his part Wavell later sent Frau Rommel a copy of his lectures on generalship inscribed 'to the memory of a brave, chivalrous, and skillful opponent.'

Much of the credit on the German side must go to Rommel himself, who had strong feelings about correct behavior and observance of the 'soldier's code' – feelings that were shared by most officers in the regular German Army (with a few notable exceptions). He was also lucky not to have any SS troops attached to his command and to be a continent away from headquarters.

Perhaps because of their early successes in the hostile desert environment most people believed that the Afrika Korps was an elite volunteer unit, specially trained in desert warfare. On the contrary, the men of the Afrika Korps had, for the most part, been plucked out of the Balkans and set down in Tripoli with no preparation at all. They were typical German soldiers – strong, brave, well-trained and disciplined. They were not well-suited to the desert. Many, especially the very young, the very blond and the older veterans of World War I, could not adapt to the new, rigorous conditions as well as did the British colonial troops or even the British regular troops. Few had ever been out

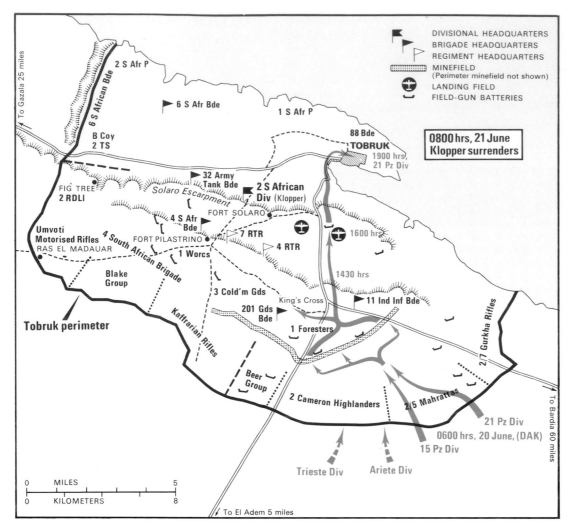

LEFT: Map of the fall of Tobruk.

BELOW LEFT: Rommel and his staff observe the fighting during the Crusader battles in December 1941.

BOTTOM LEFT: The crew of a German medical truck rest in the streets of newly-captured Tobruk.

ABOVE RIGHT: Following the fighting at Ras el Madauar on 30 April 1941, the first British prisoners to be taken outside Tobruk are marched into captivity.

BELOW RIGHT: German infantry climb aboard a Panzer III to continue their advance.

of Europe before and they lacked the British experience with foreign lands. It was difficult, for example, to teach the troops not to drink untreated water. German doctors knew less than their British counterparts about tropical medicine and German field hospitals were far inferior. Sickness, especially dysentery and jaundice, took a heavy toll in the early days of the campaign.

The Afrika Korps had some definite advantages as well. Though they had less transport, their weapons outclassed those of the British, especially in the beginning, and they understood more about using them effectively. The men had better prospects of leave and received more news from home (even publishing their own paper, *Oase*) – all of which improved morale. In addition, they were a homogeneous group, in distinct contrast to the Eighth Army, which was a mixture of divisions from every part of the far-flung British Empire.

With all this it was Rommel who, by sheer force of personality, turned the Afrika Korps into a tough, resilient and self-confident fighting unit. He taught each man to give 150 percent and never to admit defeat, so that even as they were marching down to the prisoner-of-war ships in 1943 they were able to hold their heads high.

Life in the desert was unfamiliar and rigorous, but Rommel found it no problem becoming 'desert-worthy' (a British term that came to be applied to anyone and anything that functioned effectively in the desert). Though no longer young, he was in fine physical condition, with a Spartan streak that made him take pride in the stoic acceptance of discomfort and fatigue. As one of his officers put it later, 'he had the strength of a horse . . . he could wear out men 20 and 30 years younger.'

He did not need much sleep nor did he care much about what he ate. He insisted on getting the same rations as his men, which

adequately camouflaged minefield. At the end of the day he would eat dinner in about 20 minutes, listen to the news on the radio and write his daily letter to his wife. Official papers or letters to the survivors of his World War I battalion (with whom he was a faithful correspondent) took up the rest of the evening.

Rommel was fond of young people and was very definitely a 'front-line type' so it is not surprising that the men of the Afrika Korps idolized him. The younger officers admired him especially, for his concern with their problems, his tactical ideas and his skill in navigating the desert. General von Esebeck has said, 'He had a smile and a joke for everyone who seemed to be doing his job . . . he had a very warm heart and more charm than anyone I have ever known.'

His charm and sensitivity, however, were not always so apparent to senior officers, with whom he could be impatient and, on occasion, brutal. He was in the habit of giving orders directly to subordinates instead of following the chain of command and would fly into a rage if his orders were questioned. He also tended to rely on his own judgment much more than his superiors would have wished – and the fact that he was so often right probably did not make the pill any easier to swallow. His relationship with his nominal Italian superiors was difficult, while he made no secret of the fact that he considered Halder and many others on the German General Staff fools who had no practical experience of war. Even Hitler, who liked him personally, would become angry at his 'veiled' reports to headquarters.

One of his most distressing habits was that of dashing around the battlefield, often taking his Chief of Staff with him and leaving no one with authority at headquarters. While his officers fretted in the rear, Rommel would be racing around the front.

In fact, his system of command was not haphazard. He and his commanders did not lead attacks from the front line out of a

were not too good (the food that arrived on the supply ships was usually much too heavy for the desert and did not include fresh fruit or vegetables). He was appalled when he discovered that there were three 'classes' of rations in the Italian army – for officers, noncommissioned officers and enlisted men. His reading was limited to newspapers or books about military topics. Though he did have a mild interest in North African history, the story that he was an avid classical scholar and archeologist was fabricated by the German propaganda machine.

Most days he was awake by 0600 hours, and by 0630 hours – always shaved and in uniform – would be off on his daily round of positions. Sometimes he took to the air, piloting his own Storch but more often he drove himself around the desert in his command car. He would arrive at the most isolated post without warning – and it was an unlucky officer who was caught in bed after 0700 hours. Nor were the visits mere formalities. He missed nothing, from a badly positioned machine gun to an in-

ABOVE: German troops observe the sand and smoke raised by an artillery bombardment.

LEFT: A Messerschmitt 110 takes off from a North African airfield. Conditions such as these meant that special air filters had to be fitted to engines and other modifications made.

love for histrionic heroism, but because of their knowledge of armor tactics and troop psychology. Time and again a tank crew who had halted their vehicle would hear a loud knocking on the side. Opening the turret they would discover Rommel's aide, Lieutenant Freiherr von Schlippenbach using a crowbar as a knocker, while the General, standing up in his car, shouted, 'On your way! Attacks don't succeed by standing still!' Though he took great personal risks, his uncanny instinct for what the enemy was going to do saved his life on several occasions.

His admirers will point out that this personal command was one of the main reasons why the Germans were consistently ahead in the speed of decision making and velocity of movement. Even his harshest critics will admit that he was extraordinarily brave, wonderful with his men, generous with praise and willing to admit when he was wrong. In sum, he was the best possible commander for the desert war at that time.

Since he was frequently outnumbered Rommel's main strategy was to keep his troops concentrated in the open and to use the vast desert for wide maneuvers to strike at the flanks or rear of the enemy, dividing their forces so that they could be more easily disposed of. The British frequently appeared to be cooperating with this strategy. As he commented to one captured brigadier near the end of Operation Crusader, 'What difference does it make if you have two tanks to my one when you spread them out and let me smash them in detail? You presented me with three brigades in succession.'

His main contribution to tank tactics was the use of a screen of antitank guns to shield his Panzers as they advanced, withdrew or refueled. His most valuable weapon was the 88mm gun with

ABOVE RIGHT: Unloading precious supplies for the Afrika Korps from a Ju52.

RIGHT: A German *Kubelwagen* seems to have got stuck in the sand.

high-velocity, armor-piercing shells that could inflict serious damage on both tanks and aircraft. Wherever possible artillery, rather than tanks, was used for defense, to help keep tank losses down. The tanks themselves – mainly 22-ton Mark IIIs with 50mm guns – were superior to Allied tanks. German tank recovery operations, too, were much better organized than those of the British.

Rommel used every ruse he could think of to deceive the enemy or keep them off balance. The first order he issued upon landing in Tripoli was for the construction of dummy tanks. Transport trucks – some with airplane engines mounted on the back - were often used to raise dust and create the illusion of a major army on the move. Captured vehicles were used not only for extra transport, but also to confuse the British.

Another innovation was the formation of 'combat groups.' These were about the size of a battalion and consisted of a tank company, a mixed company of antitank artillery and flak (50 and 37mm antitank guns and 20mm flak) and a column of armored reconnaisance trucks and radio cars. These groups proved to be the ideal fighting unit for the desert and Rommel had several under his personal command, constantly flinging them into the hottest parts of the battle.

Mines were a major weapon for both sides. Probably in no other theater did they play such an important role. Air support was important too, for it could seriously damage the enemy's supplies and communications lines. However in the desert it had limited effectiveness against front-line strength. It could hamper enemy movements but it could not check an advance on the ground.

The real battle in the desert war was for vital supplies, especially gasoline and water. The drivers of the supply trucks on both sides are the, largely unsung, heroes of the campaign. Doggedly they drove their three-ton trucks across burning sands when tires burst like balloons, through freezing nights and through sandstorms, where visibility was reduced to about a yard and lookouts had to lie along the front fender clinging to the radiator, to shout directions to the driver. In the Afrika Korps the motor-cyclist was the jack-of-all-trades, fetching ammunition, directing the artillery and carrying the wounded to dressing stations – all with a vehicle that could not have been more inappropriate for the terrain.

During 1941 and 1942 the campaigns in North Africa were inconclusive. In January 1941 the British took Tobruk, along with

the rest of Cyrenaica, from the Italians. On 31 March Rommel, who had been told to submit plans for a counteroffensive by 20 April, sent out a reconnaissance raid in force. The British front collapsed in front of him and within 12 days, to everyone's surprise, he had recaptured Bardia, only a few miles from the Egyptian frontier.

He had recovered all the territory the Italians had lost except Tobruk, which he had under siege, and which the British were determined to hold at all costs. The British were embarrassed. Their prestige sank to a new low in the United States and the Soviet Union, and their future seemed dark indeed. More important, they found themselves with a very precarious hold on the eastern end of the Mediterranean, and it became obvious that now they were going to pay for their neglect of tanks and tank warfare between the wars. The British tanks were too slow and their guns too weak to compete with the best of the German equipment.

While Rommel turned his energies to asking Hitler – in vain - for four more Panzer divisions, Churchill had no such reservations. North Africa was no sideshow to the British; in fact, it was to become the focus for the greatest single military effort of the Empire. On 12 May a large convoy survived the risky journey across the Mediterranean and delivered 238 tanks to General Wavell. Wavell, knowing that Rommel was short of supplies and fuel, launched an immediate offensive (Operation Brevity) to relieve Tobruk. However, instead of retreating, Rommel counterattacked and chased the Eighth Army back into Egypt.

With his tanks outnumbered four to one, Rommel had to come up with a way to keep the British off the coast road to Tobruk. He deployed his small forces to create a bottleneck where they could stall the next offensive until he had time to bring up his reserves. Meanwhile, he joined Admiral Raeder in pressing for a decisive offensive against Egypt and Suez – a concept which Hitler did not even begin to understand. The Führer continued to give Barbarossa (the campaign against the Soviet Union) top priority.

The British offensive, Operation Battleaxe, came on 14 June. It was Wavell's last chance if he wanted to hang on to his Middle East command – and it failed. By the end of the day he had lost almost half his tanks in Rommel's trap. True to form, the Germans counterattacked on 15 June. The result was another stalemate.

Churchill immediately removed Wavell and sent General Sir

Claude Auchinleck as his replacement, giving him everything he had denied his predecessor – men, materiel, and time to prepare. By the time Auchinleck launched Operation Crusader on 18 November 1941 he had an unprecedented superiority in men and equipment – almost three times as many planes, twice as many tanks and tens of thousands more men. The British neutralized their numerical superiority by dividing their force up into several attack groups for speed and flexibility – which the wily Rommel simply dealt with one at a time.

The result was another draw. Though Rommel could blunt Crusader with his skillful flanking movements and unexpected counteroffensives, he was not strong enough to defeat it. With no prospect of reinforcements in the near future, he decided to conserve his forces and withdraw to safety in Tripolitania. The siege of Tobruk was abandoned on 7 December and the Axis forces moved back across Cyrenaica, their withdrawal punctuated by a series of sharp, savage battles that took a heavy toll among the (mostly Italian) infantry units.

On paper it looked like a major victory for the British. However they were exhausted and their supply lines were long and weak, while Rommel was sitting at his home base in strong, well-prepared defensive positions. At about the same time the Germans belatedly realized that Malta was the key to the North African supply routes and began immediate steps to neutralize it. In August 1941 some 35 percent of Rommel's supplies and reinforcements had ended up on the ocean floor. In October about 63 percent had been lost and by November the flow was down to a trickle. However, in January 1942, after a concentrated effort by the Luftwaffe, not a single ton of supplies was lost. At this time also the British forces were being weakened by the withdrawal of troops to face the recently-begun attacks of the Japanese in the Pacific.

Rommel had no thought of remaining on the defensive a moment longer than necessary, and the arrival of several dozen tanks on 5 January was enough to start him planning the next offensive – over the strenuous objections of his nominal superiors. Near the end of the month the worst weather in many years – alternating sandstorms and heavy rains – offered the perfect cover for a surprise attack. The Panzer Army Africa emerged from its defensive positions in one of Rommel's most brilliant displays of opportunism and agility.

Benghazi, with its large supply of fuel and ammunition, fell on 25 January but by 8 February the Axis impetus was spent.

Rommel was brought to a standstill at a line stretching from the coast just west of Gazala, south to the British-held oasis at Bir Hacheim. As both sides settled down to build up their resources, activity dwindled to a series of harassing operations as the British Long Range Desert Group and German frontier patrols stabbed at each other's lines.

Thus, in spring 1942, little had changed since the beginning of the year. The Eastern Front was still static after the long winter. In the Pacific the Japanese continued their string of victories. In North Africa Axis and Allied forces still faced each other at the Gazala Line, some 50 miles west of Tobruk.

The Gazala Line was a 40-mile-long stretch of minefields from the coast to Bir Hacheim. Minefields alone cannot stop tanks for long, so Auchinleck and Ritchie had studded the line with a series of static field dispositions, called 'boxes.' These strongpoints stood alone, like medieval castles. They were usually circular barbed-wire entanglements about two miles in diameter, enclosing a minefield with listening posts, machine-gun nests and gaps covered by artillery. The garrison, about the size of a brigade, was supplied for long-term defense and had two jobs: to guard the minefield so that the enemy could not clear a path through it at leisure and, in the event of a breakthrough, to form pockets of resistance to harass his flanks, rear and communication supply lines. The armored and motorized units ranged around behind the boxes, ready to fall on the enemy forces while they were tied up by the defenses of the strongpoints.

On paper it was a brilliant defense system, but it made the same mistake as Crusader, splitting up the forces into small groups. Rommel, by consolidating his forces, was able to trample through the defenses in one great sweep before the superior British numbers and newly arrived American Grant tanks began taking their toll.

For his Tobruk offensive Rommel fielded 561 tanks, though the only really effective ones were 280 German medium tanks – the 228 Italian 'sardine tins' and the German light tanks hardly counted. The British Eighth Army had some 850 tanks, including 167 Grants, with 75mm guns that out-shot everything on the battlefield except Rommel's 19 Mark III Specials. Rommel's 50mm and 88mm artillery pieces were far superior to the little British two-pounders. In the air the German Luftflotte 2, with 542 aircraft, opposed the 604 planes of the Desert Air Force.

RIGHT: Italian artillery shells the retreating British columns after the fall of Tobruk.

LEFT: Those who surrendered at Tobruk are taken into captivity, 22 June 1942.

On 26 May Rommel made his move. At the unusual time of 1400 hours, General Crüwell led a magnificently staged feint on the Gazala Line. In the center was the 361st Regiment of the 90th Light Division (hot-headed, hard-fighting ex-Legionaries), on the flanks were Italian infantry divisions and behind them all raced the motorized units, recovery vehicles – anything with wheels – throwing up enough sand for two entire Panzer armies. Behind all this activity, at 2030 hours, Rommel gave the code word 'Venezia,' and five divisions moved due south, navigating by the stars, toward Bir Hacheim.

As dawn broke the Italian Ariete Division split off to engage the Free French garrison at Bir Hacheim, while the rest of the force – the two Afrika Korps armored divisions (15th and 21st, with the 90th Light and reconnaissance units on the right) - moved up behind the Gazala defenses toward the coast. Soon they encountered the 3rd Indian Motor Brigade Group, newly arrived from Egypt, and within minutes an alarmed report was speeding to Headquarters, 7th Armored Division, 'We have the whole bloody Afrika Korps in front of us!'

By midday on the 27th Rommel had good reason to congratulate himself. His force was making considerable progress against various British armored units, in fulfillment of his first principle of desert warfare: concentrate your own forces and split the enemy's, destroying them at different times. Later, led astray by faulty intelligence, he decided that he had disposed of the British armor and could safely attack the rear of the enemy infantry positions. It was a costly error. His divisional commanders, throwing caution to the winds, flung themselves into the attack without adequate artillery support. Suddenly they were attacked on all sides by British armored units – including the new Grants and six-pounder guns. By late afternoon the armored units were encircled in the north and the 90th Light immobilized in the east, both cut off from their supplies and transport. Tactical cohesion broke down and the attack foundered in the desert south of the position known as Knightsbridge. By nightfall the 15th Panzers were completely out of gasoline and the 21st was only slightly better off.

All through the 28th Rommel worked desperately to get supplies up to his strike force, which was continually being harassed by British tanks and all the British air power in the area. Typically, he never once thought of withdrawal. During the night General Crüwell was ordered to try to break through the main Gazala Line to help, but before the operation could begin his plane was shot down and he was captured. The day was only saved from total failure by the Italians. The Ariete abandoned their attack on Bir Hacheim and made their way up to Bar el Harmat where they set up an effective antitank screen to cover the supply columns. Meanwhile, the Trieste and Pavia divisions had managed to clear preliminary gaps in the minefields from the west, where they were crossed by the Trigh el Abd and Trigh Capuzzo caravan routes. Unfortunately both gaps were covered by the 150th Brigade Group box at Got el Ualeb – of which Rommel was yet unaware.

Rommel spent all day on the 29th sneaking supplies to his stranded armor, while the delayed attack on the main Gazala Line failed to break through the South African and 50th Division positions. The tank action that day around Knightsbridge, in blazing heat and blinding dust storms, was some of the fiercest so far in the campaign. At sundown both sides fell back exhausted and Rommel pulled his forces into a close defensive formation between the Sidra and Aslagh ridges – the area that came to be known as 'the Cauldron.'

On 30 May Rommel decided that his only hope lay in breaching the British minefields from the east, to regain contact with his main supply bases. Thus, on the 31st, he massed his artillery to protect the minefield gaps. Ritchie, thinking the strategic withdrawal was a retreat, cabled Cairo: 'Rommel is on the run!'

Rommel was not retreating but consolidating. For the next two days he tried in vain to knock out the 150th Brigade box. If the British had mounted a decisive armor attack immediately they would have had the Afrika Korps virtually at their mercy. Instead, they softened up the air offensive and launched a series of ill-coordinated jabs at Rommel's antitank guns. Those guns had been set up on the ridges in accordance with Rommel's second principle: everything possible must be done to protect one's own supply lines and to upset, or better still, cut the enemy's. Ariete and 21st Panzer were well dug in and resisted all attacks. By the time a major attack was launched on 5 June, it was too late. Got el Ualeb had been overrun, almost before Ritchie realized what was happening.

Rommel's brilliant improvisation had turned a near-fatal encirclement into a wedge driven deep into British territory – and once again the British had been defeated by their inability to move their forces rapidly, as a unit.

Next, Rommel turned his attention to Bir Hacheim – the southern key to the whole Gazala Line, and a serious threat to his flanks and rear. That battle lasted a week, and turned out to be the hardest fought so far in the campaign. While it was still going on, the tank commanders of the Afrika Korps in the north – by now used to Rommel's tactics – reacted to the British attack against the Ariete at Got el Ualeb on 5 June with a fierce counteroffensive on 6 June and another on the 7th. Though both these attacks were repelled, the British suffered heavy losses and it was clear that the balance was shifting in Rommel's favor.

Finally, on 10 June, the Free French outpost fell. It was an important event: not only could Rommel's supplies now move freely, but a large number of tanks, artillery pieces and planes were released for the next move – to Tobruk itself.

Immediately he gathered most of his force for the move north. On 13 June Ritchie sent a force to the southwest for an attack on the Axis flank, but Rommel, concentrating his heavy artillery, lured the British forces into an ambush. In the heaviest blow struck so far by either side, about 300 British tanks were lost, compared to about 70 for the Axis. The engagement marked the final turning point in the battle. By 15 June Rommel had cut the coast road just west of Tobruk, and the British were forced back to their third defensive line near El Adem and Rezegh. This stand did not last long; both El Adem and Rezegh were abandoned by 18 June.

In 1941 Australian troops had held Tobruk for nine months, until Rommel's withdrawal to the west. That winter the Middle East Command in Cairo had decided that without naval support it would be impossible for the fortress ever to be held again in isolation. London had been informed and had – Cairo thought – agreed, but on 15 June Auchinleck received a telegram from the Prime Minister, 'Leave as many troops in Tobruk as are necessary to hold the place for certain.' At length a compromise was reached. Tobruk was to be 'temporarily' invested while a new strike force was built up near the frontier.

The main part of the garrison was to be formed by the 1st South African Division with General Klopper – a major general of one month's standing – named commander of the stronghold. The port's physical defenses, while not in good shape, were hardly weaker than they had been in April 1941. The barbed wire, tank traps and well-placed gun emplacements were still there. Equipment was, if anything, a bit better. There were two partial medium artillery regiments and the garrison was strong in field artillery. Although there were no antitank regiments, there were about 70 antitank guns, including 18 six-pounders. In antiaircraft guns – 18 3.7in and a number of Bofors – the strength was about the same, and there were about 55 tanks. The strength of the garrison was also about the same – some

TOP LEFT: British prisoners waiting to go into camps after the fall of Tobruk.

ABOVE LEFT: Tobruk harbor in flames.

RIGHT: British troops prepare to reenter the city following the German withdrawal after the Battle of El Alamein.

LEFT: General von Vaerst (right), commander of 15th Panzer Division talking with Lieutenant Colonel Westphal. Note the Afrika Korps armband worn by Westphal. Photo taken July 1942.

BELOW: The most feared weapon in the German armory, the famous 88, in action against British tanks.

35,000 men. There was one important difference – and it was one which Klopper, none too sure of himself or his position, was ill-equipped to deal with. This time the defending troops were exhausted, their morale was low, and the camp was filled with a feeling of insecurity and impermanence.

As Tobruk prepared for battle the South Africans took up their positions along the western and southern perimeter from the sea to the El Adem road. East from there were the 2nd Camerons, 2/5th Mahrattas and 2/7 Gurkhas. Near the Palestrino Ridge in the center were the 201st Brigade headquarters, the 3rd Coldstream, and the Sherwood Foresters. Meanwhile, the rest of the Eighth Army made their way toward the defenses at the Egyptian frontier.

As usual, Rommel had devised a ruse for capturing Tobruk. Only his infantry approached the western perimeter, while his mobile forces swept on past, to give the impression that he was heading straight for the border as he had done the year before – and sending messages in clear to reinforce the illusion. Just before Bardia he and the 90th Light Division turned back to join the Afrika Korps assault divisions and the XX Italian Motorized Corps, who had been waiting southeast of the city. He was using the same plan he had intended for 23 November 1941.

Rommel's zero hour was 0520 on 20 June. As the first rays of sunlight began to creep over the desert the long black lines of tanks, trucks and infantry slowly started to move forward. From far away there came a faint drone. As it grew louder small black dots appeared on the horizon which, as they drew nearer, resolved themselves into a wave of Stukas and Ju 88s. Every airworthy Axis plane in North Africa had been pressed into service for the battle. As the heavy artillery began to fire, the planes released their bombs and quickly got out of the way of the next wave, operating a shuttle service between the defense perimeter and El Adem airfield, 10 miles away. They pounded open a gap 600 yards wide. Behind them, under cover of the artillery barrage and half-hidden by smoke and dust, German and Italian sappers raced forward to lift the mines and bridge the tank traps, and tanks and infantry raced through the gaps. As they moved forward they lit red, green and purple flares and the Stukas dropped their bombs just ahead of the advancing, multicolored smoke screen while the other planes and the artillery blasted the enemy's rear with bombs and shells.

The timing of the entire operation was perfect. Panzer Army Africa might well have been on maneuvers. The first shock troops broke into the fortress from the southeast. A second group breached the defenses in the south, along the El Adem road, soon after. As tanks poured into the city they fanned out and headed for the harbor to disorganize the defenses and protect the supply dumps from demolition.

Inside Tobruk the situation was chaotic. General Klopper – his headquarters bombed out, his radio and telephone wrecked and his code book destroyed, lost the last vestige of control. Disconsolately he and his staff watched the Panzers race past their headquarters on their way to capture the fuel dumps in the harbor. Some British troops broke out to the east. Others fought grimly on, while still others, like the South Africans in the west and south-west, hardly realized anything was happening until the 90th Light came up on their rear.

By dawn on 21 June Tobruk was a pile of ruins. The streets were a maze of rubble and in the harbor the masts and funnels of sunken ships rose pathetically from the water. General Klopper gave his compass and staff car to seven young men from the South African 6th Brigade who were determined to escape, saying, 'I wish I was coming with you.'

A few hours later a small party of officers set off in a truck, a little white flag fluttering over the hood, and at 0940 on the Via Balbo Klopper officially turned the city over to Rommel. Soon after, a large white flag was hoisted over 6th Brigade Headquarters.

The signal to surrender created even more confusion. Some units never got it. Others, like the 3rd Coldstream, decided to ignore it and try to escape. The Cameron Highlanders, along with the remnants of some of the Indian brigades, held out for more than 24 hours – surrendering only after being told that if they did not the Germans would concentrate every piece of artillery in Tobruk on their position. Finally giving in, they marched down to the prisoner of war cage in parade formation, with the pipes skirling 'The March of the Cameron Men.' As they approached every man along the way – prisoner and German sentry alike – snapped to attention.

After two years in British hands Tobruk had fallen in two days – and despite Rommel's anger at the extent of the destruction effected by British demolition squads on vehicle parks and fuel dumps, he still had captured enough to carry him on his drive to Egypt. The fall of Tobruk came as a shattering blow to the British public (as Churchill had known it would), as well as to the Australians and South Africans. General Klopper came in for most of the criticism, but he was not entirely to blame. The decision to defend Tobruk at all had been, in General Bayerlein's phrase, 'a fatal decision.' Though a more experienced general might have made more progress toward pulling the garrison into shape in time, there was also confusion among the British High Command. For example, Auchinleck realized full well that Rommel was almost certain to stick to his original plan and attack from the southeast but when Ritchie flew into Tobruk on 16 June to confer with the defenders, he warned Klopper to pay special attention to the western perimeter.

On the Axis side there was great enthusiasm. Mussolini, hitherto anxious to move slowly and consolidate positions, flew to North Africa with a white horse to ride when he entered Cairo at the head of his troops. Hitler was ecstatic, calling the victory an 'historic turning point' of 'decisive import' for the whole war. On 22 June Rommel received a message from the Führer informing him that at the age of 49 he had just been appointed Germany's youngest Field Marshal. He celebrated that night with canned pineapple and a small glass of whisky, but after dinner he wrote his wife, 'Hitler has made me a Field Marshal. I would much rather he had given me one more division.' Still, he was in unusually good spirits – it was the high point of his career as well as for the North African campaign.

Typically, he saw it not as an end, but as the springboard to a new Egyptian campaign. True to his cardinal rule – never give the enemy a breathing space – he did not celebrate too long. The next day his Order of the Day read, 'Soldiers of the Panzer Army Africa! Now we must utterly destroy the enemy! During the coming days I shall be making great demands upon you once more, so that we may reach our goal.' Gathering the tired but triumphant Afrika Korps together he set off in pursuit of the Eighth Army and that ultimate goal – the Nile.

He would never get there. Hitler, by discontinuing the attack on Malta and refusing to send Rommel adequate supplies, would make defeat in the desert inevitable. Later, the Field Marshal would find himself presiding over another fiasco – the defense of Normandy – and still later would come involvement in the plot against Hitler and, eventually, suicide.

All this was in the future; in June 1942 the Desert Fox was as he is still best remembered – dashing, resourceful and brave, racing across the desert with the tanks of the Afrika Korps, heading for the pyramids of Egypt.

CHAPTER EIGHT

MONTGOMERY

AND THE BATTLE OF EL ALAMEIN

IN THE last week of June 1942 the entire British position in the Middle East seemed to be on the verge of collapse. The battered Eighth Army was in retreat, racing for the Egyptian frontier before, beside, and sometimes even behind Rommel's victorious *Panzerarmee Afrika*. The loss of some 80,000 men since 26 May and the wreckage of two armored corps testified to the triumph of German professionalism over superior numbers. The victory seemed so complete that Rommel, even though he had orders to halt on the frontier and await the capture of Malta, was given the go ahead to continue the chase and take advantage of the panic and resulting disorganization of the British Army.

On 25 June the Commander in Chief for the Middle East, General Sir Claude Auchinleck, flew to Mersa Matruh from Cairo to take over personal command of the Eighth Army from General Ritchie and begin a planned, more orderly withdrawal to the defenses at El Alamein. By 30 June this had been accomplished and the two armies had begun arranging themselves, with Auchinleck hurriedly organizing the defensive positions for a last-ditch stand while Rommel pulled his exhausted troops together for another major effort. If the seemingly indestructible Afrika Korps could overcome this obstacle there would be little to stand in their way as they drove toward the Nile and the Suez Canal. Less than a hundred miles away, in Alexandria, papers were destroyed and government offices evacuated with a speed the Desert Fox himself would have envied, while the Royal Navy hurriedly sailed out of the harbor.

Waiting in the wings was another actor – a complex, often abrasive character who would soon achieve a reputation in the desert that would equal Rommel's and receive the impressive title, Field Marshal the Viscount Montgomery of Alamein, KG. In July 1942, of course, he was simply Lieutenant General Bernard Law Montgomery, a largely unknown career soldier in the Home Army, with more than a month to go before his first appearance on the desert stage.

Montgomery came from a large family (the fourth of nine children) that had no military tradition. Born in 1887 in Moville, county Donegal where his father was an Anglican bishop, he lived in Ireland for two years before the family was moved to Tasmania, Australia. From all accounts, including his own, he had a very unhappy childhood which he describes as 'a series of fierce battles, from which my mother invariably emerged the victor.' He was, again in his own words, 'a dreadful little boy' - a loner, in constant rebellion against an unusually strict, methodical mother, given to rudeness, bullying and hysterics.

In 1902 the Montgomeries returned to England, and young Bernard became a day pupil at St Paul's School where he asked to be enrolled in the 'army class.' This involved no commitment to the military; the 'army class' was simply designed for those more inclined to practical than academic pursuits. His mother's overreaction to the news decided him – from that moment on he was determined to be a soldier. At home he remained surly and morose, but at school he was energetic, good at cricket and other games (where his agility and stamina earned him the nickname 'Monkey'), and a confident, effective leader. He had no hobbies, no intellectual interests, and very little scholastic ability but he did have a driving ambition.

At the age of 19 – in January 1907 – he entered the Royal Military College at Sandhurst. The year began well and after six weeks he was among the few outstanding cadets promoted to lance corporal. The honor gave him an overinflated sense of power and he soon became the ringleader of a gang that persecuted other cadets. Following an unfortunate episode in which Montgomery set fire to someone's shirt tails, resulting in severe burns, he was demoted and was not allowed to graduate with the rest of his class. This reverse finally gave him the impetus he needed to settle down and work and for the first time he began to demonstrate the concentration on and devotion to minutiae, the passion for precise detail, that was to play such a large part in his future professional life.

On leaving Sandhurst he joined the Warwickshires – primarily because they had a good reputation but also because he liked their cap badge. He was anything but a typical officer – he was not good on a horse, had no military connections or social graces, and showed only intermittent respect for authority.

In 1913 back in England after a tour of duty in India, the young officer began for the first time a systematic study of the art of war. However, within three weeks after World War I began he was in France learning about war on a much more practical level. Badly wounded in his first major action, he was sent back to England, promoted to captain, and awarded the DSO – one of the highest honors the British Army can bestow for sustained gallantry in the face of the enemy. For a subaltern to win it was very rare at that time, and generally meant that he had just missed the Victoria Cross.

During the 1920s and 1930s he began to stand out as a radical crusader for military efficiency – a quality badly needed in the British Army at the time. In 1927 he married Betty Carver, a widow with two sons. The next year their son David was born and Montgomery's life was completely changed. He and his wife were inseparable and she used affection and gentle mockery to soften his rough edges. Her death, only ten years later, 'utterly defeated' him for the first time in his life. From that time he built a wall around himself which was impenetrable and he began living only for his work.

By 1938 he was established in his first senior command, with the 8th Infantry Division in Palestine, where the flood of Jews fleeing Nazi persecution in Europe had led to a state of emergency among the native Arab inhabitants. This grounding in Palestine was useful. He was noted for his insistence on methodical operations from a firm base (though he was fighting guerrillas), his egotistical view of his troops and their operations, and his ability to make sure that 'his' achievements were known and recognized in the proper quarters. He was also ruthless with the incompetent or inefficient.

LEFT: General Montgomery sports one of his morale boosting devices – an Australian style hat decorated with the cap badges of a selection of the units under his command.

RIGHT: Another of Montgomery's characteristics was his emphasis on meticulous preparation and training. He is seen here discussing a tactical problem with a group of senior officers.

When World War II began Montgomery went to France with the British Expeditionary Force, in command of the 3rd Division. With his usual energy he immediately began strenuously training his men, instilling a professional attitude toward war that helped immeasurably in maintaining order during the British retreat to and evacuation from Dunkirk. At this time too he made a great impression on his corps commander, Alan Brooke – which was to be of great value to him in his future career.

After Dunkirk he was stationed in England, climbing the ladder of promotion fairly rapidly, despite his abrasive personality and his unfortunate habit of displaying an insolence that approached insubordination toward officers he did not respect (a group which included General Auchinleck). By 1941 he was a Lieutenant General in charge of the South Eastern Army – England's main anti-invasion force, the post he still had at the beginning of July 1942.

Meanwhile, in Egypt, Auchinleck and the Eighth Army were racing against time to prepare for Rommel's arrival. The area chosen for their final defense was a narrow neck of land, about 40 miles wide, between El Alamein on the Mediterranean and the Qattara Depression in the south. The northern half of the passage was featureless, so much so that almost imperceptible rises in the ground were to assume great tactical significance in the months that followed. South of the long, low rise called the Miteirya Ridge and the rocky, austere Ruweisat Ridge came the smooth swelling of Alam Nayil, with the Alam Halfa ridge some

ABOVE: from left to right, Mr Anthony Eden, General Brooke, Air Chief Marshal Tedder, Admiral Cunningham, General Alexander, General Marshall, General Eisenhower and Montgomery with Winston Churchill in the center at an Allied conference.

14 miles to the east. These were followed by a series of abrupt escarpments. Further south the going got even worse as the rocks disappeared in a stretch of eroded channels and soft sand – 'devil's country' that continued to the edge of the great Qattara Depression and the steep cone of Mt Himeimat, which although it only rose to 700 feet, dominated the landscape like a great pyramid.

Auchinleck had chosen well. If they were properly disposed, there was no way the defenders' flanks could be turned in that narrow passage, especially since the rough going in the south would drastically hinder the movement of Rommel's armor. It was just as well, for the British had their backs against the wall. With such a small area for maneuver, the loss of even a little territory could be vital in the defense of Egypt. Rommel, on the other hand, could afford to lose much more ground without really damaging his position. Similarly, in the race for supplies and reinforcements, gaining a slight advantage would not materially affect Britain's position. Even if they could push Rommel back to the border and ease some of the pressure on Alexandria, it would not be enough for them to destroy him altogether. For the Axis, though, even a small increase in men and materiel might be enough to allow Rommel to make a temporary breakthrough, which could be all he needed to clear the way for his dash to the Nile.

So, Auchinleck threw everything he could muster into the breach at El Alamein. It was just enough. Time and again during July Rommel sent his tired troops against the British line only to see them thrown back. The balance of forces was too even to allow either side to launch a successful counteroffensive.

Meanwhile, behind the lines, the race for supplies went on. Britain had by far the longer and more dangerous supply route, but thanks to President Roosevelt a stream of men and equipment – including American tanks and planes – flowed steadily into Alexandria. Rommel, for his part, could obtain little from a country already strained to its limits by the demands of the Russian campaign. In air power, he could not match the Desert Air Force, now supplemented by American forces. Though possession of the port of Tobruk helped ease his supply lines it was attacked almost nightly. His convoys, too, were under constant bombardment by planes and submarines, as German air strength was diverted from attacking Malta to the Eastern Front.

Once again, the attitudes of the Axis and Allies toward the North African campaign were to be the deciding factor. Hitler never really appreciated its significance, always putting it second to his Napoleonic dreams of conquest in Europe. Even before Italy entered the war in June 1940, the Mediterranean and the Balkans had played a major role in British strategic planning. After America entered the conflict in December 1941, it was agreed at the Arcadia conference that one of the Allies' primary aims must be to 'tighten the ring' around Germany – and the southern section of that ring ran along the North African coast.

Thus, Auchinleck was under considerable pressure to do more than fight a holding action. Churchill, not the most patient man at the best of times, was having political difficulties at home and was anxious for a spectacular victory to bolster his fading popularity. In addition 'the Auk,' as the Commander in Chief for the entire Middle East, could not give his full attention to affairs in Egypt, and was frequently distracted by developments in Iraq, Syria and elsewhere. In short, his command was too large and complex and there was too much expected of him in too short a time – a fact Churchill subsequently admitted when it was too late.

There were, however, some severe problems within the Eighth Army, and Churchill fastened on them eagerly. There were indications that Auchinleck's command organization was not working harmoniously or effectively, and he seemed reluctant to change it in any way. Furthermore, morale was at a new low. The ups and downs of the desert war had sapped the battle-hardened veterans' confidence in their ability finally to defeat the Afrika Korps. The uneasy stalemate in July, with its frequent orders for attacks that turned out to be futile, accompanied by unfortunate, if necessary, precautionary plans for withdrawal, further weakened morale.

Churchill decided that only a drastic change could restore the Eighth Army's confidence. Early in August he visited Cairo with General Brooke (now Chief of the Imperial General Staff) and after a whirlwind tour of several Eighth Army units the two concluded that 'a new start and vehement action were needed to animate the vast but baffled and somewhat unhinged organization.' The Prime Minister's temper was not improved on this visit by Auchinleck who, lacking Montgomery's facility for public relations, made few provisions for his comfort or entertainment and left him more or less to his own devices.

Churchill's plan embodied changes in both organization and personnel. On the organizational side, Persia and Iraq would retain the name 'Middle East Command' while Libya, Egypt, East Africa, Palestine, and Syria would be detached to form the 'Near East Command.'

Within this new organization, he proposed, Auchinleck would take over the Middle East, with communication lines running back to India. For the Near East he had a new team: General Sir Harold Alexander would be installed as Commander in Chief, headquartered in Cairo; General 'Strafer' Gott would take over as commander of the Eighth Army (though Gott himself felt that he was too tired and lacking in new ideas to handle the job effectively); and Brooke's protégé, Montgomery, would be named British Task Force Commander for Operation Torch (the Allied landing in North Africa, scheduled for early November). The day after the decision was made, the plane in which Gott was returning to Cairo was shot down and the general killed. Thus two unknown Luftwaffe fighter pilots can take credit for bringing together what was to become the winning British command team. Montgomery was given Gott's job as Commander, Eighth Army, while General Anderson took his place with General Eisenhower.

Alexander – considered by many to be the best strategical brain in the Empire – was the ideal man for the labyrinthine politico-military atmosphere of wartime Cairo. He had a wealth of battle experience, having participated in most of the major battles of World War I and in many minor operations from the Baltic to India's Northwest Frontier; from this he had developed not only sound military judgment, but also a real knowledge of British and Indian soldiers that helped him avoid psychological mistakes when dealing with them. Above all, he was an ideal supervisor – good at decentralization and knowing not only how much freedom to give his subordinates, but also when and how to step in if things were going wrong. He was a perfect superior officer for Montgomery.

The new commander of the Eighth army stood out in distinct contrast to his urbane superior officer. He was not a likeable character – still less the sort of 'decent chap' so highly prized by the upper echelons of the British army. His conspicuous lack of some of the more civilized virtues led many of his contemporaries to see him as a vain, opinionated showoff, an overrated general and a thoroughly unpleasant human being; even Churchill once referred to him as 'a little man on the make.'

To many of the men who served in the ranks in the desert or, later, in the Normandy landings he was an almost god-like figure. In addition, many of his superiors considered him to be a first-class leader who took no risks and was the epitome of the dedicated professional. This professionalism was one of his best qualities – along with his ability to instill it in the men under his command. He had the great gift of being able to explain the most complicated plan so that it appeared simple and when he had finished a briefing everyone present knew exactly what he had to do – and more importantly why he had to do it and how his job fitted into the overall operation. In fact, Montgomery had more flair than the rather diffident Alexander when it came to talking to men and officers in public. His high-pitched rasping voice could hold an audience spellbound.

In his work, Montgomery was devoted to precision, caution and control. His plans – which usually relied more on overwhelming force than on skillful maneuvering – left nothing to chance. Most of his experience had been gained in the staff room rather than on the battlefield, and where Alexander deplored useless loss of life for humanitarian reasons, Montgomery hated it because it reflected poor organization.

Though he could with justice claim that he never lost a battle, he often made disastrous miscalculations. Some of these stemmed from his naturally unpredictable, eccentric state of mind, but also especially since the death of his wife, the world outside his work had become shadowy and unreal. This narrow view often hampered his decision-making capability. As will be seen later, the battle of Alamein is a good example of a certain victory that was very nearly turned into defeat.

Upon their arrival, the new command team faced three major challenges: to improve the Eighth Army's morale; defeat Rommel's next attack, which intelligence sources predicted for 26 August; and prepare their own offensive (codenamed Operation Lightfoot), which was to be co-ordinated with Operation Torch.

Montgomery immediately plunged into the work of training and reorganizing the worn-out army, directing all his energies toward making it an efficient, professional and above all tidy organization. His first move was to establish communications with all levels of the army, so that when the time came each of the tens of thousands of soldiers would not only know what to do, but would have the incentive to do it.

He was the first British general consciously to project an 'image' to his troops. Every unit was visited, and as the general's cold gaze balefully fell on the idle or incompetent, as the rasping voice explained, questioned, or ordered, he was striving to leave an impression on every man's mind. Even his studied informality of dress and his famous hats (an Australian slouch hat carrying all the 9th Australian Division badges or a black Tank Corps

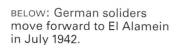

LEFT: A German 88mm gun bombarding British tanks. Far fewer 88s were actually in use than Allied soldiers of the time would have believed.

BELOW: German soliders move forward to El Alamein in July 1942.

BELOW RIGHT: British prisoners of war near El Alamein, summer 1942.

beret) were carefully calculated to make the 'new boy' part of the desert world as soon as possible. Pressmen and photographers appeared in unprecedented numbers and the Army public relations staff began working overtime.

In addition to his famous 'no bellyaching' order, Montgomery stressed in his talks to the troops that there were to be no plans for withdrawal, and that in the future there would be fewer risks, no short cuts and – most important – no more failure. The organizational changes he announced included training the X Corps, under General Lumsden, as a mobile *corps de chasse* to rival the Afrika Korps, and the relocation of Eighth army Headquarters from the eastern end of Ruweisat Ridge to the seashore at Burg el Arab – for closer cooperation with the Desert Air Force and for greater comfort. His firm line was usually well received. Some of the men were too disillusioned to accept this unknown general, who had just arrived from England with his 'knees still pink,' at face value, but most were at least content to give him the benefit of the doubt.

The next problem, preparing for Rommel's expected attack in August, was easier to solve. Soon after his arrival Montgomery had several conversations with Auchinleck, with General Ramsden (commander of the XXX Corps) and others – all of whom described their plans for the defense of the British position. In talks with Churchill and Brooke on 19 August, these became Montgomery's plans – but in fact the prelude to Alamein, the battle of Alam Halfa, was eventually to be fought on a plan constructed by General Dorman-Smith (first Auchinleck's principal Operations Officer and then, until Montgomery's arrival, Deputy Chief of Staff) and approved and initiated by Auchinleck, and utilizing fixed defenses which had for the most part been dug before he ever left England.

By the end of August Rommel was still at a disadvantage., despite the reinforcements that had arrived earlier in the month. He still had only 200 German tanks, and was so short of fuel that, though he still planned to sweep around the southern flank, he had then to use a much shorter turning radius than he

would have liked. The British, by contrast, had 713 tanks in the forward area (including 164 heavy Grants). All infantry and artillery divisions now had 6-pounder antitank guns, and the Desert Air Force had achieved complete control of the skies over Alamein. In addition, Rommel was so ill that he could not get out of his truck. He was not only under constant medical supervision but had a replacement ready on the spot at all times. Gause, his Chief of Staff, was also sick – none of which helped morale in the Axis army.

Nevertheless, after nightfall on 30 August, Rommel's four veteran divisions – the Afrika Korps and the Italian XX Corps – began to work their way through the British minefields. The barriers were thicker than they had expected, so that as dawn broke on 31 August they were only just emerging instead of being already in position in front of Alam Halfa Ridge.

Almost from the beginning it was obvious to Rommel that the offensive would not succeed. In fact, he considered a withdrawal at 0800 hours on 31 August but he allowed himself to be dissuaded by General Bayerlein. The only doubt in Montgomery's mind was whether Axis troops really were committed to an attack from the south. By 1100 hours it was clear that this was the case, and British forces were rearranged accordingly. At 1300 the Panzer Army stopped to refuel and then, instead of swinging out to the center and eastern end of Alam Halfa in an encircling movement, they turned sharply north and drove straight for the heavily defended western end – a move dictated by the shortage of fuel and the time they had lost in the minefields.

The attack stalled and that evening Allied aircraft inflicted heavy damage on both equipment and personnel (for the first time US pilots in Liberators, Mitchells, and Kittyhawks were flying alongside the RAF). The next night, 1-2 September, saw more of the same. By dawn – battered and almost completely out of fuel – the Afrika Korps began to edge away to the west.

At this point Montgomery, by launching a counter-offensive across Rommel's communication lines, could probably have encircled all the Axis armor and finished the Battle of Alamein before it ever began. With his usual desire to avoid any risk of failure and his unwillingness to deviate from a set schedule, he declined pressing the issue. By the night of 3-4 September the opportunity had passed and the Panzer Army was executing another of its skillful withdrawals. On 6 September they were out of danger, and in addition had established a bridgehead on the eastern edge of the British minefields, astride Mt Himeimat.

In later years Montgomery was to claim credit for devising the defensive tactics that prevented British armor from being destroyed piecemeal as in previous engagements. However, according to General Renton, Gott (ordered before his death to prepare a detailed defense against the German attack) had never intended 'unleashing the armor.' Despite this, and despite the missed opportunity, Alam Halfa was a model defensive battle that reflects great credit on both the planners and the field generals (Montgomery and Gott's replacement, Horrocks) who executed those plans.

Characteristically, Churchill wanted to follow up Alam Halfa with an immediate offensive in mid-September. Equally characteristically, Montgomery refused, determined to do nothing until the odds were overwhelmingly in his favor. Eventually the Prime Minister gave in, but he did so with bad grace. He insisted that the Eighth Army must have a decisive victory over Rommel before Operation Torch was launched on 8 November.

Much has been written about whether or not the battle of Alamein was really necessary. From a strictly military point of view, it probably need not have been fought at all. Rommel

would have had to withdraw as soon as Operation Torch began, and would have found himself sandwiched between two forces almost immediately. There were several political reasons for a strong British offensive: to dispel any feeling in the United States that American boys were being killed to salvage British prestige in an obscure colonial backwater; to influence the French population in Morocco and Algeria; and to help Churchill quell the atmosphere of distrust that marked his dealings with Stalin.

Thus, throughout September and October, Allied naval and merchant vessels delivered supplies and reinforcements to Egypt. Workshops hummed, supply depots swelled and spread and camps were crowded with pale-skinned soldiers.

Rommel knew that a major attack was imminent, but did not have enough transport with which to withdraw to a better position at Fuka. All he could do was dig in and make his positions as strong as possible. In the weeks before he went on sick leave his Italian and German sappers laid half a million mines across the entire front, in a honeycomb pattern. Within the cells of the pattern they planted 'Devil's Gardens' – patches of mines and any other booby traps they could devise, such as harmless-looking wooden poles attached to huge charges of explosives. They employed other tricks too – like burying metal rods which would register on metal detectors, to camouflage the gaps in the minefields. One group actually followed a British sweeping squad, laying mines behind them, so that the reconnaissance group that came later found a nasty surprise waiting. Another

group crept into British minefields and removed detonators, then reburied the harmless mines. (Needless to say, the British sappers were engaged in many similar activities.)

German and Italian infantry units were strung out all along this line. The biggest problem to be faced, however, was deployment of the armor. There was no way Rommel could obey his own cardinal principle and concentrate the armor because he did not have enough fuel to move it effectively to a threatened point. In addition it was too vulnerable to Allied air attack when it was on the move. Out of necessity, then, he placed his 15th Panzer and Littorio Divisions in the north, where they formed into three mixed groups; 21st Panzer and Ariete did the same in the south. His only reserves, 90th Light and Trieste, guarded the coast at El Daba against an amphibious landing. On 22 September, having done all he could to secure his position, Rommel finally left for Germany to have his swollen liver and constantly inflamed throat seen to.

By the end of September 1942 Montgomery had 195,000 men to Rommel's 54,000 Italians and 50,000 Germans. He had 1029 medium tanks to the Germans' 496, 1451 antitank guns as opposed to 800 (of which some 85 were the impressive 88s) and 908 pieces of field and medium artillery against the Panzer Army's 500. All this was in addition to virtually unlimited supplies of ammunition, fuel and other stores.

Most welcome of all the new weapons were 300 Sherman tanks – products of American tank expertise combined with British battle experience. With their powerful 75mm guns, they were a match for anything the Germans could field. Almost as valuable were the 'Priests' – 105mm self-propelled guns, on tank chassis, with a flashless charge to make them harder to locate. British antitank guns – the 6-pounders – were good weapons also.

For their part, in addition to the Panzer Mark IIIs and IVs, the Axis forces had the most formidable piece of artillery in the desert – the famous 88, with its 21-pound armor-piercing shot that could kill an enemy tank at 3000 yards. One of these guns could hold off an entire tank squadron for some time. The German infantry was armed with the Spandau, described as a 'vicious' machine gun with an intimidating sound like a racing car revving up.

Throughout September and the beginning of October, Montgomery collected more supplies, trained his army and laid his plans with his usual supreme confidence. Starting with Auchinleck's general concept of a breakthrough in the northern sector of the line (previously both sides had always swung first south, then north toward the coast in an attempt to encircle and trap their opponents), he developed his own system of organization and tactics. His would be a methodical, controlled operation; he still did not have enough confidence in the level of training throughout the army to give his forces much independence. In this he was probably justified. During their years in the desert the veterans of the Panzer Army had come to understand each other so well that they fought as a team almost by instinct. The British army, on the other hand, had always been a much more unwieldy, less homogeneous group and could not achieve that instinctive cooperation.

Just two weeks before Operation Lightfoot was scheduled to begin, Montgomery radically changed his plan of attack. Contrary to all the tenets of desert warfare, which held that armor should be destroyed first (at which the infantry would collapse almost of its own accord) he decided to have his armored divisions simply hold off the Axis tanks while the British infantry units destroyed their opponents in the main defensive system.

Four infantry divisions of the XXX Corps were to open two gaps through the German minefields: one in the north toward Kidney Ridge and another in the south over Miteirya Ridge. Right behind them would come the three armored divisions of X Corps, who would pass through the gaps and establish Report Line 'Pierson,' some two miles beyond the infantry's goal, 'Oxalic.' There they would set up defensive positions until the Axis infantry had crumbled, then chase and cut off the remnants of the Panzer Army. If the infantry had not reached Oxalic by dawn of the first day, the tanks would have to fight their own way out to Pierson.

Meanwhile, XIII Corps and 7th Armored Division would mount a diversionary attack in the south to pin down the 21st Panzer/Ariete groups. Other features of the long, elaborate campaign to deceive the Axis about the real focus of the attack included fake radio traffic and troop movements, and the building

ABOVE LEFT: Grant tanks of the British 22nd Armored Brigade advance to the front line in column, south of El Alamein.

ABOVE RIGHT: The unusual luxury of an early morning wash for two British soldiers.

RIGHT: Afrika Korps veterans push forward to Alamein.

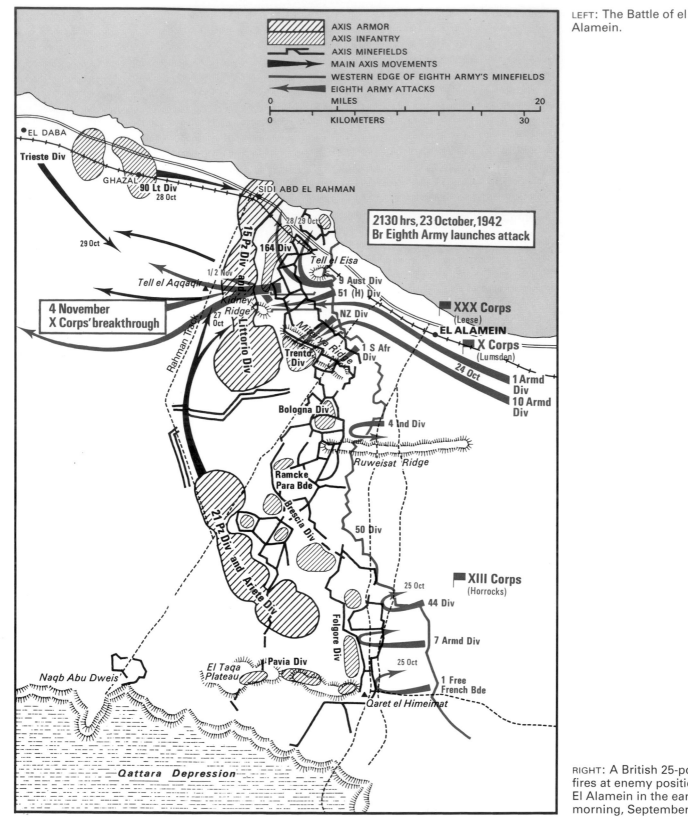

AXIS ARMOR
AXIS INFANTRY
AXIS MINEFIELDS
MAIN AXIS MOVEMENTS
WESTERN EDGE OF EIGHTH ARMY'S MINEFIELDS
EIGHTH ARMY ATTACKS

MILES 0 — 20
KILOMETERS 0 — 30

EL DABA

Trieste Div

GHAZAL
90 Lt Div
28 Oct

SIDI ABD EL RAHMAN

29 Oct

28/29 Oct

15 Pz Div and Littorio Div

164 Div

Tell el Eisa

1/2 Nov

2130 hrs, 23 October, 1942
Br Eighth Army launches attack

Tell el Aqqaqir

9 Aust Div

51 (H) Div

Kidney Ridge

XXX Corps
(Leese)

4 November
X Corps' breakthrough

27 Oct

NZ Div

EL ALAMEIN

Miteirya Ridge

X Corps
(Lumsden)

Trento Div

1 S Afr Div

24 Oct

1 Armd Div
10 Armd Div

Bologna Div

4 Ind Div

Ruweisat Ridge

Ramcke Para Bde

Rahman Track

Brescia Div

50 Div

21 Pz Div and Ariete Div

XIII Corps
(Horrocks)

25 Oct

44 Div

Folgore Div

7 Armd Div

El Taqa Plateau

Pavia Div

25 Oct

Naqb Abu Dweis

1 Free French Bde

Qaret el Himeimat

Qattara Depression

of a dummy pipeline. Even though General Stumme (who had assumed command on Rommel's departure) incorrectly believed that the attack would take place in the south, he was never in any doubt about the actual timing of the offensive, despite all the British efforts to hint at a late-November date.

As D-Day drew nearer, confidence in the British command – which had been noticeably shaky – began to improve. Their unprecedented superiority in men and materiel, their complete control of the air, and the efficiency of their intelligence operations made the outcome apparently certain.

By contrast the Axis forces were in an unhappy position – short of food, water, fuel and supplies. To make matters worse,

the German High Command appeared to have no conception of the gravity of the situation. On 23 October – D-Day – a visiting staff officer told Stumme that in OKW's opinion there was no danger of a British offensive in the near future.

But that evening, as the full moon rose, 882 guns opened fire, in Montgomery's words, 'like one battery' along the 38-mile front. The German guns, under orders to conserve ammunition, remained silent. Twenty minutes later the barrage lifted and more than 70,000 British soldiers and 600 tanks moved out toward the 12,000 men of the Italian Trento and German 164th Infantry divisions.

Most of the carefully laid traps in the Devil's Gardens had

been destroyed by the artillery barrage. Getting through the gaps should have been a simple process. However there were too many men and too much equipment packed into the narrow lanes. The infantry, with no room to fight, could not get to the western edge of the minefields. The sappers could not clear lanes for the armor and the tanks piled behind everyone where they attracted a good deal of enemy fire. Soon the area looked to General Carver like a 'badly organized car park at an immense race meeting held in a dust bowl' and into the immobile mass deadly and accurate fire continued to pour from the Axis guns. The cumbersome crowding together of infantry and armor had turned out to be a major blunder.

The problem was accentuated by the gulf of sectional pride and professional suspicion that traditionally separated infantry and armored forces in the British army. The German services achieved close cooperation naturally; their similar training and all their experience were geared toward establishing a harmonious working relationship. As Corelli Barnett has pointed out, asking the British services to do the same was, 'like asking an estranged man and wife to make love.'

All through the 24th the attack continued. The Littorio and 15th Panzer Division had moved in to form a containing line which, by fighting desperately, they managed to hold through the thunder of the artillery and the rain of Allied bombs. The X Corps (Montgomery's *corps de chasse*), with orders to fight its way through if necessary, was still 1000 yards from its objective at the western end of the northern gap. At the southern gap, the armor commanders (Gatehouse and Lumsden) were understandably reluctant to send their tanks over the crest of Miteirya Ridge and down through uncharted minefields under heavy German fire. Montgomery, however, insisted that the objectives must be met. One regiment, the Staffordshire Yeomanry, tried to get through – and lost all but 15 of its tanks. Finally, at dawn on the 25th, the British armor had either to withdraw back behind the ridge or risk being caught without cover within range of the powerful 88s. In the southern sector of the front the diversionary attack had gone astray, leaving the 7th Armored Division and 44th Division stranded in the German minefields. Already the offensive seemed poised on the brink of failure.

Early on the 25th Rommel was recalled from his sick bed and boarded a plane at Wiener Neustadt. That evening he landed at El Daba and immediately set off for the front. The report he received next morning from General Ritter von Thoma was anything but encouraging, despite the fact that his men were still

managing to hold the British off. General Stumme – a courageous soldier, but one who lacked Rommel's desert experience, instinct and luck – had been killed in the front line. Most of the Devil's Gardens had been destroyed by artillery fire. The men were becoming demoralized and much equipment had been lost as the result of bombing and strafing by Allied planes, which were flying virtually uncontested missions. The 15th Panzer had only 31 tanks still in working order and no new supplies of fuel or ammunition could be expected.

Rommel's only hope lay not in withdrawal at this point, but in a swift, violent counterattack. He immediately issued orders to mass all mobile forces in the northern sector. For a time he was afraid to bring 21st Panzer and Ariete up from the south, but it soon became evident that Montgomery was himself moving troops north. Rommel gambled, and on the 27th pulled 21st Panzer and half the artillery up to help with the attack. He also brought the 90th Light and Trieste forward from El Daba to reinforce the coastal positions.

Montgomery, meanwhile, had spent most of 26 and 27 October in seclusion, rearranging his own plans and dispositions to create a force that could break the stalemate. The 7th Armored Division was to be moved north into reserve where it would join the New Zealanders, the 10th Armored Division, and the 9th Armored Brigade. The 1st Armored Division would continue to press westward around Kidney ridge, and the Australians would begin a move on the coast road.

On 27 October Rommel launched his offensive – but this time the British stood their ground and the attack was beaten off. On the 28th he tried again. The offensive was broken up by Allied air strikes before it ever got off the ground. The Axis forces braced themselves for the British counteroffensive – but nothing happened. Montgomery was still reorganizing his troop dispositions and would not move until the last man was in his position.

The stalemate continued for some days. Though the fighting was fierce – often getting down to hand-to-hand combat in the German artillery positions – the British could make no real progress. Still, it was obvious to both Montgomery and Rommel that no amount of skill or courage could change the final outcome in view of the Allies superiority in manpower and every type of materiel.

Montgomery hoped to launch his great breakthrough, Operation Supercharge, on the night of 31 October – 1 November; but when the time came, X and XXX Corps were still too disorganized, and the main event had to be postponed for 24 hours. General Morshead and the Australians did mount a preliminary attack on the Axis coastal positions to 'keep Rommel occupied,' and managed to trap part of the 164th Division against the sea for a time, before they were beaten off by a violent counterattack from the 90th Light and a battle group from the 21st Panzer.

As night fell on 1 November, most of Rommel's men had been in action for nine days without a break. The northern front, which had been gradually pushed back until all his minefields were in British hands, had been broken in many places. The new front was being desperately defended with too few guns, too little armor and the remains of decimated divisions.

That evening Montgomery followed his well-established pattern. There was a three-hour artillery barrage, followed by carpet bombing by the RAF and an infantry attack. At 0100 on 2 November, 400 tanks rushed through the gap (there were 400 more still in reserve) to meet Rommel's 90 German and Italian 'battlewagons.' Supercharge appeared to be going well in the beginning but amazingly, as the last great tank battle of the desert war developed on 2 November around Tell el Aqqaqir,

the attack stalled. The Desert Fox was fighting one of the best tank actions of his career. In fact, at one point his counterattacks almost broke through the British salient. Behind the German lines, however, the infantry units had begun slipping away toward Fuka, while von Thoma prepared to continue the delaying action – with less than a third of his men and only 35 tanks remaining to face the reserves which Montgomery now threw into the breach.

All through 3 November the British X and XXX Corps attacked over and over again. It seemed that the Afrika Korps would never break. While the veterans of the German and Italian armored divisions were carrying out their phenomenal defense, held together by loyalty and the force of Rommel's personality, the rest of the Panzer Army was continuing its withdrawal. It was a difficult day for Rommel, but when he saw that, 'the enemy was operating with . . . astonishing hesitancy and caution,' he considered that he had a good chance of pulling through.

On 3 November, however, in response (he thought) to a message he had sent Hitler regarding the withdrawal, Rommel received a personal telegram from the Führer – containing one of his famous 'stand fast . . . victory or death' exhortations. Rommel hesitated, but eventually decided that he, who had always insisted on unqualified obedience from his own men, could not depart from that principle himself. All orders for withdrawal were cancelled. Montgomery had received help from an unexpected source.

At 0800 on 4 November Montgomery threw 200 tanks against the northern sector of the line, held by the 90th Light and the remaining 22 Afrika Korps tanks. Shortly before noon von Thoma was captured. In the center another 100 tanks descended upon the battered, badly equipped survivors of the Italian Tank Corps who, though outflanked, fought until their last tank was destroyed. At 1730 Rommel finally decided to pull his men out against orders.

The battle of El Alamein was over and the chase, which would finally end in Tunisia, had begun. On 5 November an exuberant Montgomery held a press conference to announce his 'complete and absolute victory.' Victory it was, but the fruits of that victory, which Clausewitz has said must be gathered in vigorous pursuit, were not to be forthcoming. Again, Montgomery had a chance to destroy the Panzer Army – but again he chose a cautious, methodical approach that kept the huge British war machine lumbering along one step behind Rommel. Of course, he had laid plans for a pursuit, but adequate provision had not been made for the problem of getting several divisions, under two different corps commands who were not on the best of terms, through the narrow salient. In addition, the men were physically exhausted after 12 days of hard fighting, and were disinclined to snatch the initiative even if Montgomery had ordered it. His staff were mentally fatigued and simply not up to coordinating operations.

By the time Montgomery could mount a full-scale chase, Rommel and the Afrika Korps already had a day's head start. Worn out and pounded down to less than 5000 men, some 11 tanks and about 25 antitank guns, they were still the masters of desert warfare – and proved it as they conducted their skillful, fighting retreat. Bringing up the rear, as usual, were the sappers – blowing up roads, laying mines, and setting booby traps almost under the Eighth Army's noses, eventually leading Radio Cairo to report that, 'the advance of the Eighth Army is meeting little resistance, but is seriously hampered by the . . . engineers.' With no transport, much of the German and Italian infantry had been overrun. Tens of thousands were captured,

RIGHT: Ammunition supplies lie ready beside a British 5.5-inch gun, El Alamein November 1942.

BELOW RIGHT: A mixed column of Afrika Korps transport and fighting vehicles. A command half-track, distinguished by its frame radio antenna is at right.

BOTTOM RIGHT: A Stuart tank burns in the background as German medical staff tend to what are probably its crew members.

but others made it back – like the Ramcke Parachute Brigade, which managed to hijack a complete British transport column and join Rommel at Mersa Matruh in high style.

Four times Montgomery sent his pursuing troops on tight turns toward the coast, hoping to trap the Axis forces – only to find that they had already gone. On 7 November the heavens opened, and heavy rains turned the sands around Mersa Matruh into an impassable bog. Later Montgomery was to claim that it was the rain that gave Rommel his chance to escape – apparently forgetting that it fell equally on both armies, and that Rommel had already left before the Eighth Army appeared.

After Mersa Matruh the two forces settled down to a 1500-mile march across the desert, with Rommel in the lead and the Eighth Army slowly and methodically bringing up the rear. The British commanders begged to be allowed to race ahead and force Rommel into a battle where he would surely be destroyed. They pleaded in vain. Montgomery was not only obsessed with order and method; to a large extent he had fallen under Rommel's spell as completely as the men of both armies. The set-piece battle was his area of expertise and the open desert was Rommel's country. Who knew what unexpected things he might do, even with only 10 tanks and no gasoline? It was much safer to stay behind, knowing that approaching from the opposite direction were 80,000 American and 25,000 British soldiers who would close the mighty pincers on the doomed Panzer Army.

The British victory at Alamein, coming as it did after a year of defeat, was greeted by ringing church bells, banner headlines and an outpouring of public adulation for Montgomery that continued, almost unabated, throughout his subsequent career as Field Marshal, leader of the British troops during the Normandy landings and commander of the British forces in Western Europe.

No reasonable person would deny that Montgomery was the victor at Alamein nor that Rommel was defeated. There is no need, on the other hand, to depict him as a savior who appeared out of the blue singlehandedly to snatch a defeated army from the jaws of disaster and disgrace. At the time he assumed command, the Eighth Army was anything but defeated. It had just stopped Rommel in his tracks and paved the way for a major offensive which, as Montgomery himself saw most clearly, they were at the time too weak to begin. As we have seen, many of the innovations at Alamein were based on planning done by Auchinleck and his staff, while many of Montgomery's own

plans led to chaos and confusion. Time and again his inability to improvise and his unwillingness to take chances gave Rommel the breathing space he needed to regroup and prolong the action.

The fight that the Panzer Army put up in the face of impossible odds is one of the great actions of World War II – and therein lies the only real basis for naming Montgomery the victor. For despite Britain's overwhelming numerical superiority in men and arms, it required one man with Montgomery's self-confidence, determination and rapport with the ranks to elicit the dogged, unremitting effort that eventually resulted in the British victory.

CHAPTER NINE

HALSEY
AND THE STRUGGLE FOR THE SOLOMONS

BY SPRING 1942 the Japanese momentum gained by the successes of Pearl Harbor and Singapore was being absorbed by lengthening lines of communication and increasing Allied resistance. With the Philippines, the East Indies and most of Burma under their control, the Japanese forces could consolidate their gains in the hope of entering negotiations from a position of strength, or they could prepare to defend those positions from the Allies, or they could push onward and outward in the hope of strengthening both their defensive position and their negotiating prospects.

The Japanese high command decided on further expansion, concentrated in the south-west. Papua, and the Bismarck and Solomon islands were to be captured. Port Moresby in Papua and the island of Guadalcanal in the Solomons were seen as key objectives in this offensive. Possession of airfields in those two places would enable the Japanese to locate and destroy any Allied seaborne activity in support of a counter-offensive. In fact, for the Japanese navy this was a main attraction of the strategy, for it might lure the US Navy into unwinnable situations.

But the first major naval encounter of this campaign, the Battle of the Coral Sea in May, was not a clear victory for the Japanese, and they changed their plans. They did land at Tulagi, on Florida Island, just ten miles north of Guadalcanal Island, but it was only in June that they moved on to Guadalcanal itself. This was a mountainous, humid, wooded island of about 90 miles length and 25 miles breadth, with the nearby Savo, Florida, and Malaita islands to the north enclosing a sea area that was destined to be known as 'Ironbottom Sound' because of the remains of ships that littered its depths. The first business of the Japanese on Guadalcanal was to begin construction of an airfield, later to be known as Henderson Field, on the northern side, close to the estuary of the river Lunga, which provided a place for the men and equipment to be landed.

An airbase here would be worth several aircraft carriers to the Japanese, offering them command of the air to provide cover for further expansion southward. An Allied reconnaissance aircraft in early July spotted the work going forward. The US commander of the South Pacific Area, Vice Admiral Robert C. Ghormley, had already made plans for an Allied thrust up the line of the Solomon Islands in accordance with instructions received from Washington. The recapture of Tulagi would help protect the vital line of communication between the USA and Australia, would be a stepping stone toward the reconquest of Rabaul (vital for the recapture of the Philippines), and would deter any further advance by the Japanese. However, the report that the Japanese were building an airfield meant that these plans had to be modified and acted upon immediately. Capturing the airfield before it was operational was essential.

In early August the US Marines landed on Guadalcanal, to find an enemy surprised and unprepared. It took less than a day for the Marines to capture the uncompleted airstrip and to pursue the surviving Japanese into the jungle. Meanwhile, a few miles away across the water, other Marines were dealing with the Japanese at Tulagi. These two very successful amphibious operations were the prelude of half a year of bitter fighting, because neither the Japanese nor the Americans were ready to

LEFT: Admiral William Frederick Halsey, Jr., 1882-1959.

BELOW: Japanese installations at Gavutu, Florida Is., under attack by US Navy aircraft, 7 August 1942.

concede a strategic victory to their oppononents here.

The success of the Marines was balanced almost immediately by a surprise naval defeat at the Battle of Savo Island. The Japanese were determined to fight hard for Guadalcanal and their first step was an attack on the US transports that had brought the Marines. They sent seven cruisers down to Guadalcanal and these for a number of reasons (including lackadaisical air reconnaisance by the Australian air force) managed to reach the island unreported. During the night they fell upon the five Allied cruisers escorting the transports. Lacking radar, but highly trained in night operations, the Japanese sank one Australian and three US cruisers and then withdrew.

Much of the subsequent naval activity was devoted by both sides to the ferrying in of reinforcements and supplies. For the Japanese, this meant the passing of swift convoys down the 'Slot,' the passage between the two columns of islands making up the Solomons chain. For the Americans, it meant bringing in troops and, soon, aircraft and aircraft supplies, by various evasive routes. By mid-August, a week after the Battle of Savo Island, the Japanese had brought in sufficient troops to begin an attack on Henderson Field. But by that time the Marines had brought it into service and, helped by their aircraft, they were able to hold the Japanese.

On balance, the Japanese had a preponderance of naval power in the area. Provided they operated at night, when the US air-craft were ineffective, Japanese heavy ships could move in to bombard US positions ashore. In late August there was a complex operation in which three Japanese aircraft carriers provided distant cover for a reinforcement mission and for the bombardment by destroyers of the Henderson Field area. This operation, accompanied by constant bombing, was intended to annihilate the US Marines on Guadalcanal.

Aware that the Japanese navy was about to start something big, Admiral Ghormley placed four aircraft carriers to protect sea communications but outside the range of Japanese land-based reconnaissance planes. In the ensuing Battle of the Eastern Solomons, the contending aircraft carriers did eventually locate each other, and US carrier aircraft sank the Japanese carrier *Ryujo* while Japanese aircraft damaged the US carrier *Enterprise*. The Japanese transports were also located and bombed so successfully that the survivors turned back to the north. The Japanese plan to bomb the airfield was carried out, but in the absence of further naval support did not obtain the expected results. That naval support had disappeared when the Japanese admiral broke off the operation to avoid further loss. Like several other battles in the Solomons campaign, an encounter that was indecisive in terms of material losses was a clear US victory in its consequences, in this case the continued US presence on Guadalcanal.

The Japanese continued, almost on a nightly basis, to des-

LEFT: A destroyer removes survivors from the stricken USS *Hornet.*

RIGHT: A Japanese plane prepares to launch its torpedo at a US carrier (off picture at left) during the Santa Cruz battle.

RIGHT: Japanese aircraft make a low-level attack on US ships off Guadalcanal in August 1942.

patch army reinforcements down the 'Slot' in destroyers. Sometimes this 'Tokyo Express' was intercepted by the Americans, but usually it got through. At this stage of the war the Americans were much less skilled at night operations than the Japanese. In the next major naval engagement, the Battle of Cape Esperance in October, this American disadvantage persisted, despite the possession of radar. What happened was that a force of three Japanese cruisers moving to bombard Henderson Field was spotted on radar by one of four US cruisers. But the ship with radar did not report the sighting for a quarter of an hour. Thus it was only while he was engaged in reversing the course of his ships that the US commander learned of the Japanese presence, by which time the enemy was only four miles distant. The Americans still had the advantage of surprise when they opened fire at the unsuspecting Japanese at this short range, and one Japanese cruiser was sunk and another damaged but, recovering quickly, the Japanese heavily damaged a US cruiser and then escaped to the north, leaving the Americans firing on one of their own destroyers.

The Japanese, unsurprisingly, remained confident of their naval superiority, and in the following nights their battleships and cruisers hurled hundreds of shells against the Marines at Henderson Field. All the same, thanks to US naval interventions the Japanese had still not succeeded in recapturing Guadalcanal.

Admiral Ghormley, directing the activities of several subordinate admirals who had minds of their own, and trying to do what was necessary with far too few resources, coped well with his situation. But the precarious and costly hold of the Marines on Guadalcanal, the continuing ability of the Japanese to ship reinforcements to the island, the night battles in which the US Navy too often seemed outclassed or outwitted by the Japanese, all led to demands for a fresh commander in this area. Admiral Nimitz, Commander in Chief of the Pacific Area, decided to replace Ghormley by Halsey in mid October.

Vice Admiral William F. Halsey had spent much of his career in destroyers after graduating from the Naval Academy in 1904, but in the mid-1930s he had qualified as a naval airman and at the time of Pearl Harbor had been commanding the Pacific Fleet's aircraft carriers. He had participated in almost all the carrier engagements of the war, although in the summer of 1942 he had been sick, with dermatitis. On recovery, he was sent to the South Pacific to replace Ghormley.

Halsey became popularly known as 'Bull' Halsey, and although this was an invention of the press it did express his reputation as a fighting admiral. His experience with destroyers had provided him with a certain tactical mind, a mind happy with the quick dash in and the quick dash out, and this offensive spirit was what was required in these difficult months of 1942. But Halsey had other bullish qualities, including a propensity to charge at the first whiff of the enemy. It was ironic that the sailors who cheered his appointment were men whose lives were safer under Ghormley than under Halsey.

As Commander in Chief, Halsey took over a headquarters housed in Noumea, the capital of the French colony of New Caledonia. He was responsible not only for the naval side, but the entire theater, and it was not a seagoing appointment. He installed many of his own staff officers; this gave him men whom he knew and could trust, but it meant the departure of several officers whose experience in the theater would have been valuable. As is so often the case in war, the new appointee was granted many of the resources for which his predecessor had begged in vain. New battleships were despatched to the theater, as well as Flying Fortress bombers. The latter had the range to reach Guadalcanal from an airfield further south, at Espiritu Santo.

When Halsey took command the task and the problem had become clearer. Both the Japanese and US high commands had decided that Guadalcanal was vital, but neither had been able to ship in enough troops to clear its enemy from the island. Henderson Field was a priceless possession of the Americans, because it could not only operate its own aircraft, but could also serve as a forward base for aircraft flown in from aircraft carriers or from airfields further south. So long as they were unable to capture the airfield, the Japanese would try to put it out of action by bombardment. Such bombardments, however, were only temporarily effective, for the Americans had landed a strong contingent of constructional specialists (the 'Seabees') who were adept at repairing cratered runways. For the US Navy, the task was to deliver troops and supplies to Guadalcanal while preventing the Japanese landing their own reinforcements. For the Japanese command, the tasks were similar, but because of US air superiority they were reluctant to operate in the enclosed waters around Guadalcanal in daylight.

In the previous naval battles the Japanese had proved superior in night actions. The American ships, hastily assembled into task forces or battle groups, lacked experience either in working together or in taking full advantage of technological advances like radar (or even, some critics implied, like radio). The first major naval action after Halsey's appointment came at the end of October, with the Battle of Santa Cruz taking once again the form of a contest between distant aircraft carriers. It was initiated by the Japanese, although the actual course of events was certainly unplanned. The Japanese operation was intended to coincide with the expected capture of Henderson Field, and was somewhat compromised when a false report of that capture was received and led the several Japanese naval commanders to begin prematurely their plan of advancing south to annihilate the US supply ships and their escorts that were expected to approach Guadalcanal.

Halsey, who had a fairly accurate intelligence appreciation of what the Japanese were doing, concentrated his two aircraft carriers nearly 300 miles north-east of Espiritu Santo, and then routed them north of the Santa Cruz islands in order to make an unexpected descent to the southwest in the hope of surprising the Japanese forces. This offensive commitment of his only aircraft carriers was risky, especially in view of the four aircraft carriers at the disposal of the Japanese. The air-strikes exchanged between the Japanese and US carriers resulted in the loss of USS *Hornet* and damage to USS *Enterprise*, while two Japanese carriers were badly damaged. The carrier forces thereupon withdrew, with the Japanese having won an apparent tactical victory. But probably this battle benefited the Americans most. So many Japanese carrier aircraft had been shot down that the remainder were not sufficient to mount a successful attack on

Henderson Field, which remained operational and in the hands of the Marines as the Japanese heavy ships, running short of fuel, retired to their bases in the north. Although the Americans remained in a critical situation on Guadalcanal, the Japanese had still not gained that clear command of the sea that would enable them to run transports safely down the 'Slot' and to block US transports arriving from the south.

The turning point came in November 1942, the same November that brought turning points at Alamein and Stalingrad. The Battle of Guadalcanal was really a series of battles extending over three days, at the end of which Halsey's disposition of forces had led to a definite defeat for the Japanese navy and a resurgence of confidence among the Americans. But it was a hard-fought battle, and at times the Americans were still throwing away tactical advantage by slow reactions and by their commanders' inability to find a balance between inflexible battle discipline and aimless individualism.

This battle became inevitable as soon as both sides, almost simultaneously, decided that the situation in Guadalcanal called for decisive action. Halsey, as was his habit, evolved an uncomplicated plan while in faraway Truk the Japanese Admiral Yamamoto's staff was engaged in scheduling, or rather choreographing, a series of complex movements intended to win naval supremacy, and hence land supremacy, in the Solomons. Halsey aimed simply at taking men and new weapons to the weary formations fighting on Guadalcanal, with the escorting cruisers and destroyers then utilized to hurl hundreds of high explosive shells at Japanese shore positions.

However, reports of Japanese transports and warships accumulating to the north led Halsey to doubt whether his escorts would be strong enough both to take the US transports safely in and to prevent the Japanese landing substantial reinforcements. He therefore decided to send in his two modern battleships *South Dakota* and *Washington*, accompanied by the almost-repaired carrier *Enterprise*.

The US troop convoys, escorted by cruisers and destroyers, were despatched from Noumea on 8 November and from Espiritu Santo on the 9th. The two convoys arrived safely off Guadalcanal on 11 and 12 November, although disembarkation was accompanied by attacks by Japanese bombers based in Rabaul. The commander of the convoy from Noumea, learning that Japanese forces were approaching from the north, broke off the disembarkation. Meanwhile four US cruisers and some destroyers moved to seek out the Japanese and during the night came across a Japanese bombarding force consisting of two battleships (*Hiei* and *Kirishima*) and destroyers.

Although the US cruiser force had radar, and was aware of the Japanese well before they were within visual distance, this advantage was thrown away by a delay in opening fire. When battle was finally joined, the Japanese were prompt in the use of their searchlights and the US cruisers were showered with well-directed shells. Communication between the US ships was on a single waveband, so that urgent orders were squeezed out by inconsequential chatter, and with their lack of experience in nightfighting the US ships tended to mask each other's fire or even shoot at each other. One US cruiser and four destroyers were sunk, and a second cruiser fell victim to a submarine the next morning. However, the battleship *Hiei* had been hit by so many medium caliber shells that it became an easy victim for torpedo aircraft from USS *Enterprise* the next day. More important, the attempt to bombard Henderson Field had been abandoned, so that base was free to despatch aircraft the next, vital, day. Also, in view of this failure, the planned landing of Japanese reinforcements was postponed for a day. In the close-

ABOVE: US Marines operating in typical Solomon Islands terrain.

RIGHT: US Marines in action toward the end of the Solomon Islands campaign, on Bougainville Island in late 1943.

run fighting on Guadalcanal such a postponement was of supreme importance, enabling the hard-pressed Marines to recover, re-form, and re-supply.

The most powerful of the naval forces at Halsey's disposition was Task Force 16, with its two battleships and *Enterprise*. At dawn on 13 November it was about 350 miles south of Guadalcanal, and Halsey decided that the battleships should move in if necessary. No doubt remembering his loss of USS *Hornet*, he decided that USS *Enterprise* was too vulnerable to risk, especially as any action would most likely be fought at night. Even committing the two new battleships in the restricted waters of Guadalcanal was a risk, but risk-taking had become habitual for both sides in the contest over this strategic island.

By afternoon it had become clear that Japanese transports, as well as strike forces, were once again approaching Guadalcanal from the north, and Halsey ordered his two battleships to advance so as to be off Guadalcanal at nightfall. But this was an order that could not be carried out; the two battleships were too far away to reach Guadalcanal in time. As a result, when the Japanese sent heavy cruisers to carry out another night bombardment of Henderson Field they were opposed by nothing more than a couple of motor torpedo boats. In a 40-minute bombardment, fifty US aircraft were destroyed or damaged, but the high-explosive shells did little damage to the airstrips, and next morning the airfield was still operational. Its aircraft, reinforced by some flown off the distant *Enterprise*, harried Japanese southbound transports and the naval groups supporting them. By the

ABOVE LEFT: Donald Runyon, a high-scoring Wildcat fighter pilot aboard USS *Enterprise*.

LEFT: The aircraft carrier USS *Wasp* sinking after a Japanese submarine attack off the Solomons in September 1942.

TOP RIGHT: Japanese Zero fighters, by then outdated, based in Rabaul in early 1943.

CENTER RIGHT: Beached Japanese transports burning on Guadalcanal in November 1942.

LOWER RIGHT: Japanese infantry, killed by US Marines' small-arms fire on Guadalcanal end of the day, seven Japanese transports and a heavy cruiser had been sunk for the loss of only five US aircraft. Nevertheless the surviving transports plodded determinedly southward, their commander hoping that he would at least be able to beach them on Guadalcanal. *Enterprise* narrowly escaped detection by Japanese aircraft and after this victorious day Halsey decided that she would be best left to rest on her laurels and ordered her back to the safer waters of New Caledonia. But meanwhile the two battleships stayed 100 miles south of Guadalcanal, seeking to avoid detection while preparing to move in after dark.

In fact, the Japanese knew that the two battleships were in the vicinity, but this was no deterrent to their plan to stage another, unprecedently heavy, bombardment of Henderson Field on the night of 14 November. Equally discounted by the Japanese was a US radio message they overheard, reporting that the Japanese bombarding force had been sighted. Indeed, a secondary part of the Japanese mission was the destruction of any US naval opposition that it might encounter, and previous engagements had shown that the Japanese were quite capable of dealing with the US navy in night operations.

The bombardment force consisted of the battleship *Kirishima* and two heavy cruisers, with attendant lighter ships. Admiral Lee on board USS *Washington* had *South Dakota* and four destroyers in company. His ships had not worked together before and he had not had time to issue an operational plan. He had not been allocated any radio call-sign, and this almost led to an attack by US motor torpedo boats off Savo Island. Halsey, some

RIGHT: The south-west Pacific zone, showing successive stages of the US advance.

LEFT: USS *Hornet* at the Battle of Santa Cruz. An air-launched Japanese torpedo splashes down on the right.

LEFT: US destroyers and cruisers bombard the island of Kolombangara.

BELOW: The cruiser USS *New Orleans* rests under cover at Tulagi after the Battle of Tassafaronga.

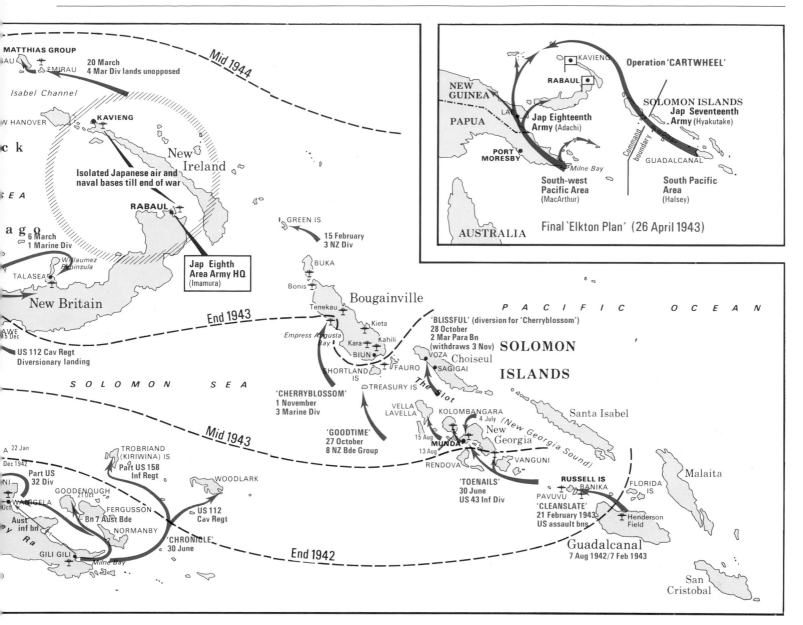

of whose staff officers had not favored sending in such valuable ships to take their chance in narrow waters, had given Lee complete freedom of action once he reached Guadalcanal.

Lee decided to patrol Ironbottom Sound, from which any bombardment of Henderson Field would be made. A Japanese light cruiser, an advance scout of the bombardment force, was the first target picked up by the American radar, and escaped amid a hail of 16-inch and 5-inch projectiles. Soon the US and Japanese destroyers were engaged in confused actions while the US radar aboard the battleships sought larger targets. But this was difficult with unsophisticated sets and inexperienced operators, especially as there were so many fast-moving and un-identified blips on the screens. At this critical time *South Dakota* suffered an electrical breakdown that, among other things, put her radar out of service.

At about half an hour before midnight, the four US destroyers were out of action, *South Dakota* could be considered as out of action until her main electrical circuit had been reinstated, and USS *Washington* was confused by the radar echoes reflected by so many ships and also by nearby islands. The Japanese were in a somewhat better situation. Their enemy was not scattered and they knew, more or less, the whereabouts of their own ships.

After a few minutes *South Dakota* restored her circuits and was capable of action. She fired a few salvos in the direction of a Japanese light cruiser, in the process setting fire to the aircraft

stowed on her own stern. Soon she was illuminated by Japanese searchlights, and from only 5000 yards the enemy battleship and cruisers poured heavy and medium caliber shot at her. Luckily the torpedoes that were also aimed at her either missed or failed to explode, but she took heavy damage.

But *Washington*, whose radar was working faultlessly and which had not been spotted by the Japanese, was preparing to join in. When the Japanese heavy ships exposed their searchlights they formed perfect targets. The American guns, 16-inch and 5-inch, were at first concentrated on the *Kirishima*. Of the 75 16-inch shells that *Washington* had time to fire, nine found their target and the Japanese battleship was reduced to a flaming cripple. The Japanese heavy cruisers also received a few shots, including some from the damaged *South Dakota* before the latter retired from the fight. Without radio, *South Dakota* was unable to inform Lee what she was doing, and he, hoping for the best, and especially that his consort battleship was at least buoyant, pressed on by himself, confident that his radar would keep him out of trouble. In fact, his continued advance disturbed the Japanese. They diverted additional ships to cover their transports, and ordered a general withdrawal. Lee soon learned of these new dispositions, realized that the Japanese transports would not reach Guadalcanal during the night, was confident that he had saved Henderson Field from a bombardment, and so decided it was time to retire and find his consort. The two battleships joined up after dawn. *South Dakota* was so badly damaged that she had to return to the USA, but *Washington* was virtually unscathed. Meanwhile, the Japanese had been compelled to scuttle their battleship *Kirishima*. And so ended one of the few battleship versus battleship encounters of World War II.

This had been the climax of the Battle of Guadalcanal. Of the Japanese reinforcements sent down the 'Slot' in the transport convoy, probably only about 2000 men ever reached the island. The Japanese navy, unlike the American, had few reserves, so the loss of two battleships, a heavy cruiser, and eleven transports was a serious blow. Even more serious was the loss of trained aircrew, for Japanese air losses had been considerably more than the American. Thanks largely to Halsey's willingness to risk his battleships and to Lee's skill in action, the US Navy now believed that it had the upper hand. There was an uplift in morale that cancelled out the depression caused by the heavy losses of the earlier naval battles.

Such an uplift was all the more necessary because the remaining naval engagements in the Guadalcanal campaign would show that the Japanese were still superior in fighting skills. On the last night of November, at the Battle of Tassafaronga, the Americans suffered one of the worst humiliations of this campaign. Eight Japanese destroyers loaded with supplies for the land forces set out down the 'Slot,' with their movement tracked by US signals intelligence. Halsey sent a force of five cruisers and six destroyers to intercept them. Using their radar, the Americans surprised the Japanese commander who, however, soon recovered himself. He ordered half his destroyers to continue to Guadalcanal to dump their supply containers, and attacked with the remaining destroyers. His torpedoes hit four of the US cruisers, sinking one (USS *Northampton*).

In this encounter the Americans demonstrated once more their lack of clearly understood tactical principles for night actions. The performance of the few Japanese destroyers against this superior force contrasted with the courageous but vain flounderings of the US destroyers, which were kept close to the cruisers and not given a chance to attack on their own initiative.

As for the cruisers, the Japanese later reported that the US gunfire was wildly inaccurate. Halsey preferred to allot the blame for the defeat to the destroyers' commander.

Despite this success, the Japanese admirals recommended the abandonment of Guadalcanal, since it was inflicting more losses than they could replace. An evacuation was decided upon, and transports were assembled, with covering naval forces. US intelligence interpreted these movements as the prelude to another massive attempt to land reinforcements, and Halsey decided to send in more troop transports. These would be covered by the very strong naval task forces that he now commanded. One of these, Task Force 18, was intended to move in close to Guadalcanal and then, when the convoys were safely unloading, seek out the Japanese transports advancing from the north.

TF18 consisted of six cruisers and two new light aircraft carriers, and was ordered to make a rendezvous with a destroyer group before starting on its offensive action. Slipshod staff work meant that it could reach the rendezvous in time only if it left its rather slow aircraft carriers behind. This it did, but before it met the destroyers it was attacked by Japanese torpedo aircraft. They began their attack at twilight, and then continued to attack by the light of flares. The cruiser *Chicago* was crippled, and was finished off by further attacks the next day. By that time the US ships had retired, mission unaccomplished. Halsey blamed the commander of TF18 for this defeat.

The Japanese were successful in evacuating Guadalcanal without the Americans being aware of their departure. Obviously, though, victory lay with the Americans, and especially with the US Navy, which had made Japanese efforts to sustain their presence far too costly in men and ships. For this success Halsey deserved much of the credit. His aggressive spirit certainly heartened his men at a critical time and this might have been decisive. But his risky tactics, born of an unjustified contempt for his enemy, paid off only once, at the Battle of Guadalcanal. His failure to carry out staff work impeccably, and his assumption that the US Navy's officers and men were naturally superior to

LEFT: A burning Wildcat fighter is rescued by US Marines after a Japanese bombing attack on the Guadalcanal airfield.

ABOVE RIGHT: A 500-pound bomb is loaded aboard one of the USS *Enterprise*'s aircraft off Guadalcanal in August 1942.

RIGHT: A light anti-aircraft battery in action aboard a US aircraft carrier.

the Japanese, cost a great many ships and lives.

In the following months the Americans moved northward up the chain of Solomon Islands, with Halsey showing increasing skill in this 'island-hopping' style of operation. In June 1944 he was appointed commander of the powerful Third Fleet, where he had plenty of scope for his aggressive tactics. At the Battle of Leyte Gulf in 1944, his impetuous approach nearly brought disaster, and his nickname 'Bull' seemed entirely appropriate. On the other hand, at that stage of the war he had also shown himself to be quite perceptive, possibly because by that time the capabilities of the enemy had been worn down to the level at which Halsey had always perceived them. In the preparations for the US invasion of the Philippines, it was he (albeit on the basis of misinterpreted intelligence) who correctly suggested that Mindanao could be by-passed, and in the same period, when attacking Formosan airfields, he was cunning enough to use two of his damaged cruisers as bait for Japanese aircraft, which were thereupon shot down by the score. Evidently he was an intelligent man, but it is also evident that he too often allowed his feelings to swamp his intelligence. But at a time when depression and defeatism were all too pervasive, Halsey with his slogan 'Hit Hard. Hit Fast. Hit Often' was a priceless asset. He is an interesting, although not unique, case of a responsible commander who sometimes could be more dangerous to his own side than to the enemy, but whose part in victory was yet undeniable.

CHAPTER TEN

CHUIKOV
AND THE SIEGE OF STALINGRAD

IN POPULAR imagination the Battle of Stalingrad ranks as the turning point of the war in Europe, and rightly so. For it was the first really crushing defeat suffered by the German army. It is true that the Battle of El Alamein, occurring at the same time, also showed that the Germans could be beaten, but Alamein was a relatively small encounter. Only in the USSR did the *Wehrmacht* suffer losses on a scale promising ultimate defeat.

General Vasilii Chuikov, in many ways a run-of-the-mill commander, won renown in this battle for his handling of the battle in the city itself. Under his auspices the technique of street fighting developed into something quite different, the technique of city fighting. Without his speedy acceptance of new tactics for a new situation, it is unlikely that Stalingrad would have been held long enough to draw the German High Command into crushing defeat.

The first year of the war between Hitler's Germany and Stalin's Russia had been unsatisfactory for both sides. The Russians, thanks to their ideological attachment to the offensive war, had been unprepared and untrained for retreat. They had failed to make use of their biggest strategic asset, space, and had been surrounded time after time so that when they finally came to make a stand outside Moscow and Leningrad they had lost most of their strength. The Germans, on the other hand, had failed to take either of those cities before winter came to rob their blitzkrieg of its momentum.

For the Germans, 1942 required the evolution of a winning plan. For the Russians, it demanded the modernization of their army not just materially but in terms of attitudes and organization. They had to learn how to retreat with minimum loss. They had to learn how to command, for the joint command of units by the military commander and his political commissar had often led to disaster. New instructional manuals took care to explain how retreats were best organized, and the baleful influence of political commissars was reduced, firstly, by removing some of the most incompetent and, secondly, moving toward one-man command of units. Meanwhile, factories that had been moved from the war zones to the east began to re-start production. Modern designs, especially of aircraft and tanks, came into full production and slowly narrowed the technical gap between the Soviet and Nazi forces.

Hitler wanted the 1942 campaign to concentrate on the capture of the Caucasian oilfields. His generals agreed that this was an acceptable target, even though it meant very extended German lines of communication. But Hitler also decided that the campaign into the Caucasus should be covered by a drive on Stalingrad. He regarded this city as a vital strategic point, mainly because it commanded the Volga. In reality, it was not that vital, but probably had an obsessive attraction for him because it was 'Stalin's City,' the capture of which, he imagined, would be a demoralizing blow to Soviet morale. In a sense he was right, because Stalin did have nostalgic memories of the siege of Stalingrad in the Russian Civil war, and his insistence that it be held at all costs predated the Soviet counter-offensive plan in which its retention was an essential part.

Inwardly, the German generals feared that this division of effort would mean that neither of the two objectives would be gained. As things turned out, they were right, for although the Germans would reach both Stalingrad and the Caucasian oilfields, they would not succeed in holding them.

Von Bock's Army Group, with Hoth's 4th Panzer Army, was entrusted with the drive toward Stalingrad. In May it was delayed for some weeks by an offensive launched by the Soviet General Semyon Timoshenko near Kharkov. This ended, however, with yet another major encirclement of Soviet forces. But soon after, while Hoth was handicapped by fuel shortages and poor air reconnaissance, other Soviet formations were able to make withdrawals over the Don.

General Chuikov, who arrived on the scene at this point to take over one of the Soviet armies, was horrified by the apparent chaos and panic of the Soviet retreat across the Don. What he did not realize, being new to the European war, was that this was a great step forward insofar as the Soviet troops had managed to extricate themselves in good time. Chuikov had been serving as military attaché in China, advising Chiang Kai Shek's forces in their long struggle against the Japanese, and had been recalled only in 1942. His battle experience so far as Russia was concerned dated from the Civil War and the war against Poland in 1918-20. He had studied the Western Front campaign of World War I quite closely, and much of his strategic and tactical knowledge came from that source. He soon found he had a lot to learn, and the ability to change his conceptions, almost overnight, was perhaps the most valuable ingredient of his subsequent success at Stalingrad.

Chuikov, coming fresh to the scene, was without the bitter weariness that 1941 had inflicted on many other generals. He was appointed commander of the 62nd Army at an interview with the commander of the South East Front and the latter's political

LEFT: General Vasili Chuikov. After the Stalingrad battle Chuikov's 62nd Army was redesignated 8th Guards Army and he led it to the end of the war.

RIGHT: Chuikov's opponent, General Friedrick Paulus (left) in conversation with General Pfeiffer.

commissar, Nikita Khrushchev, in September. Hitherto Chuikov had been with the 64th Army, one of those defending Stalingrad from the south. He had had one small success against the Germans, and that had been noticed, so when the commander of the 62nd Army, which had become the main formation holding the city itself, had shown signs of cold feet, he was replaced by Chuikov. The latter assured Khrushchev that he would, indeed, hold Stalingrad or die.

Probably Stalingrad would have fallen in the summer had not Hitler decided to divert Hoth's Panzer Army to the Caucasian campaign. When it got back, in early August, it advanced on Stalingrad from the south but after reaching Kotelnikovo began to experience stronger Russian resistance. Meanwhile, another German army, Paulus' 6th Army, crossed the Don at Kalach and then advanced along the tongue of land separating the Don from the Volga. When it linked up with Hoth's forces at Kotelnikovo in late August Stalingrad's defenders were in a semi-encirclement, with the Volga at their backs and the Germans at their front and flanks.

The Volga at Stalingrad is wide, although the width varies according to the season. On average it is a mile wide, and Stalingrad is located on its western bank, a long straggling city measuring about 18 miles from north to south but only a mile or two in width. High bluffs rise from the riverside on the western bank, and these are intersected by gullies running across the width of the city, as well as by the bigger rift carved out by the river Tsaritsa, that flows into the Volga.

Bringing supplies and reinforcements across the river into the beleaguered city was difficult even in the beginning, for from late August onwards, in daytime, there were almost continuous raids by German high-level and dive-bombers. At night, as soon as the Germans had their guns and observers in position, the river could also be covered using artillery guided by the light of blazing buildings. The singletrack railroad bringing supplies from the north-east was especially at risk, and it became necessary to unload freight trains many miles from the city, sending their contents to the jetties by less vulnerable motor transport.

The Soviet armies north and south of Stalingrad, sometimes using only partly-trained troops, made desperate attacks on the Germans to delay their advance and thereby make time for the defenders of Stalingrad to organize defensive positions and receive reinforcements from across the river. Chuikov's appointment coincided with the realization by Stalin and his advisers that Red Army forces were too weak to stop the German advance. But there was a chance that if the city was held long enough, drawing in and wearing down German strength, it might be possible to accumulate sufficient forces for a massive counter-offensive from north and south. But it all depended on the city being held.

In early September the two main defending armies, the 64th and 62nd, were pressed back to their final defense line. By this time both had virtually become skeleton formations, with some of their divisions containing fewer than 200 men each. Stalingrad was divided into three sectors, of which Chuikov's 62nd Army held the most important, the central sector which included virtually the whole city. At this stage Chuikov had about 50,000 men with some 100 tanks. Most of the latter were of the light and vulnerable T60 and T70 types.

The concept of a defensive line was about to disappear, as an irrelevance, because at the end of the first major assault there could be little talk of continuous positions, only of a scattered and sometimes coherent patchwork of strongpoints. That assault began at dawn on 13 September with massed artillery preparation and waves of Ju87 dive-bombers, followed by an attack against the central sector made by three infantry divisions, two Panzer divisions, and a motorized division. Chuikov's HQ was on a commanding height, the 102-metre Mamayev Kurgan, an ancient burial ground, but by the end of the day he had been forced to move, his line communications having been cut and most of his bunkers destroyed. His new HQ was in the so-called Tsaritsyn Bunker, with one exit in the bed of the Tsaritsa River and a second at street level. Here, paradoxically, he was closer to the Germans than were the HQs of the divisions he was directing, but his communications staff had more protection.

By the end of that tumultuous and confused day the Germans had made gains, but had not attained their objective of reaching the river and thereby splitting Stalingrad and its defense. In the small hours of the next day Chuikov ordered counter-attacks but these were soon quelled by German gunfire.

On 14 September the attack gained even more devastating force, with what was left of Chuikov's line being subjected again to mass shelling and dive-bombing. Tanks and assault infantry again broke into the city, with the attacks coming from several directions and aiming at different objectives. Heavy casualties were suffered by both sides in desperate close-range fighting as the Germans slowly but steadily moved toward the Volga, block by block. They captured the vital Mamayev Kurgan and, near the main railway station, they captured a big building that commanded the main river landing stage, thereby threatening Chuikov's link with the rear.

Chuikov, whose HQ was within half a mile of the German positions, decided that the threat to the landing stage justified throwing in his last paltry reserve of 19 tanks, which succeeded in killing the German machine-gunners in the building. Mean-

ABOVE: German officers confer in the early days of the Stalingrad campaign.

RIGHT: Watchful German infantry occupy part of a wrecked factory in the north of Stalingrad.

LEFT: A heavily-laden German infantryman makes his way through the wreckage of Stalingrad.

time he summoned help. On the other side of the river was the elite 13th Guards Division. This had about 10,000 men, although not all possessed weapons. After dark, it was brought down to the river in small parties. The burning city, and a burning barge, helped the German gunners, and only a proportion of the division reached the other side. By daylight it was ashore, at grips with the German positions, and about to be mercilessly dive-bombed. It could hardly be termed a division any longer, but it had succeeded in blocking, at least temporarily, a German attack that had seemed likely to carve up the city.

The main railway station changed hands four times during the morning of 15 September. Mamayev Kurgan, lost the day before, could not be recaptured. The following night some more of the 13th Guards Division succeeded in crossing the river and with this reinforcement two regiments stormed that height and

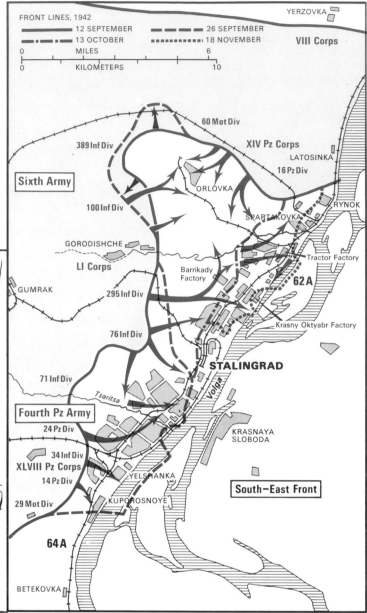

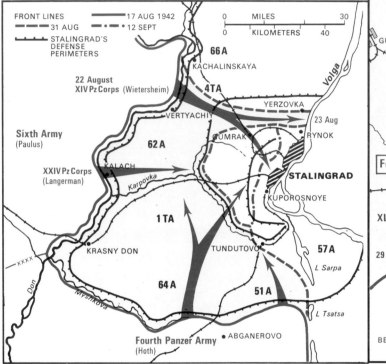

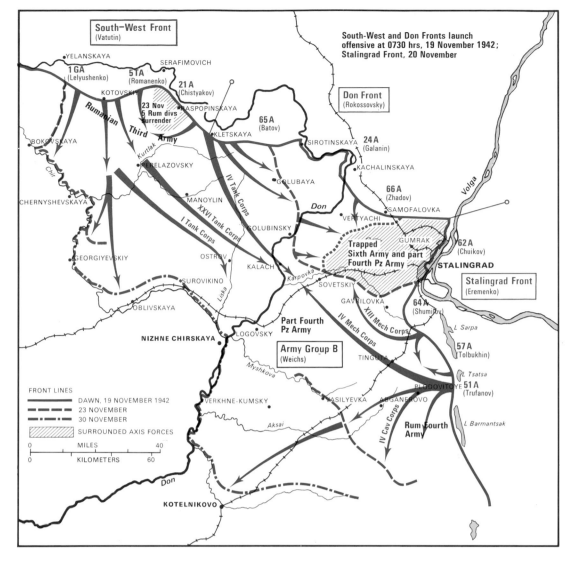

FAR LEFT: Map showing the German advances toward Stalingrad.

LEFT: Map of Stalingrad, showing how the long, straggly, city was divided between the Soviet 62nd and 64th Armies, the former being commanded by Chuikov.

RIGHT: Map showing the start of the Soviet offensive in November.

BELOW RIGHT: The final phase, with the Germans besieged in Stalingrad.

BELOW LEFT: The Stalingrad industrial area after German bombing.

six men succeeded in reaching the top and surviving there. Henceforth this hill would be the scene of repeated attacks and counter-attacks.

On 17 September Chuikov reported that to hold out he needed two more divisions. German reinforcements seemed endless and, although the enemy were taking heavy casualties, they continued to outnumber the defenders. Chuikov was not allowed those two divisions; with the scraping together of reserves for the coming counter-offensive all that he could be afforded was two brigades. As for Chuikov, his HQ had become far too close to the German positions, and he was given permission to move to the north, close to the landing stage serving the Krasny Oktyabr factory. Here, bunkers and trenches had been built just below a row of oil storage tanks.

On 18 September, with the fight for the railway station and Mamayev Kurgan still raging, and with dive-bombing and artillery attacks showing no sign of slackening, Chuikov was making one improvization after another. It was at this point that he received orders to prepare a counterattack to coincide with offensives by the Russian forces outside Stalingrad, offensives designed to take pressure off the city itself. With great difficulty he did mount a counterattack to clear the Germans from the center of the city, but this was only partially successful, while the offensives outside the city soon petered out, their only effect being to divert the dive-bombers away from the sreets for a few hours.

But on 20 September the dive-bombers destroyed the railway station and its surviving defenders flitted from one building to another until, finally, the last 40 survivors entered and held a

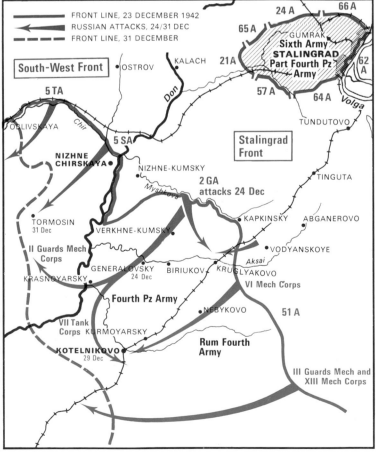

building for five days. Eventually German tanks demolished the building, and only six Russian defenders managed to find their way to safety.

From the experience of the first days of fighting, Chuikov drew several conclusions about the best tactics to be used. Although a few feeble street barriers had been built before the Germans closed in, there were no really substantial defense works. Buildings were seldom intact, the wooden ones had been burned by shells and bombs while the others had been gutted, if not dismembered, by the same weapons. The big factories in the north of the city were also heavily damaged, but groups of workers, even at the height of the battle, carried on with their work, which was mainly the repair of weapons, including tanks. These factories raised their own armed militia, much of which was subsequently merged with regular army units in the guise of reinforcements.

Although Soviet troops might defend every house in a street, floor by floor, Chuikov favored the creation of what he called centers of resistance. These were patterns of strongpoints, usually masonry buildings, that were linked with each other by communication trenches. The latter, more often than not, were hardly trenches but ditches carved out of rubble. Burned-out stone buildings made the best strongpoints, not least because they could not be set on fire. Each strongpoint had to have an all-round field of fire, obtained if need be by breaking holes in blind walls. Each building was meant to be defended by at least a section of infantry, but platoons or companies were often used, although these were seldom up to strength (and nor were the battalions that were sometimes thrown into a strongpoint).

It was considered important to provide each strongpoint with anti-tank rifles or guns, and larger pieces of artillery were provided for a few. Some had light tanks, often placed in a key situation dominating one or two streets, and buried up to their turrets in rubble. Soldiers were also provided with anti-tank grenades and Molotov cocktails. Supplies were sufficient to allow a strongpoint to fight independently for several days. It would usually have specialist soldiers, including snipers and sappers, the latter being valuable in demolition work and, occasionally, in undermining enemy positions. Most strongpoints

ABOVE: German infantry trying a highly unorthodox method of delivering anti-aircraft fire.

ABOVE RIGHT: Red Army men go into the attack in the central area of the city.

LEFT: Ju52 transport aircraft loading supplies for the Germans cut off at Stalingrad.

RIGHT: Soviet sappers cut their way through German barbed wire.

had a medical orderly or nurse too. A major strongpoint, typically centered on a substantial building in the city center, might have, apart from rifles (which were increasingly outnumbered by sub-machine guns, far more suitable for close-range work), flame-throwers, mortars, machine guns and light artillery. The basement and ground floor were used for weapons firing along the streets, while on the upper floors were weapons for firing downward; tanks were quite vulnerable to downward fire, especially around their engine grilles. Tanks, heavy machine guns and light artillery were placed at the side of the building, or behind it. Obstacles were built in the streets,

covered by concealed machine guns and artillery. German infantry typically advanced along a street behind tanks, and the recommended tactic was to separate the men from the machines and destroy each individually.

For their part, the Germans evolved their own, not dissimilar, tactics, although they had the advantage of ground-attack aircraft on call. As they advanced, they created their own strongpoints. When they penetrated into Russian-held streets they often seized a building or two and converted them into isolated, advanced, strongpoints.

Conventional infantry tactics were very costly in these situa-

ABOVE: One of the new German Fw189 aircraft hurriedly pressed into service for the campaign.

ABOVE RIGHT: Handling a Heinkel bomber on a Russian airfield. Local climatic conditions made simple operations very time-consuming.

LEFT: General Rokossovsky, organizer of the Soviet counter-offensive.

tions, as the attackers inevitably exposed their flank to one or other enemy strongpoint. The Russians, in particular, developed successful infiltration tactics, where very small groups of men would slip between enemy strongpoints to attack carefully-reconnoitred buildings. The daily tasks of Chuikov's men, holding their own strongpoints, capturing the enemy's, and destroying advancing enemy troops, led to the development of small task forces, called storm groups. These were infantry sections accompanied by tanks and artillery, and with sappers and chemical warfare specialists. The sappers were employed offensively to blast through walls behind which enemy troops were sheltering, and the chemical warfare men, trained in smoke-screen tactics, used their skill to smoke Germans out of their strongpoints. The unpredictability and surprise tactics of these storm groups, apart from gaining objectives, also kept the enemy in a constant and therefore very wearing state of tension. Chuikov impressed on his storm groups the importance of acting offensively wherever possible, for the side which held the initiative was the side which made the gains.

As the battle developed, so did tactics need to change. After the first weeks, when the Germans managed to establish strongpoints in the city and weld them into centers of resistance, attacks by single storm groups became less successful simply because the opposition was stronger and more integrated. Storm groups henceforth tended to act together, with their movements coordinated by a central plan based on knowledge not only of the enemy's whereabouts, but also of his habits. Until the Germans learned from their mistakes, it could happen that the Russian storm groups would enter a building while most of the defenders were in the basement, having their supper.

A later refinement was to divide the storm groups into three semi-specialized sections, one for assault, another for reinforcement, and the third as a reserve. The assault section was often divided into parties of half a dozen men each, who would enter the targetted building at several places simultaneously. The hand grenade was their key weapon. Coming to a doorway, they would hurl a grenade past it, and then move in to the room, sub-machine gun at the ready. Precautionary treatment of rooms by hand grenade was also a German technique. One of its consequences was that the few civilians still in Stalingrad, and usually sheltering in basement rooms, had little chance of survival if their building should become an objective.

Other weapons carried by the assault sections were knives, and entrenching spades sharpened on one edge to serve as axes. The reinforcement section would enter a building as soon as the assault parties were safely inside. It had somewhat heavier weapons, and its job was to set up firing positions to prevent the enemy sending reinforcements to help the Germans still resisting inside the building.

Careful study of the building and the way its occupants defended it was an essential preliminary for an assault. Then, it was surprise and meticulous timing, plus luck, which led to success. Typically, a multi-storey building would be cleared in about 20 minutes or half an hour. Sometimes there would be a preliminary barrage in the form of machine-gun and light artillery directed against the enemy's firing positions. Then, before the enemy had time to recover, the assault parties would go in. If there was no preliminary bombardment, the assault parties, concealed close to the building, would rush up and throw grenades through the ground-level windows before jumping inside. Because of the general state of the terrain, with its covering of rubble and ruin, it was fairly easy for men to approach unseen. Once in their jumping-off positions they were relatively safe, because one of the first things the Soviet troops in Stalingrad learned was that the closer they were to the enemy the less likely they were to be attacked from the air.

FAR LEFT: Bulgarian troops on the Eastern Front. They proved to be less effective than their German allies.

LEFT: German troops on the march in the Caucasus, a campaign closely linked with the Stalingrad offensive but physically very different.

RIGHT: German officers during a more successful phase of the Russian campaign.

BELOW LEFT: A German soldier inspects knocked-out Soviet T34 tanks in the Ukrainian steppes.

BELOW: Earlier in the Russian campaign, a German infantryman takes stock in a village fired by the retreating Russians.

In early October air attacks set ablaze most of the oil storage tanks. Burning oil floated on to the river and helped to disturb Russian boat communications (most of the bigger river craft had already been destroyed by guns or bombs). The oil tanks above Chuikov's HQ were among those hit, and a wave of burning oil surged toward his position. Luckily it passed close by without destroying it, and for a day or so the HQ, as well as some other positions, enjoyed a dense smokescreen that covered it from air attack.

Toward the end of September the Germans, who still seemed able to pour in fresh troops to replace their heavy losses, reached the central landing stage. This interrupted the Russians' communications with the east bank and split the 62nd Army as well as the city itself. Stalin, aware of the danger, and especially of the likelihood that the Germans could now force their way north and south along the shore to cut off the Soviet units fighting within the city, sent messages that were not helpful. Chuikov was ordered not to retreat, and counter-attacks were suggested.

Chuikov established a new line of communication through a landing stage near the factory area in the north. It was to here that the Germans shifted the main weight of their attacks in October, with the increasingly devastated Krasny Oktyabr, Barricady, and Tractor works, as well as the nearby railway freight yard, forming a rubble-strewn battleground on which the Germans gained a few yards each day, and the Russians a few yards each night. Throughout the area of the 62nd Army, the width of the defended territory had diminished to a point where Chuikov, after much argument, was allowed to shift his artillery to the eastern shore. From its new positions it succeeded in putting up a long and heavy bombardment on German troops collecting for a new massive assault on the Soviet occupied part of the city.

As time passed, those German troops who had survived from the early days began to show acute signs of physical and psychological exhaustion. The German Chief of General Staff, Kurt Zeitzler, recommended that the Stalingrad operation be called off, and the local German commander, Paulus, seemed to share that opinion. However, both were overruled, and on 14 October what was intended to be the final assault began. By this stage the area held by Chuikov amounted to little more than a small zone around Rynok in the north, part of the factories zone, some parts of the city around the railway station, and the north-eastern side of Mamayev Kurgan (the Germans held the other sides, but nobody could really hold the exposed top). Chuikov, who had been receiving trickles of reinforcements throughout the battle, still had about 50,000 men and 80 tanks. But the German assault troops numbered around 90,000, and they had about 300 tanks. The big factor in the Germans' favor was still the air. Although Chuikov nominally had almost 200 aircraft, their technical condition was poor and they were completely dominated by the thousand or so aircraft that the Luftwaffe was devoting to this battle.

The German command, pushed by Hitler, sought to use this air superiority to change the form of the battle. Instead of house-to-house fighting, the aim henceforth was simply to destroy all the buildings. This made it difficult for the Russians to apply their new strongpoint tactics, but they soon adapted themselves to conducting their battles among rubble. At the same time, that rubble held up the enemy advance, so the new German approach was not especially effective.

By the time of this new German assault, Chuikov had shifted his HQ once again, and was now working near the river, only partly protected by the bluffs. His communications personnel had to send signals to the eastern bank, from where they were relayed back to the scattered units fighting in the city. On 15 October, with the Germans advancing everywhere and his units isolated and running short of ammunition, Chuikov asked permission to remove his HQ to the eastern bank, but this was refused. On 17 October he was forced to move again, first to a gully that proved to be in the line of German machine gun fire, and finally to an open space on the riverside near Mamayev Kurgan.

Although in retrospect 14 October was the most critical day, heavy fighting continued for several days, with the Russian positions slowly being pushed even further back. The Tractor Plant was irrevocably lost, but by the end of October the Germans found that they could sustain the effort no longer. They had won most of the city, but they had not won the battle because the Russians were still there.

In their two months of dour resistance, Chuikov's men had given the Soviet High Command time to assemble its forces for a great counter-offensive. This began on 19 November, with Rokossovsky's army breaking through the Rumanian formations covering the German flank and then advancing to Kalach. From the south, Eremenko broke through more Rumanians, gained Kotelnikovo, and linked up with Rokossovsky's troops. The besiegers thereby became the besieged, and although Göring promised Hitler that he could keep Paulus' troops supplied, in practice this proved impossible and on 2 February Paulus surrendered.

The Stalingrad campaign cost the Germans their 6th Army, and much more besides. It was a defeat from which they never really recovered, although it took more than two years for the Red Army to fight its way to Berlin. Chuikov took a leading part in the capture of that city and, something of an expert on urban fighting, he was somewhat critical of the way his superiors misused their tanks in those final days at Berlin. As an officer he was perhaps hypercritical, but this ability to detect faults had not come amiss in the Stalingrad campaign and had helped him to see that the tactics that had been taught were not necessarily the tactics to be used. This tactical flair, plus the stolidity that enabled him to work under fire for week after week, had been his great contribution to the victory at Stalingrad.

ABOVE LEFT: The Germans experience the misery of retreat over Russian roads in the Russian winter.

ABOVE RIGHT: Field Marshal Paulus, photographed soon after his surrender. Later in the war, under Soviet auspices, he willingly took part in anti-Nazi propaganda campaigns.

RIGHT: Soviet infantry, with their customary unrefined tactics, goes into the attack.

CHAPTER ELEVEN

MANSTEIN
AND THE KHARKOV OFFENSIVE

THE GERMAN campaign against Russia had a good beginning but a very bad end, and Erich von Manstein, who emerged as the star general of that campaign, was perhaps lucky to be dismissed before the situation became hopeless. His classic counter-offensive at Kharkov in early 1943 was the last of the major German successes of this campaign and for a few weeks seemed to suggest that the Russian victory at Stalingrad had not been quite so decisive after all.

Manstein, who early in life took the name of the military family that had adopted him, was commissioned in the infantry before World War I and in 1914 served first on the Western Front and then on the Eastern, where he was badly wounded. Later he served as a staff officer under General von Lossberg, and was involved in that general's design for a defense-in-depth system. After World War I, seeing how army officers seeking to influence events had often only made matters worse, he decided that officers should stay away from politics, a decision that may have been wise but which later enabled him to serve Hitler with a clear conscience.

When Germany remilitarized in the 1930s his advancement was fast, and seems to have been based on real ability rather than on useful connexions. By 1935 he was head of the operations section of the General Staff, and became Deputy Chief of Staff the following year. However, the upper reaches of the German Army were turbulent areas, with both personal and inter-departmental jealousies distorting both appointments and policy-making. Manstein was soon caught up in these currents, and in 1937 was removed from the General Staff. But on the eve of the 1939 Polish campaign he became Chief of Staff to General Rundstedt, who directed that campaign.

Later, still with Rundstedt, he had his own ideas on how to conduct the imminent campaign against France and Belgium, and these were very different from the somewhat orthodox plans of the General Staff. Obviously regarded as too clever by half, he was soon shifted from staff duties and sent to command an infantry corps in January 1940. However, Hitler heard of his ideas, which seemed closer to his own than did the plan put forward by his generals, and in the end it was a modification of Manstein's proposals that became the operational plan (known unofficially as the 'Manstein Plan') for the Western campaign. The opposing forces were to be drawn into a battle in Belgium, and then cut off by an unexpected powerful thrust through the Ardennes. In this campaign Manstein's corps played only a minor role at first, but in the second stage it made the first break in the French line along the Somme. The mobility of Manstein's troops was outstanding, and they were the first to cross the Seine.

In the Russian invasion of 1941 Manstein commanded a Panzer Corps, with which he managed to reach and cross the River Dvina in only four days, having covered 200 miles, but this rapidity was squandered when he was ordered to stand for other units to catch up. He was soon promoted, and in September was leading his 11th Army in the south, where he succeeded in crossing the strongly fortified Perekop Isthmus into the Crimea.

When Hitler dismissed his Commander in Chief, von Brauchitsch, many officers hoped that Manstein would be offered the job, but Hitler assumed this office himself and did not, as many had hoped, appoint Manstein as his Chief of Staff. Manstein was not a person who would subordinate his own judgement to Hitler's intuition and, unlike so many other generals, he was not afraid to argue with Hitler, both privately and at conferences.

His capture of Sevastopol in 1942 was a demoralizing defeat for the Russians and was achieved with great skill. He was then switched to the north, in the hope that he would repeat this success and capture Leningrad. But he was diverted to help retrieve the threatening situation at Stalingrad, where Hitler's decisions had created the conditions for a major defeat. Manstein's plan for a thrust to relieve the Germans cut off around Stalingrad would probably have succeeded, if it had been launched in good time. But it was not, and he managed to force his way only to within 22 miles of the beleaguered German troops.

At the beginning of February 1943 the German 6th Army surrendered at Stalingrad. As some of Hitler's generals had forecast, the decision to go for both Stalingrad and the Caucasus in the 1942 campaign had resulted in neither being taken. Moreover, in addition to the crushing defeat at Stalingrad, an even greater reversal threatened the Germans, for their six corps in

LEFT: Field Marshal von Manstein, regarded by many as the ablest general of World War II.

RIGHT: German troops equipped with skis pass beside a Do17 on a wintry Russian airfield.

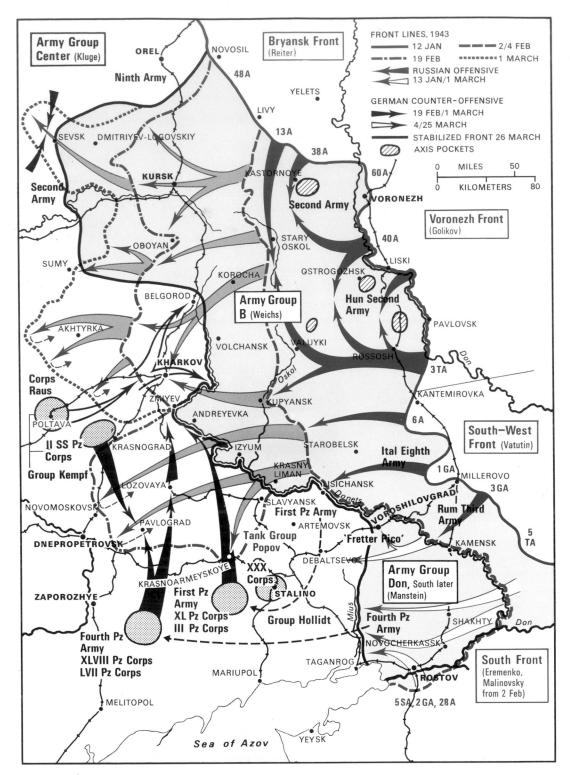

UPPER RIGHT: General Zeitzler, the German Chief of Army Staff, and Manstein's superior officer.

LOWER RIGHT: Russian partisans plan an attack. Such partisans, often including Red Army men cut off in the retreat, put a constant strain on German resources.

the North Caucasus could easily be cut off by Red Army advances from the north. Those six corps had two possible lines of communication, either through Rostov or through the Crimea. The Russians managed to capture Krasnodar, commanding the North Caucasus escape route, but the Germans' 1st Panzer Army was able to scrape through before Manstein was forced to abandon Rostov. The rest of the German forces in the Caucasus took refuge in the Crimea, while Stalin and his *Stavka* decided to make a second attempt to cut off the Germans as they retreated, this time on the River Dnieper.

Manstein, as commander of Army Group South, was therefore responsible not only for the secure deployment of his own troops but also, indirectly, for those of Army Group A from the Caucasus, who could so easily be left marooned should Manstein retreat too far or too soon. Hitler was well aware of this situation and, moreover, was opposed to the abandonment of

positions in the basin of the River Donets. Hitler always found it difficult to abandon territory to the enemy. Unlike trained army officers, he seemed unable to grasp the concept of retreating in order to be better able to attack, a concept which in the situation facing Manstain meant simply that it was better to save the army than try to save territory. Also, the Donets Basin was Russia's main coal-mining and metallurgical area and Hitler was convinced that his possession of these resources was not only beneficial to the German war economy but also fatal to the Soviet. Like many other strident anti-Bolsheviks, he had very little idea of what actually had been going on inside the USSR, and was unaware that Soviet war production could be maintained from resources in, and east of, the Ural Mountains.

Manstein, who had shifted his HQ to Stalino, conferred with Hitler in the week after the Stalingrad surrender. He had by this time found all kinds of ways to lessen the consequences of

Hitler's interference in his operations, and especially of the Führer's inability to comprehend the merits of a strategic withdrawal. In particular, in the disastrous days following the start of the Russian counter-offensive at Stalingrad he had contrived to ignore Hitler's demand for rigid, and rigidly-held, defense lines which, he knew, were costly and not necessarily successful ways of defending territory. Elasticity, Manstein realized, was what was needed at this critical time and he was not afraid to move units back, and occasionally forward, to achieve this. His technique was to inform the Supreme Command that unless he heard from it by a certain time he would act according to his own discretion, a reservation which, in the prevailing situation of bad communications and long deliberations in the Supreme Command, usually enabled him to do what he wanted.

His meeting with Hitler, therefore, was not altogether welcome for Manstein. He had also risked Hitler's wrath by requesting, earlier, a wholesale and immediate retirement to a new defense line along the River Mius, as well as by presenting a long shopping list of needed reinforcements. But, to Manstain's surprise, Hitler was in a humble and conciliatory mood, expressing remorse for the failure of the Stalingrad operation and agreeing with Manstein's requests and comments. However, although he approved of a withdrawal to the River Mius, Hitler was not really convinced that the eastern Donets basin should be evacuated, as Manstein wished. But Manstein soon afterward ordered the withdrawal to enable him to transfer the highly experienced 4th Panzer Army to his western flank and thereby reduce the risk of his Army Group South being encircled. Hitler and Manstein parted, therefore, amicably, and the meeting was an exemplary demonstration of winning minds and influencing

people although, as things turned out, whose mind was won and who was influenced is not entirely clear-cut.

Within a few days, one of Manstein's anxieties, the weakness of Army Group B, his immediate neighbor to the left, was exacerbated by the decision to eliminate that Army Group. Most of its forces joined Army Group Center of General Kluge, not one of Manstein's favorite colleagues. That part of it which did not go to Kluge, three highly-rated SS Panzer divisions, was used to form a group at Kharkov under General Lanz, who was intended to answer to Manstein. Manstein concluded, more or less correctly, that this arrangement would not work so long as his communications with Lanz were so scanty, and it would be some time before his signals units would be able to set up reliable radio and telephone links. This was especially troublesome because Lanz's group was covering Kharkov, which Hitler, true to form, was determined to hold irrespective of the general situation, in line with his 'not-a-step-back' strategy. Manstein would be responsible for those three Panzer divisions but would have difficulty in communicating with them.

In that same second week of February, Manstein's Army Group South was under heavy pressure, and at times parts of it were in disorder. What was especially worrying was the penetration by Soviet formations deep into the German-held territory, so that the Mius line was in danger of disintegration. About three Soviet cavalry divisions had got as far as the railway junction of Debaltsevo and not only slaughtered two trainloads of German reinforcements but also positioned themselves to cut the best rail supply route. At about the same time, Soviet mechanized troops had fought their way into Krasnoarmeisk, which commanded another vital rail route from Dnepropetrovsk. A multilingual SS division of Scandinavian and Baltic volunteers was sent against these Red Army mechanized forces, but took so many losses that it ran out of interpreters and thereby lost cohesion and failed in its task.

Thus, by mid-February Manstein's Army Group South was out of touch with its neighbor to the north, Lanz's Panzers at Kharkov, and had itself been divided into three parts by the Russian advances to Debaltsevo and Krasnoarmeisk. Then, despite Hitler's orders, repeated by Lanz, the SS Panzer divisions abandoned Kharkov just as they were being transferred

LEFT: The German army depended very much on horse haulage, which in Russian climatic conditions often proved more reliable than mechanical transportation.

RIGHT UPPER: German tanks move in on a burning Russian village.

RIGHT: German infantryman carrying one of the versatile MG15 light machine guns.

from Army Group B to Manstein. To the north, Manstein discovered, there was now a 100-mile gap between his Army Group South and Kluge's Army Group Center, a gap vacated by Lanz's Panzers who were now under his command but not under his control.

This situation prompted an unanticipated visitation by Hitler, and Manstein was subjected to a three-day argument at his new headquarters in Zaporozhe; the fact that this HQ was close to Soviet positions and in fact was only thinly defended did not deter Hitler, who was alarmed at the apparent collapse of German positions. It seemed that he regretted the leeway he had allowed Manstein. As usual in a crisis, his emotions told him that any retreat would be fatal and so, not for the first time in the Russian campaign, he ordered his general to stand fast, whatever the consequences. Manstein's flexible defense was, he said, simply conceding territory and leading to a collapse of morale and prestige. Manstein, he claimed, was allowing half his troops to sit quietly behind the fighting areas yet simultaneously demanding reinforcements. The Panzer divisions should be up to strength by this time and no time should be lost in recapturing Kharkov, but without the help of Lanz, who was to be dismissed. A frontal attack with those Panzers would be quite enough to win back Kharkov.

Manstein's reaction to Hitler's harangue deserves to stand among his best feats of generalship. Although he could not persuade Hitler to agree to do what he wanted, he did at least prevent him ordering an immediate recapture of Kharkov. More-

over, he convinced Hitler that however threatening the Soviet advance might look on the map, in reality the Red Army could have only one possible object, and that was to push back and outflank Army Group South until it was pinned against the Black Sea. As the Red Navy commanded that sea this would amount to an encirclement. If Manstein was to hold his existing extended front of 470 miles with his 32 divisions his defense would be so thin that the Russians could penetrate it at any point. Hitler was persuaded of the dangers of a Soviet out-flanking movement and not only decided to provide more men for Manstein, but also accepted that some withdrawals might need to be made to free formations for blocking a Soviet attempt at encirclement.

With Russian tanks about to arrive within range of the air-field, Hitler at last flew off, having conceded a little and, equally important, having acquired a much better understanding of the real situation of Manstein's army group.

Manstein calculated that the Russians could assemble forma-tions to give them an eight-to-one numerical advantage, but he realized that the Red Army, as yet inexperienced in long, broad, advances, was unlikely to muster the supplies or achieve the mobility that exploitation of its position would require. Where-as the Germans had supply dumps behind their positions, the Russians had already advanced for many miles, outpacing their supplies and wearing out their tanks. Although the Germans were outnumbered, their elite Panzer troops were far better than the Red Army formations, whose commanders were un-likely to show any flexibility, and which in any case would be im-mobilized by muddy roads as soon as the thaw came. The best plan would be to prepare for the anticipated Soviet attack on the river crossings over the upper Dniestr. Using the SS divisions to strike south, and the 4th Panzer Army to strike north, it would be possible to cut off the advancing Soviet formations. Having

dealt with the latter, Kharkov would fall with hardly a struggle, and there would then be at least a month of relative tranquility when the thaw set in, a month in which the German units could reform and consolidate.

The inflexibility of the Russian commanders was already evi-dent in their reluctance to change plans when Manstein did not react in the way they expected. With their advanced troops at Debaltsevo and Krasnoarmeisk, they anticipated that the Ger-mans would make partial withdrawals in order to smooth out the Soviet salients. But Manstein did not do this. He was content to maintain his untidy defense line while he completed his pre-parations, and the Russians did nothing to exploit this.

Manstein's preparations included a very neat re-positioning of his withdrawing formations. Hoth's 4th Panzer Army, which consisted mainly of the 48th and 57th Panzer Corps and which had been located north of the Sea of Azov not far west of Tagan-rog, moved north-westward and within five days was in position south of the Dnepropetrovsk-Krasnoarmeisk railway. On 21 February this Army began to move against the Soviet troops holding Krasnoarmeisk and also, by advancing northward, cut at right angles through the Soviet 1st Guards and 6th Armies, which had been pushing southeast toward Pavlograd. These Soviet armies were already tired and depleted, and the thrust by Hoth shattered them, inducing them to break up and retreat as best they could.

This process of disintegration was accelerated when the second element of Manstein's pincer began to move on 23 February. This consisted of the Waffen SS Panzer Corps, and Panzer detachments that had once been commanded by Lanz. Assembled west of Kharkov, part of this force moved south-east to complete the pincer, while part moved east to put pressure on the Russian line around Kharkov.

The resultant rout of the two, once-confident, Soviet armies

UPPER LEFT: The Russian Ilyushin-2 aircraft, a formidable ground-attack machine.

LEFT: Soviet T34 tanks. This was probably the most successful tank design of World War 2, and was put into production on the eve of the German invasion.

RIGHT: One of the later versions of the German HeIII bomber, as used in the Russian campaign.

was due almost entirely to Manstein's superb grasp of space and time, enabling his blows to materialize at precisely the right place at precisely the right time. A supplementary factor was a technological advantage that he enjoyed, for two of the SS formations had received the new Tiger tank. This mounted the 88mm gun, which could master the hitherto all-triumphant Soviet T34 tank, and moreover it could travel over soft ground impassable to the T34. In this battle it was employed in numbers insufficient to make it a dominant factor from the material point of view, but it had a damaging influence on Russian morale.

It took about a week for Manstein's pincers to close, and the meeting was not altogether significant in any case, because whereas he had enough tanks for his purpose he was very short of infantry, and without infantry it was impossible to make a tightly-sealed encirclement. As a result, many small groups of Red Army men managed to get away and cross the frozen River Donets. Compared to previous encirclements, very few prisoners were taken by the Germans. But to those 9,000 prisoners had to be added perhaps 23,000 Russians killed and about 600 Russian tanks destroyed or captured.

Moreover, the Red Army formations were so demoralized and off-balance that Manstein was in a position to push further east, over the Donets, and perhaps capture Kupyansk and even Orel. If he had been confident of Kluge's support he might well have used his victory to push back the Soviet salient (the 'Kursk Salient') between Orel and Belgorod. But, aware that the thaw might catch him any time, he resisted these temptations and concentrated on capturing Kharkov. He mounted a pincer operation against this city, and managed to capture it with little bloodshed because Stalin's *Stavka*, recalling disastrous encirclements in the past (and notably the Kharkov encirclement in spring 1942), evacuated the city in good time. The Red Army left Kharkov on 13 March, and two days later also found it expedient to evacuate Belgorod and move to a new defensive line behind the Donets. All in all, Manstein, despite the disasters of the intervening months, had succeeded in restoring the southern front line to where it had been in summer 1942.

Although this operation had been relatively small and short, it was a classic example of victory snatched from defeat. In little more than three weeks Manstein had seemed to demonstrate the German army's remarkable power of recovery and its continued technical superiority. Confidence returned to the German high command and correspondingly diminished in the Soviet high command. In Moscow, the *Stavka* had to abandon its dreams of a continuous advance and contemplate the likelihood of yet another German offensive in the summer of 1943.

The recapture of Kharkov may not have been the climax of Manstein's career, but certainly everything that followed was anti-climax. In the summer of 1943 he was closely involved in the operations known as the Battle of the Kursk Salient, which

ABOVE: A German bomber airfield is overrun by the Russians.

LEFT: Civilians shot by the retreating German security forces are identified by their relatives.

RIGHT: Prowling tanks and burning villages were constant ingredients of the Russian campaign.

resulted in a crushing defeat for the German armored formations. That this defeat occurred in spite of rather than because of his generalship was small consolation.

The victory at Kharkov had given Hitler renewed confidence and encouraged him to ignore two lessons of that operation. One lesson was that Manstein's victory had been accomplished thanks to the mustering of reserves obtained by a shortening of the defense line (obtained notably by the evacuation from the Caucasus). From this it would have been evident that future successes, or the avoidance of additional defeats, depended on further reduction of commitments so as to enable sufficient strength to be concentrated at the key points. Secondly, the SS Panzer formations that had distinguished themselves in the Kharkov operations had been units that had recently rested, re-formed, and re-equipped. While it was plain that man-for-man the German units were far superior to the Soviet, this advantage was likely to disappear when tired and depleted German units went into battle, and this was likely to be increasingly the case in future unless commitments were reduced.

Hitler, however, sought a grand victory in summer 1943 to restore his prestige, and Manstein's success at Kharkov encouraged him in this aim. The wish gave birth to Operation *Zitadelle*, whose object was to push back the Kursk Salient while destroying the Soviet forces within it. Manstein had himself wished to flatten back this salient, but he wanted to do so as soon as the thaw came to an end, for he had learned by experience that the Russians moved rapidly when they needed to strengthen a threatened sector. Any delay, he knew, would simply enable the Russians to bring in reinforcements and prepare strong defensive positions.

The *Zitadelle* plan envisaged a southward advance from the Orel area by the 9th Army, which at Kursk would meet a northward advance from the Kharkov direction undertaken by Manstein's Army Group South and mainly entrusted to Hoth's Panzer army. This would, once again, encircle the Russian formations and permit their methodical destruction. The plan was quite attractive, but many of the generals responsible for its execution soon became disillusioned. General Model, for example, said that more troops were needed because the Russians were stronger than the staff appreciations indicated. Guderian, the tank specialist, was wary of the plan because it would inevitably use up tanks, and his prime task, as he saw it, was to amass tanks for the expected Second Front. Kluge and Manstein, for once seeing eye-to-eye, lost enthusiasm when delays accumulated, and tension was so great that at one point Kluge challenged Guderian to a duel. Hitler, with his exaggerated faith in new technology, put off the battle until more of the new Panther tanks could be made available. In the end, the operation was begun only on 4 July, by which time the Russians were expectant and ready.

In the face of successive lines of Russian defense works, both arms of the German pincer made very slow and costly progress. Moreover, the new German tanks and self-propelled guns did not perform well, and the German dive-bombers could not wreak their usual havoc because of the strong Soviet fighter opposition. Unexpected rainfall also hampered the Germans. The great tank battle of Prokhorovka began on 12 July, and at first was indecisive, although highly destructive to both sides. While it was still at its height Hitler decided to withdraw his SS Panzer units, for transfer to Italy where the Allies had just landed. At this point Manstein, who had opposed the beginning of the operation, had to oppose its ending as well. He realized that the withdrawal of the Panzers meant, in effect, a disengagement, and he believed that the Germans were on the point

of winning. Whether he was right or wrong cannot be determined; all the signs were that the Russians would hold their ground and would therefore win the battle, but Manstein was a general of exceptionally good judgement and it is more than possible that his appreciation was on this occasion again an accurate one, but overruled.

Having made the decision to disengage, the German high command had opened the way for the carefully prepared Soviet counter-offensive. This was directed mainly against Manstein's Army Group South, which lost Kharkov and had to withdraw to the line of the Dniepr. Some months later, in March 1944, Manstein was dismissed. Hitler, quite clearly, was tired of listening to his urgings for a substantial withdrawal in order to win space and time for the German Army's recovery. He had been distrusted for a long time already by leading Nazis. In the previous November Goebbels had written disparagingly of him in his diary, mentioning that Himmler regarded Manstein as a 'first-class defeatist,' and that the trouble then besetting Army Group South was a consequence of Manstein being a man of low caliber.

From 1944 Manstein was effectively out of the war, a living example of the Nazi regime's congenital inability to work with first-rate professionals. He was arrested by the victorious Allies in 1945, but his trial for war crimes was delayed. In the end, few of the charges against him could be upheld, but enough offenses were contrived to win him a long prison sentence from which, however, he was released in 1952. With his remarkable strategic sense, he was probably the ablest of Hitler's generals, and he was especially notable in that although he was not a tank specialist he had a very sure understanding of what tanks could, and could not, achieve.

UPPER LEFT: General Vatutin, commander of the Soviet Voronezh Front in the Kursk Salient.

UPPER RIGHT: General Konev (nearer camera), commanding the Soviet Steppe Front in the Kursk operations.

LOWER LEFT: General Kluge strikes a pose.

LOWER RIGHT: Manstein (left) discusses the situation with Hitler's ally, Marshal Antonescu, dictator of Roumania.

CHAPTER TWELVE

EISENHOWER

AND THE NORMANDY LANDINGS

SUPREME COMMANDER of the biggest military enterprise of World War II, subsequently US President, Dwight D. Eisenhower seemed to possess none of the obvious qualities of greatness. This led many commentators to suggest that this was a man who had greatness thrust upon him. But this is to ignore the question of how to define greatness. If it is the performance of great tasks with a success difficult to envisage with other commanders, or if it is the taking of fateful decisions cooly and correctly, then Eisenhower qualifies as a great leader. If, on the other hand, it consists in the leadership of men in battle, sharing perils and quickly seizing opportunities to turn defeat into victory, then Eisenhower never had the chance to qualify.

It was not his fault that he was denied battle experience in the field. He graduated from West Point two years before the USA entered World War I. In many ways he had been an ideal cadet, getting on well with his equals and superiors, staying in the top third of his classes, and making the football team. As a football player, he was tough and determined, so much so that he sustained a knee injury which took him out of the game for life. This was probably fortunate, for the time he might otherwise have spent playing he could devote to football coaching. The latter occupation encouraged him to develop what was perhaps his most valuable talent, showing people the best way to do things without causing resentment. As a commander, Eisenhower was remarkable for his ability to observe the line between guidance and interference.

This made him an ideal choice for the work of instructor, training men who would form part of the US Expeditionary Force in France. In this role he proved so invaluable that, despite several requests, he was never himself posted to Europe.

At the end of World War I, however, he was training the new tank corps and soon he made friends with Colonel George Patton who, like him, saw that the tank should not be treated simply as an infantry weapon but as an arm in itself, capable of revolutionizing warfare.

There followed three years as a staff officer with a brigade stationed in Panama. His commanding officer, luckily and rarely, had a good library, and Eisenhower spent much of his spare time reading military history. Having proved he was very capable in staff duties, in 1925 he was posted to a one-year staff course, and graduated first in his class. He went to join General Pershing's staff, had a period at the War College, and then served in the War Department, where he studied ways of mobilising industry in a future war. Here he soon became assistant to the Chief of Staff, Douglas MacArthur, and went with him when MacArthur became military adviser to the Philippine government.

These successive appointments were achieved not only because Eisenhower showed great competence, but because he had an ability to get on well with people. Appointment followed appointment because his superiors willingly helped him forward. By the time World War II broke out he had, with the one exception of active war service, an unrivalled record that extended from experience of dealing with recruits to contact with very wide military, political, and industrial affairs.

As soon as Britain and France declared war on Germany Eisenhower regarded the eventual involvement of the USA as almost inevitable. Wishing to be where the action seemed most likely (one of his few misjudgments, as it turned out), he asked to leave the Philippines and return home. Soon he got what he wanted, actual command of troops, in this case an infantry brigade in California. But because of his proven ability he was soon returned to staff work, and by early 1941 was Chief of Staff of the Third Army, where he was dealing with virtually untrained officers and men. Here his ability to sift the grain from the chaff while still remaining popular with both stood him in good stead, and when Japan attacked Pearl Harbor he had reached the rank of brigadier-general.

LEFT: General Eisenhower, pictured in 1943 during his assignment as Supreme Allied Commander in the Mediterranean.

BELOW: Colonel Eisenhower (left) during 1941 maneuvers, before the US entered the war.

Because he knew the Far East, and perhaps because he knew the best way of dealing with MacArthur, within a few days of Pearl Harbor Eisenhower was transferred to the War Plans Division in Washington, charged with examining Far Eastern strategy. His recommendation that, whatever further disasters might ensue, the USA should keep open its communications with Australia and set up a base there, was characteristic; he was a sure judge of the essential. He was then entrusted by Marshall with working out a sensible command system for the Southeast Asian theater, where not only different arms but different nationalities needed to be welded together. This was Eisenhower's introduction to what was to become one of his strongest fields, the formulation of chains of command that would accommodate the needs, and often the vanities, of several parties while maintaining fast decision-making and unimpeded execution.

The immediate problem in Southeast Asia, and a continuing problem throughout the war, was the conflict between the British preference for commanders of equal authority for each of the three services in a given theater, and the American concept of unified command, with one man directing all arms. Helped by Eisenhower's study, the American view was accepted, with the supreme commander in the theater reporting to a new body,

the Combined Chiefs of Staff, an Anglo-American committee based in Washington.

This set the command pattern for the later inter-allied operations and, although it was not spectacular, in real terms it was a war-winning development. An effective command system is the first necessity for successful operations, and it is not easy to construct. The Axis powers failed in this respect, with Italian and German operations frequently failing through non-cooperation, and with rivalry between armies and air forces compromising strategic decisions. Post-war evaluations of Eisenhower as a 'good committee man' are serious undervaluations. He was much more than that. He achieved, in 1942 and later, command structures that reconciled the seemingly irreconcilable, and through good judgment and respect for officers as people managed to keep them working together even in the most tense and divisive situations.

Eisenhower was now head of the War Plans Division, and was soon to be promoted Major General. He upheld and provided arguments to support Roosevelt's and General George Marshall's decision that logic, and logistics, dictated that the main US effort should first be concentrated against Germany, leaving Japan to be defeated later. He was entrusted with the initial

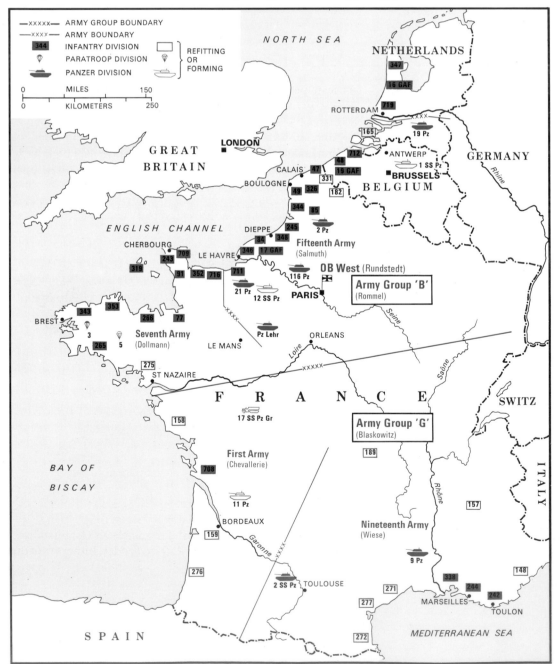

LEFT: The German dispositions in France, with Rommel's Army Group B concentrated along the Channel coast, and southern France left with only light cover.

RIGHT: The location and planned movements of the Allied formations allocated to the invasion. The logistical problem was the funnelling of widely-spaced formations into the relatively narrow channel of attack.

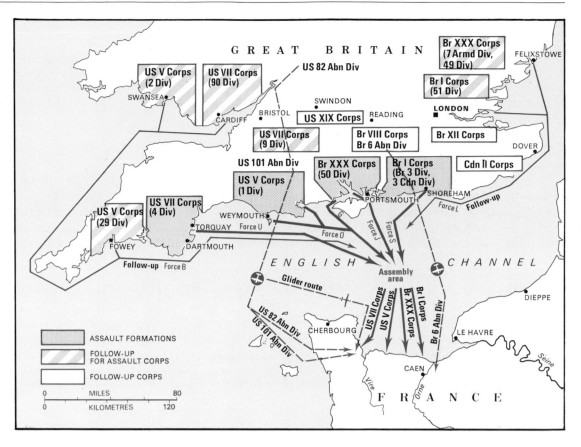

planning for a landing in France in 1942, and right from the beginning insisted that the US forces in Europe should have a unified command, with one officer directing the army and navy and their respective air forces. In May 1942 he went to Britain to discuss the movement of US forces to that country, and although he attended some demonstrations he appears to have spent most of his energy in trying to persuade the British that their command system would not work well in a combined operation in continental Europe. He suggested several alternatives, all variations on the theme of a supreme commander answerable to the Combined Chiefs of Staff and below him the respective British and US army commanders; how the air and naval commanders would fit in was negotiable.

This question was still not solved when Eisenhower, shortly after his return to the USA, was told that he had been appointed to command US forces in Britain. Nor was it certain when an invasion would take place. In fact the British war cabinet had already, unknown to Eisenhower, decided that a 1942 operation was unlikely, if only because not enough shipping was available. Attention was shifting to another strategy, less risky but still big enough, it was hoped, to take pressure off the Russians. This was the proposed invasion of French North Africa.

For some weeks Eisenhower continued to plan the cross-channel invasion and, even when he learned of the British unwillingness, continued to argue that although its success was far from certain, it was worth doing because even if it was unable to make headway it would still serve to keep Russia, reeling at the time, in the war. Nevertheless, he set willingly to work on the planning for the North Africa operation, 'Operation Torch.' It soon became clear that US troops would be most suitable for the initial landing because of the political situation. Morocco, Algeria and Tunis were French territories and had not declared for De Gaulle's Free French. It could be expected that the authorities, and the considerable French forces there, might take the Allied side soon after the landing, but this would be less likely with obvious British participation – Britain was still suffering the unpopularity of its 1940 assault on the French navy in North

African ports. Since the army operation would be largely American, an American Commander in Chief was appropriate, and Roosevelt nominated Eisenhower.

Conscious as always that the key to a successful campaign was a command structure with one top commander, acting through separate service commanders, responsible for the whole operation, Eisenhower spent much of the early planning period trying to persuade his political masters to agree to his command outline. He was only partially successful. As Allied Commander in Chief, he had control of the armies and navies that he required, but the air strength was divided between the local commanders and the Commander in Chief. In practice, this proved unsatisfactory but not disastrous. As his naval commander Eisenhower had Admiral Andrew Cunningham. Most of the naval resources employed were British, and Cunningham had a fine record as a fighting admiral. He proved also to be an intelligent admiral, sensitive enough to see that Eisenhower, faced with a task of unprecedented complexity and lacking any fighting experience, needed moral support as well as technical help.

The North African landings went well, and after two days the French decided to cooperate. However, the aim of taking Tunis before the Germans could enter Tunisia from Libya was not achieved. The Allied forces around Tunis were soon in difficulties, faced by bad weather and German air superiority. For a time Eisenhower moved his headquarters near to this sector and made some tactical decisions, but always with the knowledge and concurrence of his commanders. Towards the end of this campaign, which ended with the expulsion of the Germans from North Africa, Eisenhower's wish for a single air Commander in Chief was granted; Air Marshal Arthur Tedder, hitherto not one of Churchill's favorite RAF officers, was sent to him. This team of General Harold Alexander (army), Cunningham (navy), and Tedder was also to serve Eisenhower for the next campaign, the invasion of Sicily and Italy.

Eisenhower left the planning of these next operations to his subordinates. He was busy with overseeing the African operations, securing the supplies his forces needed, and negotiating

ABOVE: US troops training for D-Day on a British beach.

LEFT: British infantry use a lake for a night landing exercise. Live ammunition is fired close to the training soldiers to add to realism.

UPPER RIGHT: US troops make the most of limited transatlantic troopship capacity.

LOWER RIGHT: British Valentine tanks inside their canvas flotation screens. Amphibious tanks were an important part of D-Day plans.

with the French. But he did approve the eventual plan that was presented to him. Moreover, it was he who had to give the final order for the Sicily operation to begin. This was not easy, because on the eve of the planned assault a strong wind developed. This threatened the landing operations, but on the other hand there were not many days when the moon and tide would be equally suitable. In the end, when the meteorologists forecast a slight improvement, he gave the go-ahead, and events justified this decision.

His deliberate policy of letting his commanders make the decisions once battle was joined was wise, but occasionally led to errors of omission. In the Sicily campaign, such an error was the failure to prevent the German defenders evacuating to the Italian mainland after they had lost the battle for the island. Later, but much more questionably, Eisenhower was criticised for cancelling an airborne landing near Rome at the time of the Italian surrender. This would, it was said, have prevented the Germans taking over that city. On the other hand it would have been a risk, and Eisenhower was always sensitive about risk-taking. Earlier, in the North African campaign, he had decided not to mount an airborne landing to prevent the Germans getting to Tunis first. Here again, the risks were obvious, and so were the gains. Eisenhower was a man of exceptionally good judgment, and moreover had the knack of ensuring that his judgment was accepted by others. But inevitably, as with all persons of good judgment, there were times when he did less well than a gambler might have done.

In the fighting on Italy's mainland he was content to let his three British commanders direct the campaign, although it was he who had the ultimate responsibility for the Salerno landing, a risky enterprise that succeeded only at a heavy price. Otherwise his interventions were rare, and often consisted of making sure that his US generals saw the need to take orders willingly from their British superior, and to cooperate with the British. This was not always easy with the impetuous Patton, but the other Americans went along, realizing that the British commanders in chief had equally willingly subordinated themselves to the American supreme commander.

By this time, summer 1943, the British had agreed that a cross-channel invasion should be mounted in 1944, and had accepted the proposal for an American supreme commander for this operation, 'Operation Overlord.' Marshall was the anticipated commander, but Roosevelt was unwilling to part with him, so Eisenhower was chosen instead. Roosevelt called on him to tell him this on the way back from the Teheran Conference with Stalin and Churchill in late 1943.

Eisenhower arrived in Britain in January, to find that the basic planning for Operation Overlord had already been accomplished by an Anglo-American planning group whose plan, based on a three-division landing force, had been expanded by General Bernard Montgomery into a bigger and broader assault. The landing was to be in Normandy, with the Americans on the west so as to move on to Cherbourg and Brest, and the British and Canadians on the east to block enemy reinforcements coming from the east and southeast. Eisenhower approved this plan, and left it to his subordinates to accomplish the immensely detailed work involved in transporting, placing, supporting and training all the units required. Eisenhower's own tasks were ensuring that the command structure was set up the way he wanted; allotting resources and, often, begging for them; studying the political problems posed by an invasion of France in the presence of De Gaulle; putting some order into the plans for air support; and making his contribution to strategic planning decisions, which at the time revolved mainly about the question of whether to go ahead with a proposed landing in the south of France ('Operation Anvil'). True to form, Eisenhower strove to keep this as an option as long as possible. In the end, it was postponed so as not to interfere with Overlord.

The problem of air support was intertwined with that of command, and the struggle which Eisenhower put up to get his views accepted might perhaps be rated his biggest and most important battle in this campaign. The command structure was designed on the lines of that which had proved so successful in Sicily and Italy, with Eisenhower as the supreme commander, having ultimate responsibility for all arms, and with commanders in chief of the three arms reporting to him. He willingly accepted Montgomery as army commander (Alexander was still needed in Italy) and of Admiral Bertram Ramsay as naval commander (Cunningham was by then First Sea Lord – Britain's chief of naval operations), but he was successful in keeping Tedder as air commander. Instead, Tedder was appointed to the more general post of deputy supreme com-

mander, and Churchill on the advice of his air chief of staff nominated Air Chief Marshal Trafford Leigh-Mallory as air commander.

Leigh-Mallory was disliked by many of his RAF colleagues, who felt he had stolen much of the credit for the Battle of Britain and had risen above his ability. Moreover, his experience was with fighters. The commander of the RAF Bomber Command was unlikely to cooperate with him and could conceivably obstruct him. His appointment intensified the unwillingness of Bomber Command to plan its activities according to the requirements of Overlord. Air Chief Marshal Arthur Harris, chief of Bomber Command, and General Carl Spaatz, heading the US strategic bombers in Britain, both believed that they could win the war singlehanded, that given a few more months they could bomb Germany into submission, making Overlord an expensive luxury. As both air forces throughout the war had been making blatantly exaggerated claims, their confidence in 1944 was not taken seriously, even though by this time their capabilities had vastly increased. They were unwilling to divert their bombers to targets important for Overlord, and they were unwilling to accept orders from Leigh-Mallory. But Eisenhower was insistent that all air power, including strategic bombers, should be under his ultimate control in the forthcoming operation.

Seeing no other way to persuade Churchill, he told the latter that he would give up his job if not satisfied on that point. In the end, a compromise was reached that gave Eisenhower what he wanted but not the appearance of a victory. It was agreed that Eisenhower and the British Chief of Air Staff would approve an air plan for Overlord and that supervision of this plan would be by Tedder. In this way Eisenhower ensured that the bombers would be devoted to Overlord targets and, moreover, that Tedder would in effect if not in name be his Commander in Chief for the strategic bombing forces.

It would have been highly unusual for a commander to resign on the eve of a great operation, and had Eisenhower actually acted as he threatened both his career and reputation would have been badly compromised. That he was prepared to use this threat emphasizes his determination not to give way on what he knew to be essentials. Easygoing in his manner, there were times when he dug his heels in, to the eventual benefit of all.

With the strategic bombers under his control, Eisenhower could ensure the execution of what became known as the transportation plan. This was a carefully planned bombing of French rail installations so as to deny the Germans any chance of bringing railborne reinforcements to the Normandy battlefields. So as to give no indication where the landings would be, all lines serving the north of France had to be attacked. Bomber Command, perhaps in a bid to avoid this unwanted task, had told Churchill that this plan would involve up to 180,000 French civilian casualties, a horrifying figure that impelled Churchill to ask if the plan could be modified. It was not, and in fact French casualties proved to be only a small fraction of the forecast.

In the weeks before this bombing operation began the British

ABOVE: The invaluable and ubiquitous Jeep, shown here as used by special forces behind German lines in France.

UPPER RIGHT: Sections of the concrete Mulberry Harbor under construction in London.

LEFT: Eisenhower encourages his paratroopers shortly before take-off.

RIGHT: General von Rundstedt, whose forces bore the brunt of the Allied invasion.

and American strategic bombers had continued their assault on Germany. The British bombed by night, choosing cities as their targets because they were hard to miss, and in the belief that German morale could be broken. The Americans attacked selected industrial targets by day. They achieved considerable success against the oil industry, but little against the aircraft industry. However, the bombers were so well-protected by recently-introduced long-range escort fighters that intercepting German aircraft were shot down by the thousand. Unrealized by the bomber commands, and therefore unknown to Eisenhower, German air power had been shattered by these raids and would be unable to oppose the Allied air forces in Normandy. Thus perhaps the most important battle for Normandy had already been won, weeks before the invasion fleet sailed. Another prerequisite for victory, the maiming of rail junctions, was already achieved by D-Day. On the other hand, because of the bad blood surrounding Leigh-Mallory, planning and briefing for close air support of the troops had been only cursory. In fact, the basic air plan for the support of the armies was finally fixed only a day before the invasion fleet set sail.

Apart from settling the question of air command, and arriving at an acceptable compromise over the landings in southern France, Eisenhower was occupied in these pre-invasion weeks

with ensuring that training went ahead, that the attack plan was refined to take account of the latest developments and intelligence, and that the enormously complicated details of the attack were properly coordinated and feasible. With five divisions making the first assault, on separate beaches and not (because of differing tides) at precisely the same times, timetabling was elaborate and therefore vulnerable. All the time, too, it was essential that the Germans were given no clue as to where the landings would take place. From signals intelligence, some of it obtained from 'Ultra' interceptions, it was clear that the Germans expected an invasion that summer and that they thought the Pas de Calais area was the most likely place for it (only the German Navy, the least influential of the German services, correctly forecast that it would be between Havre and Cherbourg). A deception scheme had been incorporated in the plan for Overlord. This provided for one army to be visibly stationed in south-east England; this was Patton's Third Army, which in the event was to land in Normandy some weeks after D-Day. The assemblies of landing craft, the paths of reconnaissance aircraft, radio deception and occasional releases of false information were all designed to reinforce the Germans' impression. So successful was the deception that for some time after D-Day the German command regarded the Normandy landings as a diversion, intended to cover a second landing near Calais, and deployed its troops accordingly.

To ensure that training was carried out effectively, and also to show himself to the troops for reasons of morale, Eisenhower found time to visit all of his divisions. Unassuming, but confident and natural, 'Ike' was liked and trusted by the officers and men of all the nationalities involved. These were mainly Americans, Britons and Canadians, but there were also sizable French and Polish contingents. He took a special interest in the US units, because he felt he had a duty to weed out any inefficient commander.

At the same time, he was constantly in touch with his masters, the Combined Chiefs of Staff in Washington. Sometimes he needed their support in decisions that were not to the taste of a particular service or particular country. More often, he had to answer, or act upon, their suggestions. Of the latter, the urge to

ABOVE RIGHT: US troops crouch in their landing craft, en route to Omaha Beach.

TOP LEFT: A fighter control unit used to direct Allied fighters against ground targets.

CENTRAL LEFT: Laying a fuel pipeline beneath the Channel.

LEFT: Beach obstacles and supply ships after the landing.

make more use of airborne divisions, a favorite idea of Marshall, caused him the most trouble. In February, four months before the invasion, Marshall urged him to make one large airborne drop well inland, to capture airfields and disturb German reinforcing movements. Eisenhower, probably rightly, concluded that such a drop would probably result in the airborne forces finding themselves beleaguered and out of reach of the main Allied units. As he regarded the seizure of a defensible beachhead, and then of a good port, as the most critical objectives, he was prepared to use airborne forces in those tasks, and to this end he agreed to send in a British airborne division to cover the eastern flank of the British beachhead, and at the same time drop two US airborne divisions in the Cherbourg Peninsula with a view to speeding the capture of Cherbourg. In this latter enterprise Eisenhower had the support of Montgomery, but had to endure Leigh-Mallory's opposition; Leigh-Mallory forecast that only 30 per cent of the airborne troops would actually get into action. In the event, this was a grossly pessimistic forecast.

In his dealings with the French, Eisenhower was perhaps at his best, evading potential disaster by tact and restraint. Although most of the Free French army had been earmarked for the later invasion of southern France, as soon as the Allies touched Normandy they would inevitably be involved in French politics. Roosevelt, who distrusted and disliked De

Gaulle, was reluctant to acknowledge that De Gaulle's cooperation was essential if the French local population was to be properly administered in the areas captured by the Allies, and if it was to support the Allies. De Gaulle represented a potential French government, and Roosevelt insisted that nothing should be done to favor one political grouping over another. In his contacts with the French Resistance, on whom important tasks had been placed for D-Day, Eisenhower had become well aware of the several French political currents that were developing, but he was also aware that at that time De Gaulle's organization was the only one which had the substance to replace the existing Vichy regime. In the end, after asking Roosevelt to express his views on De Gaulle not to him directly, but through the Combined Chiefs of Staff, and by leaving Churchill to deal with the Frenchman, Eisenhower concentrated on winning the confidence of the French liaison officers who were already being prepared by his civil affairs staff to take over local administration in France. To a considerable degree, these French officers were encouraged to divide their loyalty between De Gaulle and the general Allied cause.

The network of interlocking schedules that made up the plan for Overlord had to be ready by June 1. The precise timing of the assault was to be fixed later, but on the assumption that it would be as soon as possible after June 1. A rising tide to help the landing craft, moonlight to help the airborne troops, darkness to cover most of the invasion fleet as it neared the coast, some light to help the air and naval support bombardment were the requirements, and so far as the first half of June was concerned just three days, 5, 6 and 7, provided these in the right sequence. In the second half of the month 19 June was the first suitable day. Eisenhower chose 5 June, presumably because that would allow postponements to either of the two following days if something went wrong, but he reserved his final decision for early on 4 June, when he planned a final conference of meteorologists and commanders.

On 2 June the weather began to turn nasty, and it worsened on 3 June. At the conference on 4 June it was clear that the air forces would not be able to operate effectively unless the weather improved. Eisenhower decided on a postponement for one day, subject to later weather forecasts. Meeting again that evening, the commanders heard that there were forecasts of clear skies for at least the first half of 6 June. Ramsay, commanding the sea operations, pointed out that because of fuelling problems a decision to proceed had to be taken within the next half-hour. Tedder and Leigh-Mallory were still not very happy with the prospect.

Eisenhower realized that all his forces were in a state of tension. The men and their officers were keyed-up, and would be demoralized by a further postponement. The schedules would be at risk if some ships had to refuel. Above all, a postponement added to the likelihood that the Germans would discover where the landing was to be made. Moreover, there was no guarantee that the weather would be any better on June 7 or 19. Against these considerations was the disruption of the plans that could occur if some craft never made it to shore, or if visibility was too poor for the preliminary naval and air bombardment. In the

ABOVE: Mail distribution for US troops in France.

UPPER LEFT: British commandos in a French village.

CENTRAL LEFT: Landing craft off Normandy on June 10.

LEFT: The US Navy sets up a shore communication system on the Normandy coast. Each landing beach was allocated a Beachmaster who had total authority over all movements in his area.

TOP RIGHT: A member of an SS unit surrenders to the Allies.

RIGHT: General George Marshall, Chief of Staff of the US Army, addresses US troops in Belgium.

worst case, the invasion could fail, with grave military and political consequences. In a better case, the bad weather might mean that the objectives would be secured, but at a heavier price in casualties.

His decision to go ahead on 6 June shows him at his greatest, with the calm shouldering of an awesome responsibility and the calm appraisal of the conflicting risks. In the end, it was typical of his clear way of looking at things that determined that his decision was made not on the basis of the possible risks of an immediate go-ahead, but on the certain risks of a postponement.

The weather did in fact work against the Allies, insofar as some weapons did not reach shore. The British had invented and developed a variety of special equipment for Overlord. One of these devices was a flotation screen for tanks, enabling them to 'swim' ashore. In the event, many of these tanks, intended to provide support for the infantry from the very start, on the beaches, foundered. This was particularly damaging for the US V Corps, which lost all but two of its tanks, was pinned down on the beach, and suffered a crisis of morale.

On the other hand the bad weather had caused the Germans to relax in the expectation that nothing would be undertaken until there was an improvement. In fact, when the Allies landed many of the German officers had taken the day off. At the end of D-Day it was clear that the landing had been a success and had gone according to plan. In the east the British 6th Airborne Division had successfully landed, had seized vital bridges, and was covering the flank of the British and Canadian beachhead, which had been won by the British 3rd and 50th divisions, and the Canadian 3rd, which together made up the British Second Army. Further to the west Montgomery's other army, Omar Bradley's US First Army, had likewise established a defensible beachhead. Even further to the west, the two US airborne divisions had successfully, and at relatively small loss, established themselves.

In the following days extra divisions were poured in, and the beachheads deepened. Within a week there were more than 300,000 men ashore. Eisenhower was content to let his subordinate Montgomery get on with the job. He remained at his headquarters at Portsmouth and made his first visit to the battlefield on 24 June. He was soon engaged in holding his team of commanders together, when Montgomery's handling of the British Second Army was questioned. Montgomery regarded its role as primarily defensive, sucking in and destroying the German forces sent against it. Eisenhower had hoped that the British would be more venturesome by advancing further, and the failure to capture Caen promptly was a disappointment to him. However, he saw what Montgomery was doing, and knew that the British, who had few reserves to call on, needed to avoid unnecessary casualties. He played therefore the role more of a buffer than a commander in this phase, sheltering Montgomery from the criticism, sometimes abuse, of Tedder and Leigh Mallory, both of whom thought Montgomery was being lackadaisical and both of whom had been hurt by Montgomery's criticism of the air support he was getting.

Due to the activity of the British and US press, this controversy threatened to develop into a chauvinistic outburst, with the American public being told that the US troops were doing most of the fighting and the British public being told that the British were killing most Germans but were being deprived of the credit that was their due. Here Eisenhower made his views quite plain, and wrote to the Public Relations director of the War Department in Washington to the effect that journalists were in danger of breaking up the inter-service, inter-national, team that he had spent so much effort creating.

The battle for Normandy effectively finished when Patton's Third Army swept out toward Brittany before wheeling east and, on the way, forming one half of the claw that was to wreak destruction on the German armored forces around Falaise. For the remainder of the war in Europe, Eisenhower took a closer grip of activities, his headquarters following the line of advance.

But his principal task, as always, was holding his command structure together, no easy matter when so many of the generals were concerned with their image back home, and when two of his generals were Patton and Montgomery, both notoriously difficult characters.

Eisenhower favored a broad-front approach to the Rhine and an orthodox advance into Germany, whereas Montgomery and others believed that the war could be ended in 1944 by a swift narrow-front advance into the heart of Germany. Always willing to discuss this difference, Eisenhower nevertheless ensured that his less adventurous but safer strategy prevailed, and the war in Europe ended when his forces met the Red Army on the Elbe in 1945. On the way there had been one critical period, when Hitler launched his unexpected counterthrust through the Ardennes. Eisenhower was no more prescient than his generals in anticipating such a move, but reacted energetically. Because the

German thrust had split Bradley's US army group, he decided that for effective command two of Bradley's armies should be placed under Montgomery. That he was willing to do this, in the full knowledge that it would add fuel to the Montgomery v. Bradley debate then raging in both the US and British press, confirms that he always put the real needs of his units before considerations of image.

That he was able to end this campaign, like the African and Sicily campaigns, with his Anglo-American team of commanders still working together in the common cause despite differences of personality and attitude, confirmed his reputation as a great leader. In their scale, and in their continuing and close cooperation between national armies, the Normandy battle and the following campaign were unprecedented, and demanded an unprecedented kind of leadership. It was such a leadership that Eisenhower provided.

LEFT: US paratroopers, alive and dead, near Carentan, June 1944.

BELOW: US infantry pass an abandoned German Mk IV tank amid the ruins of a French town.

CHAPTER THIRTEEN

SLIM

AT IMPHAL AND KOHIMA

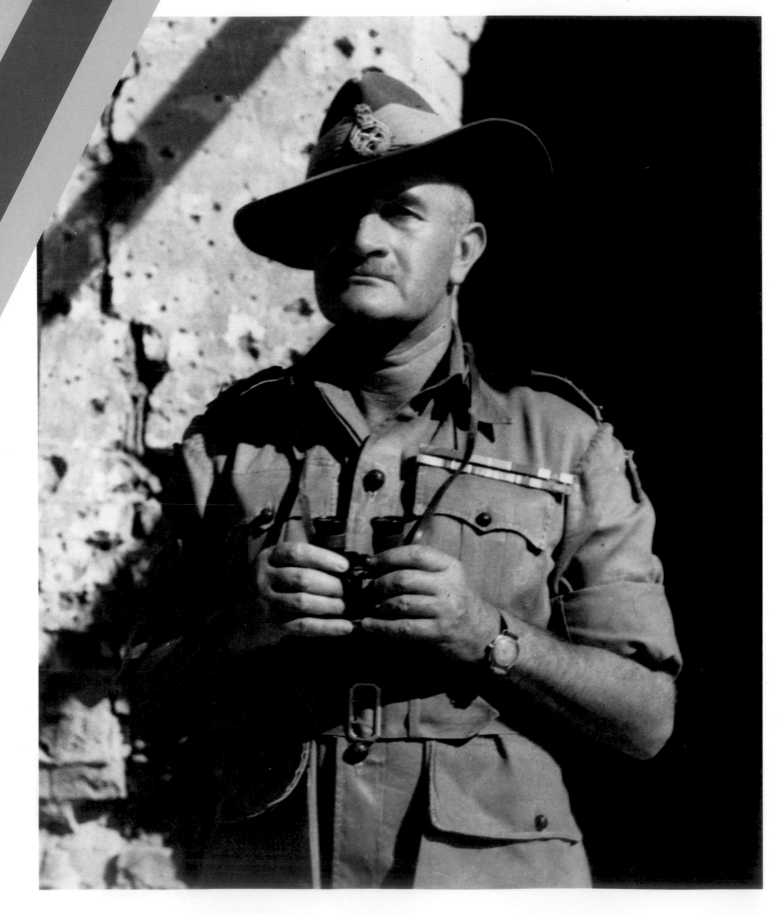

WHEN JAPAN began her Far Eastern war in December 1941 it was to secure territory that would make her economically powerful and independent. She called this territory her Southern Resources Area, and while its richest part was to be the East Indies, Burma with its mineral and oil resources was also included. To win Burma a separate campaign was necessary, and the earlier Japanese occupation of Thailand provided a threshold for this. Like Britain, Japan could never turn her main strength to this campaign, but because a successful occupation of Burma would bring her to the frontiers of India and also cut the Burma Road (China's only surface route for supplies from her western allies) the Burma campaign was regarded as strategically vital.

In January 1942 two divisions of the Japanese 15th Army crossed into Burma and advanced upon Moulmein. The British had two divisions available, but these were under strength and, moreover, had very little support in terms of supplies, transport, and air cover. A withdrawal behind the Salween River gave only a temporary respite, because the Japanese, using infiltration and surprise tactics that would be repeated time after time, crossed that river upstream and thereby turned the British flank. Another withdrawal to the Sittang River ended badly when the Japanese crossed that river before all the British forces had retreated behind it. The destruction of the Sittang Bridge which followed meant that part of the 17th Indian Division was cut off and lost (the British forces' Indian divisions were nominally two-thirds Indian and one-third British).

The arrival of Lieutenant General Harold Alexander to take command of the British forces brought no improvement. Ordered to hold the capital, Rangoon, Alexander only narrowly escaped capture as the Japanese entered the city. He took his forces northward to defend the Yenangyaung oilfield and to link up in a defensive line with Chinese formations supervised by the American Lieutenant General Joseph Stilwell. Meanwhile the British forces (the Burma Division and the 17th Indian Division, together forming 'Burcorps') were put under the command of Major General William Slim.

Slim, who became Britain's best-loved general of World War II, was a man of intelligence and sensitivity hidden behind a facade of iron self-control and rough-and-ready Birmingham-style humor. He did not win all his battles, being cautious rather than impetuous, but neither did he ever lead his men into disaster in this mountain-and-jungle campaign for which neither he nor his troops had been trained. He had not risen to command on the basis of a Sandhurst education, for he had begun his military career in the Birmingham University Officer Training Corps. In World War I he was in the infantry at the Dardanelles, where he was wounded, then in Iraq, where he was again wounded, and he ended up in the Indian Army where, between the wars, he was able to enter the Quetta Staff College. Here his diligence and intelligence combined to make a great impression on his instructors, and he began to progress upwards. In 1940 he was commanding an Indian infantry brigade against the Italians in East Africa with great competence until an Italian aircraft put three bullets (including one tracer) through his backside. A year later, having recovered the ability to sit down, he commanded an Indian division in Iraq until his transfer to Burma in 1942. He was remarkable in many respects, not least for the way in which he could speak to both superiors and subordinates on a man-to-man level without sacrificing the sense of rank that was so important in the functioning of military life. He saw his colleagues and his men as people as well as soldiers. As a commander, he would introduce his radio messages with 'This is Bill speaking,' and toward the end of the Burma campaign he was generally known as 'Uncle Bill.' This relationship was invaluable in difficult times, when morale tends to crumble. It is doubtful whether, for example, the epic retreat of Burcorps through the jungle to the Indian frontier could have been accomplished so well under a different commander.

Neither Slim nor his superior Alexander were given any general directive as to the first priority of their campaign. They were given a variety of tasks, which in total could not be achieved with the resources available, but were never told which

LEFT: General Slim in a typically pugnacious pose at his 14th Army HQ early in 1945.

RIGHT: The flamboyant Supreme Allied Commander South East Asia, Admiral Lord Mountbatten, addresses a group of US airmen at a base in India.

objective overrode all others. At this stage, in March, they were told to maintain a defense line in contact with the Chinese on their left, and at the same time defend the oilfields. The need to maintain touch with the Chinese forces who, ordered London, were never to be given cause to believe that the British would retreat and leave them in thin air, meant that the British defenses had to be spread far too thinly. As Slim was beginning to realize, this was not a conventional war of fronts. It was a war of infiltration fought under very high temperatures along rough tracks and, increasingly, spreading into the surrounding jungle.

The Chinese formations fought erratically, being under political as much as military control, and could never be relied upon. Japanese infiltration time after time brought hostile units behind or alongside British defensive positions, and it was not long before the defense crumbled. The oilfield installations were demolished and Slim ordered his troops back. Repeatedly baffled by Japanese tactics, which often placed a roadblock both behind and before them, the British struggled toward India. The end of Chinese support was a relief for Slim and his staff, as it removed one crippling restriction on their decision-making, but there were problems enough without the Chinese. Water was one of them. It was so scarce that when planning the successive defense lines the first consideration had to be not so much defensibility as availability of water.

The climax of the 2-month retreat was at Shwegyin, a small plain between mountains where the troops had to embark on river craft for the 6-mile trip to Kalewa, from where a road led into India. Organizing an ordered embarkation of the men, their supplies, and equipment was itself a staff officer's nightmare, especially after Japanese bombing had prompted most of the river crews to disappear. However, an effective shuttle service was arranged, but it was interrupted by the Japanese, who had manged to infiltrate riflemen into the commanding hillside. While weary British units tried to make an effective counterattack, Slim stayed on the jetty, doing his best to get most of the guns embarked. But at night the final boats had to cast off, leaving some guns and motor trucks behind. The rearguard infantry, or most of them, managed to reach Kalewa by a narrow path through the jungle.

The final stage into India was accomplished on foot, but the sick and injured were usually provided with motor transport. Sickness rather than the Japanese was now the main killer. The monsoon had begun, and the roads and tracks were soon muddy, with the weary and ill-fed survivors living in a constant condition of wetness. With the rain came mosquitoes, to add malaria to the dysentery that was already spreading.

On 20 May 1942 Slim handed over his ragged survivors to the officer commanding at Imphal, a military depot just inside India. He had lost 13,000 men over the previous two months, but extricating the rest had been an achievement. No preparations had been made to receive his men, and no opportunity was lost to tell him what a nuisance he was, and how his retreat was inglorious. In his postwar memoirs, *Defeat into Victory,* Slim shows a rare resentment at the way he and his men were treated by staff officers at Imphal.

A month later Slim was commanding XV Corps, one of two that were the nucleus of the British Eastern Army. He had hoped to restore its morale and to retrain it, using his recent experience to prepare it for more successful operations against the Japanese. But for some weeks he was occupied in counter-insurgency duties, as riots, strikes and the occasional murder convulsed India, the result of a campaign by the Indian Congress Party. Once this crisis was over, however, he returned to training, and introduced his new concepts.

His first concern was that soldiers should learn not to fear the jungle, and the easiest way to instill this confidence was to spend as much time on jungle training as possible. Once the jungle was regarded as acceptable operating terrain, new tactics followed. These avoided long defensive lines, and also frontal attacks. The latter, especially on a narrow front, simply enabled the enemy to concentrate his forces, whereas the aim was to force him to stretch his men thinly. Attacks were to take a hooked alignment, so as to go round the enemy. In this type of warfare, units were not to contain non-combatants; soldiers normally regarded as non-combatants would have to do their share of the fighting. New patrolling techniques, and new patterns for tank operations (for Slim insisted that tanks could take part in jungle warfare) were also introduced.

Remembering the Japanese tactics of building fortified roadblocks both before and behind an opponent, and their skill in infiltration, Slim insisted that units finding themselves cut off should stand fast and wait for relief. If Japanese troops were discovered in the rear, then those Japanese troops were themselves cut off and their presence was certainly no cause for dismay.

While Slim was preparing his corps for an eventual offensive into Burma, Eastern Command was building the infrastructure for the re-conquest. The plain around Imphal, just inside India amid mountains, became a future jumping-off point. Meanwhile, however, as the Army gathered its strength in Eastern India, Churchill was demanding that the Far East Commander in Chief, General Wavell, should make a thrust into Arakan, the Burmese seaboard territory. Slim's corps did not take part in this, and he deplored the frontal tactics that were used by the local commander. Sure enough, after some initial success the offensive came to a halt at Donbaik, where the Japanese bunkers, defended to the last man, proved lethal and, usually, invincible. Slim was asked to take a look at the situation but when he reported back his advice was not only not taken, but seemed to be resented.

But soon afterward he was ordered to take his corps headquarters to Arakan, where after a long delay he was given operational control. This was just in time to withdraw the troops, because they were on the verge of demoralization. He managed to get them back inside India and was then criticized by the commander of the Eastern Army, who said he would be dismissed. As it turned out, however, it was the Eastern Army commander who was dismissed, and Slim got on much better with the new man, General George Giffard. He began to plan a new offensive, conducted on what he regarded as sensible principles, in Arakan. But before he could achieve anything with his corps he was himself appointed army commander, Giffard having become Army Group Commander in the aftermath of the arrival in India of Admiral Mountbatten and the appointment of Wavell as Viceroy of India.

Meanwhile, Slim's concepts had received implied support by the apparent success of an operation that he himself had not especially favored, the 'long-distance penetration' of the guerilla-style but regular-army force command by General Orde Wingate. This 3000-strong raiding force, practised in jungle operations, supplied by air, and winning occasional skirmishes well behind the Japanese lines, lost about 800 men and did not do great damage, but it showed what could be done and, above all, it certainly demonstrated that the Japanese soldier was not a superman.

Slim's army was renamed the 14th Army and consisted of the IV and XV Corps. Mountbatten, pressed by Churchill, had visions of combined operations along the Burmese coast, culminating in the recapture of Rangoon. In these plans the 14th

RIGHT: General Orde Wingate (bearded) with some of his deep penetration force.

LOWER RIGHT: Wingate's men on the march inside Burma.

BOTTOM RIGHT: British, West African and Gurkha troops assemble for movement by Dakota transports.

Army had only a subsidiary role. However, it did receive logistic support because it worked in cooperation with Stilwell's Chinese formations and was therefore essential protection for the construction and operation of the new road being built to supply China. In these months, Slim worked smoothly with Mountbatten, but was engaged mainly in promoting a spirit of confidence, and a kind of togetherness, in his men. He himself later wrote of the way in which he would go around talking to all and sundry; he was rather like a parliamentary candidate, he wrote, although he differed in not making any promises. As for the Indian troops which made up so large a proportion of his Army, these did not respond to him in the same way as the Anglo-Saxons. Yet, because of his quiet confidence and direct ways, they too developed a strong sense of loyalty toward him. Having spent so much of his earlier life in the Indian Army he was, after all, almost one of them.

The proposed combined operations came to nothing, largely because all possible landing craft were required for operations in Europe. Slim then began to wonder whether his army might inflict a defeat on the Japanese before the time came for it to plunge into Burma. He was a great believer in forcing the enemy to stretch, to stretch too far, and wondered whether the Japanese could be enticed further east, across the Chindwin River which at that time was the eastern frontier of Japanese-held Burma. But before he had made any plans for this, the Japanese moved first, and in the direction he had in mind for them. The only problem was that they had made their move too early, and that his troops were prepared for an offensive rather than a defensive battle.

In 1943 the Japanese had decided that the war was not going well, and that resources must be saved by withdrawing from exposed fronts. However, the commander of the Burma Area Army, Lieutenant General Kawabe Masakazu, realized that his front would be made more secure not by withdrawal, but by an advance into India. He was expecting a British offensive in any case, and if he could anticipate this by advancing to the British army base of Imphal he would block the mountain passes by

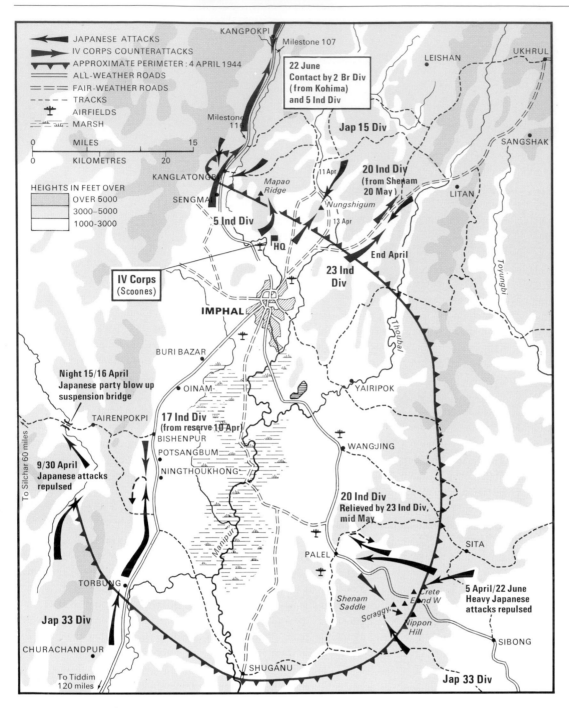

LEFT: The defensive perimeter at Imphal and the Japanese lines of attack.

UPPER RIGHT: The Durham Light Infantry meets Indian armored troops on the Imphal-Kohima road when the Japanese encirclement was broken in June 1944.

CENTRAL RIGHT: Lt. General Scoones, who commanded the IV Corps at Imphal.

LOWER RIGHT: A village devastated by battle at Kohima.

which an attack would be supplied and also disrupt the British preparations, since he knew that Imphal was crammed with supplies.

In January 1944 Slim was preparing for a possible offensive based on Imphal, and at the same time was supervising the Arakan operations that he had inherited when he took command of the 14th Army. On the latter front, the British were by this time making some progress. However, both in Arakan and on the central front pivoted on Imphal there was increasing evidence of Japanese reinforcement. A new division was being transferred from Thailand in the Imphal direction, and a new army HQ had been identified in Arakan. Slim well realized that to be attacked just at the moment when his troops were preparing their own offensive would be embarrassing, both in terms of military balance and of the morale of his men. But he still thought that a decisive battle outside the frontier of Burma might save him a good deal of difficult fighting inside Burma later.

He decided that the best thing to do would be to continue his preparations for an offensive, both in Arakan and on the central front. Should the expected Japanese attack materialize, then his

anti-infiltration tactics, so thoroughly instilled in his units, would be used. In early February the second and last struggle for Arakan began when a stong Japanese force, favored by fog, infiltrated between British units and took up its position in the rear. Judging, no doubt, from past British performance, the Japanese expected that the British reaction to this would be a confused withdrawal, but this did not happen. Instead, the British strength, two Indian divisions, was held in place, and Slim ordered long-studied plans for a supply airlift to be activated. As Japanese fighter strength was weak, and as the British advanced forces in Arakan had an airstrip, the latter were cut off only in a traditional sense. In fact, they could go on fighting while Slim moved up his reserves. In the end, the continued Japanese attacks on the two stalled but persistent divisions failed and ended in costly retreat as the British reserves were able to move up.

Slim at this time was suffering from dysentery, which was an especially cruel blow because he had made considerable efforts over the preceding year to improve the health and sanitary standards of his troops. However, fate turned out to be even-

handed, for at the height of the following Imphal struggle the Japanese Commander in Chief, Kawabe, was stricken by the same disease.

Slim's methods had justified themselves in Arakan, and the advance there continued until it was temporarily halted so as to enable one of the divisions to be airlifted to support the Imphal operations. Kawabe, and his 15th Army commander Lieutenant General Mutaguchi Renya, had counted on the Arakan operation tying down the British reserves while the Imphal thrust was taking place, but the impeccably organized airlift frustrated this hope. Even so, Mutaguchi's three divisions were considered to be more than a match for the three British divisions that the Japanese command supposed to be no better than the divisions it had routed in 1942.

The Imphal operations commenced in mid-March and lasted into June. They consisted usually of very hard-fought battles between small units, typically of company strength. In these battles the British and Indian troops proved to be just as tough and resourceful as their enemies, no fewer than six Victoria Crosses being awarded, and many more deserved.

Imphal was the center of these battles, but they were scattered over more than 100 miles. Mutaguchi's men crossed the Chindwin in March expecting a campaign lasting about three weeks, and carried rations for that period. They had no sure supply route to their rear, as the Chindwin was not bridged, so took with them a supply train of several thousand oxen and horses, not to speak of elephants to carry their mountain guns. Their main objective was Imphal, but the key to Imphal was Kohima, on the only road linking Imphal with the nearest railhead at Dimapur.

Slim planned his first preparatory moves. These consisted in the withdrawal of outlying units in order to strengthen the defensive semi-circle covering Imphal on the east. Here the timing was important, because these troops covered labor gangs constructing various defense works, and Slim and the commander of his IV Corps, defending Imphal, were a little late in making this withdrawal. The Japanese had lost none of their ability to move fast and unexpectedly, and they showed up earlier than Slim had anticipated. During March all three of his divisions were brought to battle, and there was no reserve. Moreover one division, the 17th, having been cut off by the Japanese, was fighting its way back toward Imphal only with great difficulty.

ABOVE: A Commonwealth Bren gun carrier near Imphal.

UPPER RIGHT: After the Kohima battle.

CENTRAL RIGHT: Later in the war, a Sherman tank is ferried across the Irrawaddy.

LEFT: One of Slim's tanks patrols the Imphal-Ukhrul road.

LOWER RIGHT: Commonwealth artillery in action against the retreating Japanese in Burma, March 1945.

Possibly the best description of the ensuing battle for Imphal is Slim's own in *Defeat into Victory:* '. . . back and forth through great stretches of wild country; one day its focal-point was a hill named on no map, the next a miserable, unpronounceable village a hundred miles away. Columns, brigades, divisions marched and countermarched, met in bloody clashes, and reeled apart, weaving a confused pattern . . .'

Working to the rear of the British positions the Japanese built a roadblock behind Kohima on 4 April, and another behind Imphal on 5 April. But they had learned nothing from the recent Arakan operations; this time the British would not retreat and, just as at Arakan, Slim had an airlift arranged to keep his men supplied. Moreover, Mountbatten allocated all available Dakota air transports to Slim, enabling the 5th Division to be airlifted from Arakan into Imphal during the last ten days of March, some of its battalions being thrown into battle immediately on landing.

Meanwhile at Kohima an entire Japanese division was coming into action, rather than the single regiment that Slim had expected; he had correctly calculated that nothing more than a regiment could be kept supplied there by the Japanese, but had overlooked the Japanese propensity for heroic attempts at the impossible. In the end the Japanese could not supply that division, but in the short term it was a dominating threat. Slim also concluded, logically enough, that the Japanese thrust on Kohima was simply the prelude to an attack on Dimapur, the vital rail and supply base. But in fact the Japanese command regarded Kohima as an end in itself, and was not thinking of Dimapur. Thus the two contending sides had different priorities. Slim ordered the local commander to give priority to the defense of Dimapur, while the Japanese priority was the capture of Kohima. It was only at the eleventh hour that a battalion of the West Kents was pushed into Kohima before that town was cut off.

Slim had made two miscalculations, therefore, but he was very poorly provided with intelligence. Not many Japanese allowed themselves to be captured (and senior officers never). Because of the peculiarities of British higher education, Japanese linguists were scarce. Slim's divisions probably averaged about two interpreters each, which was not enough to handle all the captured documents as well as prisoner interrogation.

But after these intital miscalculations Slim recovered fast, and handled the remainder of the battle with sureness. He had, in fact, been given what he wanted by the Japanese. They had been impelled into battle in his own territory, they lacked a sure supply line, and he had reserves on the way. At Kohima, and also at Imphal, the garrisons were in a critical situation, but reinforcements and relief were planned. Of all the defensive actions at this time, the 11-day siege at Kohima became a classic, with the dominant ridge being held tenaciously by the British. Around Imphal, where Slim eventually accumulated 100,000 men, the siege lasted for nearly three months.

Kohima was a close-run thing, and Slim enjoyed an element of luck here. But by the middle of May the worst was over, and an offensive spirit permeated his troops. At Kohima the Japanese, unwisely, refused to give up their objective, while British reinforcements in the form of the 5th Brigade moved toward them from Dimapur. The monsoon was imminent, which would render Japanese communications with their rear very tenuous. Command of the air remained with the British. Slim could now regard the destruction of the Japanese forces as the first priority, rather than the defense of Imphal. In June the Japanese 15th Army, worn down by the stress of weeks of unsuccessful battle and a general lack of supplies, as well as the inability of its commanders to develop new tactics to meet the situation, began to collapse. Eventually it withdrew back beyond the Chindwin, having lost about 30,000 dead.

This was probably the biggest single defeat inflicted on the Japanese army in World War II. Total Japanese losses probably amounted to 65,000, and by this victory the British smoothed their path for the reconquest of Burma. In December Slim's 14th Army pushed across the Chindwin in a general offensive coordinated with Stilwell's Chinese divisions in the north. By this time Slim was an expert in divining Japanese intentions and countering them. Almost alone of the Allied commanders, he concluded that the Japanese would attempt to destroy his army at the Irrawaddy crossing at Mandalay. Forestalling this, he surprised his enemy by striking suddenly at Meiktila, almost 100 miles south of Mandalay and commanding the road and railway to Rangoon. Alarmed by this move, the Japanese sent reinforcements from Mandalay and in the end lost both cities. The road to Rangoon was thereby opened, and Slim managed to get there before the monsoon, the Japanese having evacuated. With this, the campaign in Burma was virtually over. Slim would go on to higher things, his next appointment being Commander in Chief of the Allied Land Forces in Southeast Asia.

In retrospect, it is pleasing that so humane and sensitive a soldier as Slim should have emerged so triumphantly from World War II. His success had lain not so much in scintillating brilliance but in a willingness to learn, an insistence that those lessons be acted upon, and in relationships with his soldiers, staff, and superiors that even at the most tense moments were friendly. Unlike some other successful commanders, he appears to have had a well-balanced personality, and made full use of it.

LEFT: One of the Burmese guerillas organized by the British to harass the Japanese rear.

RIGHT: In the pursuit of the Japanese after Imphal, amphibious vehicles cross the River Chindwin.

LOWER LEFT: Slim's wife stands between her husband and General Scoones, after the commanders had been knighted at Imphal.

BELOW: A Dakota transport adapted for carrying mules to Imphal.

CHAPTER FOURTEEN

PATTON

AND THE BATTLE OF THE BULGE

THE BATTLE of the Bulge, often known as the Ardennes Offensive, has been called – by no less an authority than Winston Churchill – the greatest American battle of World War II. Adolf Hitler, reacting to a situation in Germany that had been steadily worsening since the Allied landings in June and the abortive 20 July bomb plot, had developed a bold, imaginative plan to recapture the initiative in the west. As a result, in one month, from mid-December 1944 to mid-January 1945, the American army lost some 80,000 men and an enormous amount of equipment opposing this last great German offensive of the war.

There were many heroes at the Bulge – most of them unsung – but of them all one name stands out above the rest, that of General George Smith Patton. Flamboyant, swaggering and controversial, he was a man of contrasts: deeply religious and fiercely profane; a hot-tempered, ruthless fighter with a kind heart; a fiery tank commander and a learned military theoretician. With the Battle of the Bulge he hit the apex of his career, amply justifying the German High Command's opinion, expressed in an analysis of Allied generals, that he was 'the most dangerous man on all fronts.'

George Patton probably never considered anything other than a military career. This was perhaps because there was a strong soldiering tradition in his family. In June 1909 Patton graduated from West Point a year behind the rest of his class, owing to his problems with mathematics. During the 1930s he devoured military studies by Erwin Rommel and Heinz Guderian, Basil Liddell Hart and J F C Fuller, on infantry and armor tactics and strategy. However, in his own reports he had to be very cautious as by this time he had made some highly placed enemies. He felt it necessary to make his points obliquely, while still paying lip service to traditional concepts.

In 1938 General George Catlett Marshall was appointed Deputy Chief of Staff, and fortune finally turned in Patton's favor. Marshall, an astute judge of character, was not put off by Patton's flamboyant eccentricity. Furthermore, he was himself convinced of the importance of armor in the new army and had read enough between the lines of Patton's reports to recognize the latter's preferences.

Patton would never have agreed that 'war is hell.' He saw it as the only area in which he could excel. In 1940, when the German blitzkrieg rumbled through the Low Countries, France and Poland, he was tremendously excited – not only by war itself, but by the thrill of seeing the armor tactics he had been studying for 20 years actually being put into practice. Immediately he began hounding Marshall for a job nearer the action and at the same time tried to obtain a commission in the Canadian army.

In July Marshall came through. The first two American armored divisions were established and Patton was sent to Fort Benning, Georgia, to organize one of the brigades comprising 2nd Armored Division. He was promoted to Brigadier General and he soon took over command of the division, and began to turn it into a polished, dashing outfit. Meanwhile, his own extraordinary personality was doing much to publicize the new service and he was rapidly gaining a reputation as America's top tank expert.

However Patton was never just a tank specialist. His extensive reading and study had given him a broad view of war that enabled him to see parallels that many others missed. He was greatly interested in weapons and tactics used by the other services, and in fact held strong views on almost every aspect of the conduct of war. His insistence on military discipline was well-known – to the extent that an especially snappy salute was often called a 'georgepatton.' Discipline, he believed, saved lives, and as for the outward manifestations, 'If you can't get them to salute when they should salute and wear the clothes you tell them to wear, how are you going to get them to die for their country?' His opinions even extended to the placement of military cemeteries. This interest in minutiae and the ability to fit them in a broader context were traits he shared with another great field commander, Erwin Rommel. The two tank men had other things in common, for instance their habit of roaming the front lines during battles.

Thus beneath the flamboyance, the emotionalism and the 'goddamming,' the discerning eye could spot Patton's dedication to his profession. One of his colleagues who recognized that professionalism was Marshall, another was Dwight David Eisenhower. The two were old friends who had served together in the tank corps during World War I. However Ike's support during the next war, often against considerable opposition, was not solely based on friendship. He saw Patton as a 'master of pursuit' – the sort of general, like Napoleon or Grant, who could spur his men on to chase the enemy even when they were dropping from fatigue. For his part, Patton had early predicted that Eisenhower would one day be his superior officer. 'Ike,' he said, 'You will be the Lee of the next war and I will be your Jackson.'

In 1942 Patton was given command of the Western Task Force for Operation Torch, the Allied landings in North Africa.

LEFT: General Patton in fine aggressive mood during a speech to a contingent from Third Army before the D-Day invasion.

RIGHT: Eisenhower and Patton discuss a tactical problem, Tunisia 1943.

Although the responsibilities of the post gave him less direct contact with the armor than he would have liked, both he and his men profited greatly from their experience in Africa, learning lessons that would be put to good use later in France. Later, at the head of Seventh Army in the dust and heat of Sicily, he demonstrated his talent for pursuit to the full. He also showed his quick temper and after hitting a soldier in public was demoted. Finally, in January 1944, he was called to England and placed in charge of Third Army.

Operations in the European Theater were controlled by Supreme Headquarters, Allied Expeditionary Forces (SHAEF) and the Supreme Commander, General Eisenhower. Under him were two army groups. The British 21st Army Group, under General Montgomery, consisted of the British Second Army and the Canadian First Army. General Omar Bradley was in charge of the US 12th Army Group – US First Army, commanded by General Hodges, and Patton's Third Army. In the Normandy landings, the First Army would hit the beaches; the very existence of Third Army would be kept secret until at least D-Day+10, when they would join the line west of the First Army positions and execute Patton's favorite type of operation – a breakthrough followed by an advance clear across France to Germany.

The choice of commanders shows that Marshall, as much as he appreciated Patton, was not blind to his faults. Although on the face of it Patton was best qualified to lead the invasion, his impetuousness, Marshall knew, would be a grave handicap in that intricate political/military situation: Patton 'needs a brake to slow him down . . . someone just above him and that is why I am giving the command to Bradley.' That Patton recognized his own limitations is shown by the fact that he accepted the news of his former subordinate's promotion with good humor. He had always considered himself more of a tactician than a strategist; in any event, he much preferred commanding at the field army level where there was more personal contact with the men.

The Third Army's embarkation from Southampton was delayed; it was 5 July – almost a month after Operation Overlord – before they finally slipped ashore in France and dug in near

Néhou, some 15 miles south of Cherbourg. While Patton champed at the bit, the transporting of men, equipment, and supplies took its deliberate course, and it was not until 26 July that Operation Cobra was ready to strike.

Following a mammoth aerial and artillery bombardment by the First Army, the Third Army took off, racing through the gap at St Lô, past Avranches on the 30th, and on through France in an extraordinary sweep that brought them to the outskirts of Paris by 21 August.

LEFT: The Siegfried Line is breached on 15 September 1944.

ABOVE: German troops captured by the 82nd Airborne Division are lined up on a road near Hierlot, Belgium.

TOP RIGHT: A German soldier examines an American half-track, which has been converted into an ambulance.

ABOVE RIGHT: A knocked out American half-track near Malmédy, 16 December 1944.

LOWER RIGHT: A wrecked German Marder assault gun.

BOTTOM RIGHT: A German StuG III assault gun is hidden in a farmyard as part of the preparations for the Ardennes Offensive.

The Third Army could easily have entered the French capital, but instead Patton was instructed to bypass the city to the north and south and continue his advance toward Germany – an order that did not sit well with the men of Third Army, who objected strongly to the news that the men of the US First Army, were parading the streets as liberators.

Their tempers were not improved by the sudden realization that their supplies were being drastically reduced. Montgomery, whose forces were some 100 miles behind Patton's, had been arguing for some time that instead of advancing on a broad front, there should be one decisive thrust – in his northern sector. Thus most of the supplies should be diverted north, while the troops in the south fought a holding action. Near the end of August Eisenhower had arrived at a compromise: Montgomery's push into Belgium would be given priority until he had taken Antwerp. Then the offensive would revert back to the 'broad front' advance.

Furious with Eisenhower, whom he felt had sacrificed an early victory to Montgomery's 'insatiable appetite,' Patton ordered his advance units to keep moving until their gas tanks ran dry – and then to get out and walk. Third Army took Verdun, surrounded Metz, and reached the Moselle River (where they linked up with the Franco-American Seventh Army under General Alexander Patch). There – about 30 miles from the great industrial complex in the Saar valley and less than 100 miles from the Rhine – they finally came to a halt at the beginning of September.

The dash across France was a triumph for both Patton and his staff – which was, at his insistence, the fastest, most efficient, and most professional in Europe. Ever since landing in Europe his orders had been to 'advance and keep on advancing' and that is exactly what his army had done – repeatedly bypassing areas where the Germans tried to make a stand, never giving the enemy time to stop and organize a counterattack. But though the attacks were violent and unrelenting, they were never wild

Patton was able to force the Moselle in several places, he had to scrap his plans for a lightning offensive and settle down to a hard, set-piece battle.

Nancy, the old capital of Lorraine, fell to Third Army on 15 September. A few days later Patton received word that he was to stop and assume the defensive while Montgomery and the 21st Army Group made another concentrated assault, north of the Ardennes. If there was one thing Patton hated, it was defensive warfare; he considered it not only a waste of lives, but even un-American. His method of defense, therefore, was to maintain a continuous series of local actions with units small enough to escape Army Group Headquarters' notice. If questioned about his actions he would reply that he was only 'rectifying the line.'

As winter drew near the weather became almost as bitter an enemy as the Germans. The Third Army was receiving minimal supplies, not only of fuel and ammunition but also of other essentials like raincoats, sleeping bags and winter clothing. Despite the efforts of the Quartermaster Corps, who commissioned what they could from local suppliers and improvised the rest, sickness (especially trench foot) began to increase alarmingly. At one point the sickness rate equalled the battle casualty rate.

Patton spent most of October hounding headquarters for permission to attack, while Bradley and Montgomery argued the merits of a single attack in the north against the Ruhr versus a two-pronged assault against both the Ruhr and the Saar basin. Eventually Bradley won his point, and Patton was called to Group Headquarters to receive the good news that the winter campaign would involve a series of assaults along the entire front with an attack on the Saar as one of the two main efforts.

Little planning was necessary since they had been working on a Saar offensive for over a month, but the precarious supply situation had to be taken into account. There were also some new troop dispositions. For this offensive, the VIII Corps would stay in the Ardennes under the control of the First Army. The Third Army would get the III Corps in its place, along with two divisions presently en route from the States, the 10th Armored and 95th Infantry Divisions. On 3 November Bradley reported that Montgomery had not yet set a starting date for his half of the attack, but would probably not be ready before 1 December. Patton, however, could go whenever he was ready.

The Third Army attacked on 8 November. Metz was under Patton's control by the 19th (though the last of its forts held out for another month). Mud and slush hindered the offensive and it

or uncontrolled; staff planning was always at least two operations ahead of the one in progress so that the army advanced with great speed, but never in haste.

The support between Patton and his Third Army staff was mutual and wholehearted, whether the battle was being waged with the Germans, 12th Army Group Headquarters, or even SHAEF. When the gas crisis was nearing its height, Patton received a bitter complaint that Third Army officers, disguised as First Army men, had stolen quite a lot of fuel. With a straight face, he replied, 'I'm very sorry to hear First Army lost some of its gas. But I know none of my officers would masquerade as First Army officers. They wouldn't stoop to that, not even to get gas SHAEF stole from us.' The merit promotions that several young officers in the Quartermasters Corps received shortly thereafter were probably not coincidental.

Antwerp was finally taken on 4 September, and Third Army's supplies began arriving again. But in the meantime the German High Command had taken advantage of the 'miraculous' – if to them incomprehensible – respite to reinforce the area. Though

LEFT: Three views of some of the 14,000 German prisoners captured during the first days of the Allied counter-attack.

BELOW LEFT: Members of the 101st Airborne who held out in Bastogne.

RIGHT: The 101st Airborne Division held out in Bastogne from the 19 to 26 December when the 4th Armored Division relieved the 'Battered Bastards of the 101st.'

became more and more difficult to maintain momentum. However, after six weeks of fighting, the Third Army had reached the Siegfried Line along most of its front and in one place had driven a wedge some 30 miles beyond it. Overall, they had advanced approximately 50 miles. Meanwhile, the northern offensive had been stopped in an attempt to take the Roer River dams and in the south the Seventh Army had reached the Rhine and turned to join up with Patton's right flank.

Although the Allies' headlong advance had been slowed down and their initial complacency had been dispelled to some extent by the Germans' stubborn resistance, it was obvious that they would come out the winners in a battle of attrition. However, as early as September Hitler had conceived an audacious plan. In one last, gigantic offensive, he would strike westward, penetrate between the First and Third Armies to Antwerp (thus depriving the Allies of their main supply port), and mop up the British and Canadian Armies along the Belgian-Dutch border. The attack would be mounted through the Ardennes, where he had made his great breakthrough in 1940. He knew that this area was thinly held by only four infantry divisions. Field Marshal Gerd von Rundstedt was called out of retirement to lead the offensive (code named Operation Autumn Fog), and the task of quietly collecting an attack force began.

In November a few high-ranking German staff and army officers were informed of the plan. The generals were astounded. They pointed out that Germany was much weaker than it had been in 1940 and furthermore was facing a much stronger enemy. Together von Rundstedt, Field Marshal Walther Model (Commander of Army Group B) and the three field commanders – SS General Sepp Dietrich (Sixth SS Panzer Army), General Hasso von Manteuffel (Fifth Panzer Army) and General Erich Brandenburger (Seventh Army) – concocted an alternative plan with more limited objectives. Hitler remained adamant. He was convinced that he could shatter the 'unnatural' Allied union with one blow – and the generals were too intimidated after the purges that had followed the July Plot assassination attempt to put up much of an argument.

On the evening of 12 December several senior German field commanders were taken to a secret rendezvous at Hitler's bunker near Frankfurt where many of them learned for the first time of the great offensive, scheduled to begin in only four days. Over 250,000 men – 28 divisions, nine of them Panzer units – had been assembled, along with some 2500 tanks and field guns. It was a puny force compared to the resources Rundstedt had controlled on the same front in 1940, but the Germans were not without some advantages.

Although the men themselves were not as fit or well-trained as the previous strike force, their ranks were stiffened by the addition of several fanatical, well-equipped SS units. In addition, the Germans still had superiority in some important weapons. The Mark V Panthers and Mark VI Tigers, for example, had thicker armor and wider tracks than the Allied Shermans and were armed with more powerful guns.

There were also some desperate problems. Allied bombing raids had left the German transportation network a shambles and there was a grave fuel shortage. Hitler was counting on his last, most important weapon to help overcome these difficulties – the advantage of surprise. Despite the lesson of 1940, Allied planners persisted in viewing the Ardennes, with its heavily wooded hills cut by deep valleys where tank advances could easily be stopped, as unsuitable for a large-scale armor action. From the German point of view, however, the forest was natural camouflage for concentrations of ground forces, while the drier high ground gave the tanks more maneuverability.

The night of 15 December was cold and a thick mist covered the German troops as they moved into position along their 70-mile front between Monschau and Echternach. Bad weather had been forecast for the next several days and was essential to the success of the operation, to protect the German supply columns from Allied air strikes. On the 16th they moved out. In the north, the main strike force, Dietrich's Sixth Panzer Army had orders to advance northwest, past Liège to Antwerp. Manteuffel and the Fifth Panzer Army, in the center, were to push through the Ardennes and then turn north to the Meuse and, eventually, to Antwerp.

The offensive came as a complete surprise to the Allies – and unnecessarily so. Third Army advance units had been keeping a faithful eye on the German troop dispositions ahead of them. As early as 4 December Patton's G-2 (Intelligence) staff had sent a Special Estimate to Army Group Headquarters that concluded, 'A large build up of troops and supplies is clearly in progress opposite the southern (Ardennes) flank of First Army.' Allied planners were blinded by overconfidence. Montgomery and Bradley were both convinced that Hitler lacked the resources for a major offensive, and that he would be forced to throw everything he had into stopping their drive toward the Rhine. An unofficial rebuff was the only reply to the Third Army's communique, and on 15 December Montgomery issued his own assessment of the situation, 'The enemy is at present fighting a defensive campaign . . . he cannot stage major offensive operations . . . . He has not the transport or the petrol . . . nor could his tanks compete with ours in a mobile battle.'

He could not have been further from the mark. In the north, where Sepp Dietrich (a good fighter, but one with little understanding of armored warfare) was in command of the attack, the Allied line buckled, but held at several key points. In the center, however, the brilliant tank commander, Manteuffel, led the

Fifth Panzer Army in a rapid advance that recalled the days of the first blitzkrieg. Despite the terrible weather, the delays in bringing up fuel supplies and occasional pockets of American resistance, it was more than 48 hours before his headlong rush was stopped, not far from Bastogne, by the US 10th Armored Division's desperate delaying action.

Manteuffel was assisted by the confusion in the American ranks sown by Operation Greif. This consisted of about 40 jeep loads of English-speaking German commandos in American uniforms, led by the famed Otto Skorzeny, whose mission was to infiltrate the American lines and turn signposts, cut communication wires, kill messengers and do anything else they could think of to create confusion. One captured commando started the rumor that a unit was on its way to kill Eisenhower with the result that the Supreme Commander was virtually immobilized in his Paris headquarters for some days, to his extreme annoyance. In the attempt to weed out the infiltrators, soldiers in the battle area were frequently required to identify themselves by correctly answering questions like 'Who won the World Series in 1938?' Bradley had to spend some time convincing a zealous sentry that Springfield, not Chicago, is the capital of Illinois.

As the German attack began on 16 December the Third Army was preparing for its own offensive, an elaborate assault on the Siegfried Line. On the 17th, when they finally got a clear idea of

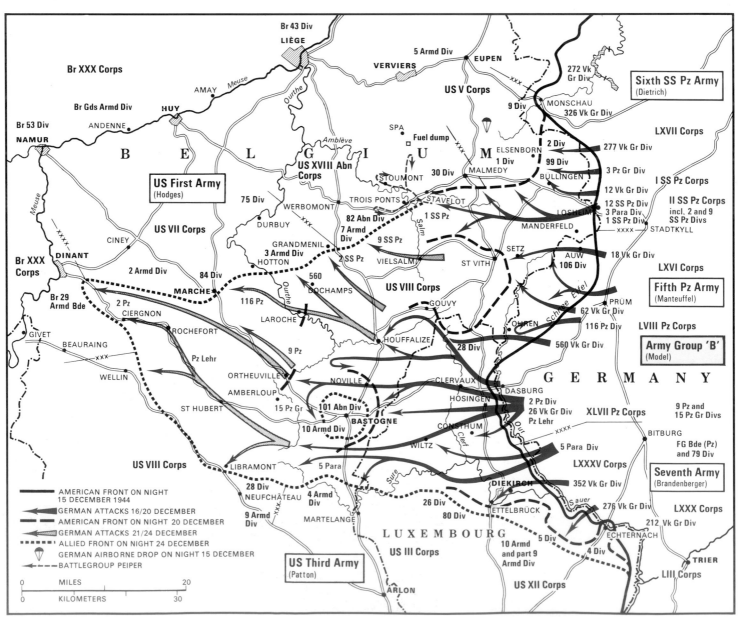

what was happening, several staff members were optimistic, thinking that the action to the north would take some of the pressure off their own operation. Patton, however, was less sanguine. Realizing that he would probably have to postpone his own plans, he set the staff working to prepare three contingency plans, in case they were asked to move north and help.

This proved to be a wise precaution. The next day he was ordered to Luxembourg to confer with Bradley, and by 19 December he was attending a meeting of senior American commanders called by Eisenhower at Verdun. Ike decided that the First and Ninth Armies, in the north, should be temporarily placed under Montgomery's command – a plan that greatly displeased Bradley. All were agreed that the Allies' first move should be a counterattack by the Third Army from the south, against the underbelly of the Bulge. There were only two problems. First, how far north could General Jacob Devers stretch his 6th Army Group to cover Patton's territory (eventually he

moved up to a point between Saarlautern and Saarbrücken), and second, how to time the attack. As far as Patton was concerned, he could begin immediately and be in position to attack by 21 December. This was no idle boast. His staff had completed their plans and were simply waiting for him to telephone a code word, telling them which of the three to put into operation.

It was eventually decided that Middleton's VIII Corps would be returned to the Third Army. Most of it was already engaged in and around Bastogne, but the remainder would be launched on the left against the nose of the German salient, toward St Hubert. The XII Corps would attack on the right, toward Echternach. In the center would be Milliken's III Corps – 80th and 26th Infantry and the 4th Armored Divisions – with their main objective the liberation of Bastogne (by now surrounded and under siege). This was a calculated risk, for it meant leaving the 50-mile north-south front, including the Saarlautern salient, in the hands of just XX Corps (two infantry and one armored division) and a Cavalry Group. Though too weak to withstand an attack in force, they were in a position to fight a strong delaying action – as well as prevent a surprise attack through that sector.

Returning to his own headquarters, Patton found his staff under a considerable amount of tension, which he characteristically dispelled as soon as possible. Standing in front of the room, he glared into the tense faces before him and after a few moments announced impressively, 'This will get the bastards out of their holes so we can kill all of them. Now go to work!'

And work they did, racing against time to shift a three-corps, north-south battle line to a four-corps line running east-west in the Ardennes and north-south in the Saar. Hundreds of units had to be moved quickly and efficiently. At Patton's orders they disregarded all blackout regulations and drove north with headlights blazing and throttles wide open. Thousands of miles of telephone wire had to be laid and an entire communications network, capable of remaining operational despite both cold and enemy attack, had to be established. A new supply system had to be set up, and thousands of tons of supplies shifted for distribution or storage in new depots and dumps. Hospitals had to be organized and stocked, maps and orders distributed, and hundreds of other details taken care of. During those busy days Patton worked as hard as anyone else, but neither then nor later would he claim credit for the gigantic effort. His staff, he said,

ABOVE: General McAuliffe, commander of the 101st Airborne Division.

LEFT: The German offensive.

RIGHT: Members of 101st Airborne Division advance from Bastogne, 29 December 1944.

had performed a miracle. (He was willing, however, to take credit for being the unofficial 'ray of sunshine and backslapper' for both his men and his superiors.) At 0600 on 22 December, right on schedule, III Corps attacked.

Meanwhile, the 'Battered Bastards of the Bastion of Bastogne' – the 101st Airborne Division along with remnants of the 10th Armored Division, the 705th Tank Destroyer Battalion and several other units, all under the command of General McAuliffe – had been grimly hanging on under the German barrage. Although it was a tiny town with a population of about 3500, Bastogne was the junction of seven major paved roads, and the key to the defense of both the Ardennes and the Meuse beyond. Theoretically the Germans could have bypassed it on secondary roads, but these were in such bad condition that during bad weather they were practically impassable for military vehicles.

On 18 December, when Manteuffel's spearheads had advanced to within 15 miles of Bastogne, there were few American troops in Bastogne. However, by that evening, when his main force arrived, the town was already occupied by the 101st Airborne. Starting the previous evening from Reims, over 100 miles away, the 'Screaming Eagles' had beaten the Germans in a decisive race. Eventually, and with some difficulty, Manteuffel got his divisions around Bastogne, but he was forced to leave a substantial force behind to deal with the junction. In addition, the delay had given the Americans time to bring up more reserves, and Manteuffel was getting no support from Dietrich's army (which had been cornered by the US First Army near Stavelot on 19 December). Although an advance guard would eventually reach the Meuse at Dinant on the 24th, they would soon be cut off and forced to withdraw.

In effect, the German advance was stalled at Bastogne where, as an anonymous GI put it, 'They've got us surrounded, the poor bastards.' On the 22nd General Heinrich von Lüttwitz, commander of the German XLVII Armored Corps, sent a message to McAuliffe demanding he surrender the city. McAuliffe's reply, 'Nuts!' is probably unequalled in the annals of military history, both for its brevity and the amount of confusion it caused in the enemy camp before it was deciphered.

The III Corps began their attack first, in the worst possible weather conditions. They were hampered by fog, a howling blizzard and below-freezing temperatures. Their winter equipment still had not arrived. They had no snow-camouflage material, parkas, hoods or fur gloves. Blankets were cut up for shoe liners, and yards of white cloth purchased from the French were run up into camouflage suits by the Quartermaster Corps. Along with their improvised equipment the men carried a prayer for good weather, composed some days before (for the Saar offensive) by Chaplain James H O'Neill.

On the east of III Corps' front, the 80th Division was attacking toward Ettelbruck and the Sûre River, while in the center the 26th Infantry Division was aiming for Wiltz. The terrain these two divisions were moving through was some of the worst in the entire Ardennes. On the left was 4th Armored Division which had orders to 'drive like hell' straight for Bastogne. The division was divided into three units, or combat commands. Combat Command A went north along the Arlon-Bastogne road. Combat Command B took secondary roads through the hilly, wooded countryside from Hubay-la-Neuve (about 5 miles west). Their orders called for them gradually to move closer to each other until they were advancing on parallel paths about two miles apart. Combat Command Reserve was held back; they were rarely committed to action.

The two 4th Armored units made good progress at first, but

Combat Command A was slowed down by an American minefield originally laid to stop the German Seventh Army. In the afternoon they ran into a German rifle company guarding the demolished bridges at Martelange, and were held up until about 0300 on the 23rd. Combat Command B met little resistance on the back roads, and by noon had advanced nearly 12 miles – to within 7 miles of the center of Bastogne. They too, however, were stopped cold until the small hours of the morning, this time by a German company holding a blown bridge at Burnon.

The next morning, 23 December, was crisp and cold with clear, sunny skies. As the air filled with the sound of Allied aircraft, a jubilant Patton shouted at one of his staff officers, 'Hot damn! That O'Neill sure did some potent praying! Get him up here, I want to pin a medal on him!' For the next five days pilots of the XIX Tactical Air Command flew until they were out of ammunition, touched down to reload and refuel, and took off again. As darkness fell a Night Fighter (P-61) Squadron took over.

Patton called Milliken and ordered the 4th Armored to 'stop piddling around' and get on toward Bastogne, by-passing centers of resistance and mopping them up later. Combat Command A followed orders. At midday they tried to go around the village of Warnach. However, the Germans put up a desperate defense of the area, and Combat Command A was not able to either take Warnach or bypass it for 24 hours. Thus by noon on 24 December they were still several miles behind the point Combat Command B had reached 48 hours earlier.

Combat Command B fared little better. At noon on the 23rd they took Chaumont, which had been under heavy aerial assault all morning, but the sun thawed the open ground, and the Shermans became thoroughly bogged down. When the Germans realized what was happening they moved an assault-gun brigade on to the hills above the village, knocked out every tank they could see, and retook the town, inflicting heavy losses on the Americans. By the end of the day Combat Command B had managed to struggle only as far as Hompre – a distance of just over five miles. They were still three miles from the Bastogne perimeter.

Patton fought the Battle of the Bulge in his own fashion – tearing around the front lines in his open jeep, which was specially equipped with a loud horn and blazoned with huge red stars. One of his cardinal rules was that 'Commanders (and their staffs) should be seen physically by as many individuals of their command as possible, certainly by all combat soldiers.' Patton, in his worn field overcoat, visited battle lines and unit headquarters, showing up at every critical point. No one saw him moving backward. He always flew to the rear, to save time and avoid the chance his 'retreat' would be seen and thereby lower morale.

On the day before Christmas the Bastogne defenders received the message from Patton, 'Christmas Eve present coming up. Hold on.' It was not to be. Though the attack had picked up somewhat once the planes were in the air, the tanks and infantry still moved slowly over the winding, icy mountain roads, battling fiercely for every foot of ground. This did not conform to Patton's theory of warfare, and he called Eisenhower several times to apologize for the delay.

ABOVE LEFT: Soldiers of the Adolf Hitler Division on the road between Malmédy and St Vith, 17 December 1944.

LEFT: A German infantryman in the early stages of the advance.

Despite its initial success the German offensive, in Rundstedt's and Model's view, was a failure by 22 December. The field commander, Manteuffel, came to the same conclusion on Christmas Eve. He knew he could not hold the narrow salient much longer. On 25 December he pulled troops from the eastward advance and turned them toward Third Army. In the east, in VIII Corps' sector, he launched powerful Panzer attacks against St Hubert, Rochefort, and Hotton; another series of heavy assaults hit Bastogne itself. In addition, to the south, General Brandenburger initiated several violent battles in the Saarlautern region.

Combat Command A and Combat Command B had each been strengthened with a battalion of infantry, and even Combat Command Reserve had been thrown into the fighting, on a line parallelling the Neufchateau-Bastogne road. Again, they could not make a decisive breakghrough. Patton's temper on Christmas night was precarious, and it was not improved when Brad-ley relayed Montgomery's suggestion that Patton fall back to the Moselle and 'regroup' (as Montgomery himself was doing). Patton's reaction was that it was a 'disgusting' idea.

RIGHT: 'For you the war is over.' German prisoners are taken into captivity.

BELOW: Changed times from this scene photographed at the start of the German advance. A massive Tiger II tank passes a column of American prisoners.

December 26 was an important day in the battle. Manteuffel finally received official permission to establish defensive positions, though Hitler was still convinced that he could ultimately take Bastogne, drive through on the Northern Front and capture Antwerp. That same day, Bastogne was relieved. In the afternoon, advance elements of the 4th Armored Division's Combat Command B made contact with the 101st Airborne Division's outposts on the perimeter, and that evening five tanks from Combat Command Reserve entered the city itself. In the afternoon Combat Command Reserve's two battalion commanders, Lieutenant Colonels Creighton Abrams and George Jacques had decided to ignore the battle plan for the day and drive straight through Assenois to Bastogne. While most of their forces engaged the Germans at Assenois, five tanks plus an infantry half-track slipped away from the battle and into the beleaguered town. The first exchange between Captain William Dwight and General McAuliffe was typical of the American command style that Germans, and other Europeans, found so difficult to understand. 'How are you General?' asked Dwight. 'Gee, I'm mighty glad to see you,' replied McAuliffe. The latter's first message to Patton was typical of the Bastogne de-

fenders' attitude throughout the conflict, 'Losses Light. Morale high. Awaiting orders to continue the counteroffensive.'

Bastogne, of course, was still an island in hostile territory, though it now had a thin, tenuous lifeline to Third Army – whose first priority had to be widening and protecting it. The Germans, who rallied with their usual speed and efficiency, launched two heavy attacks on the narrow corridor that night. Two convoys loaded with food, ammunition, medicine and other supplies were ready to go on the 27th, but the journey was still too hazardous. Instead, Patton, after much haranguing of headquarters, arranged for an airlift to drop as many supplies as possible. Though an air mission to evacuate the wounded had to be scrubbed, XIX TAC improvised their own lift. A small squad of L-5s, with P-47 fighter support, dropped several teams of medics into the town. By the evening of the 27th the corridor, though still dangerous, was passable. The siege of Bastogne was over; the battle was just beginning.

On 28 December the weather closed in again and the Germans began their next attack on Bastogne in a heavy snowstorm. In addition to the reinforcements from the west, Manteuffel had been able to call on German units in the northern sector, where Montgomery was still refitting his four armies. Within a few days, at the height of the battle, Third Army would be facing elements of 12 German divisions in the Bastogne area alone. Seven other divisions would be thrown against the newly-reinforced VIII Corps in the west and XII Corps in the east.

The German attacks were held off on all fronts. This success was due in large part both to XIX TAC, which managed to keep its planes up almost all day despite the weather, and to the artillery units. The new proximity fuze had given an added boost to the artillery, which proved to be indispensable in the days ahead. Still Hitler would not consider a German withdrawal. Despite Manteuffel's pleas that he be allowed to pull out while he still had a chance to save his army and despite Guderian's warning that the Eastern Front was a 'house of cards,' the Führer - in a harangue lasting several hours – ordered the western offensive resumed.

For the next eight days, from 28 December to 5 January, it was attack and counterattack, as Germans and Americans engaged in a series of murderous battles. On the 28th Patton launched a three-corps offensive toward St Vith, Houffalize and Echternach. The Germans quickly countered with their own series of attacks. On 30 December Manteuffel threw five divisions against the Bastogne corridor but the weather cleared for a few hours and they were beaten off with help from XIX TAC. On 1 January the Luftwaffe launched a well-coordinated attack on Allied airfields. Although they inflicted some damage, they also lost about 300 of their own planes. That same day there were seven attacks on Bastogne, and a force of eight German divisions moved against the Saar. None succeeded.

On 3 January there was another heavy attack against Bastogne, by two German corps (nine divisions). While all German eyes were on Third Army, First Army was allowed finally to make its move in the north. By the 5th it was obvious, even to Hitler, that the great Ardennes Offensive had failed. There were still some weeks of hard fighting left, but from then on the outcome was never in doubt. The Germans executed a skillful withdrawal. Operating behind infantry attacks, armored groups moved at night to avoid the worst of the air assaults and fought from prepared positions during the day. The German experience in Russia proved to be of great value; Hitler's forces were much better than the Americans at travelling through the deep snow and over the icy roads. The withdrawal was accelerated on 12 January when the Russians launched their mammoth winter offensive.

Finally, on 16 January, First and Third Armies linked up at Houffalize. It was an especially satisfying meeting for Patton, since First Army was represented on this historic occasion by a task force from his old unit, 2nd Armored Division. Now there was only mopping up to be done. On 23 January St Vith was retaken. The Battle of the Bulge was over.

Hitler had gambled and lost – and in losing, had not only sealed the fate of his armies in the west, but had also made defeat in the east inevitable. Overall, Germany lost more than 120,000 men (killed, captured and wounded) during the Battle of the Bulge, along with some 800 tanks and guns, 1600 planes and 6000 vehicles. American losses included about 80,000 men and over 700 tanks and guns. The Allies could replace their men and equipment, while Hitler had staked everything on this last throw.

There were three basic reasons for the failure of the German offensive. First, Hitler grossly overestimated his own capabilities vis-à-vis the Allies. Not only did he discount the effect of superior Allied numbers of men and equipment, but he also had little regard for the American soldiers' fighting ability. He was misled, as were many in the German High Command, by the Americans' generally casual approach to military discipline and appearance. The second reason for the failure was the Allies' overwhelming superiority in the air – and the five days of clear weather (23-27 December) that enabled it to be used to such effect. Last, but not least, was Third Army's unexpectedly quick assault on the southern flank of the Bulge. The Germans never dreamed that Patton could turn and strike so hard in such a short time.

ABOVE RIGHT: A US soldier examines the optimistic slogan written on a wall in Trois Vierges, north of Clervaux. It reads 'Behind the last battle of this war lies our victory.'

RIGHT: Mark V Panthers were the best German tanks of the war and took part in the Ardennes Offensive.

BELOW: German prisoners en route to the rear following their capture by troops of the 102nd Division.

This chapter has looked at just one aspect of one engagement in Europe, but it is one which Patton described as 'one of the greatest exploits of military history . . . executed under the most difficult and trying conditions and against tremendous odds . . .

and also without any help from anyone.' He was not praising himself, but was speaking, quite sincerely, about his army. Characteristically, he always maintained that he had had 'Damned little to do' with the victory. Speaking of himself in the third person, he emphatically told the press, 'All he did was to give the orders. It was the staff of his headquarters and the troops in the line that performed this matchless feat.' During his last staff briefing in Europe he told his men. 'There is probably no commander in Europe who did less work than I did. You did it all.'

Patton was not indulging in a show of false modesty, he believed every word he said. What he did not say, however, was that in addition to giving the orders, it had been he who turned Third Army into an efficient, well-knit team capable of carrying them out, and who kept that team functioning at peak performance under extremely difficult conditions. Though his reputation was made as a tank commander, his army's success at the Bulge depended far less on spectacular tank battles than on the superb coordination of armored, infantry, artillery, air and support forces. The arguments, the political gaffes, the eccentricities, aside, Dwight D Eisenhower has summed him up best, 'George Patton was, if nothing else, a man who knew his business.'

CHAPTER FIFTEEN

NIMITZ

AND THE BATTLE OF LEYTE GULF

ON THE Allied side, the most substantial military reputations were won by the commanders in chief of theaters. Theirs was a job that required more than the traditional military virtues, and for the most part Britain and the USA did find leaders with the combination of experience, judgment, breadth, and tact required to integrate subordinate commanders into a common endeavor. Eisenhower was the most outstanding of this elite, planning strategy and winning the cooperation of commanders who, all too often, were weighed down with a sense of their own importance. He succeeded, largely, because he knew the value of modest friendliness and hard work. MacArthur, neither modest nor friendly, succeeded because for a highly competent man who believed himself to be one of God's chosen few neither modesty nor friendliness were relevant. Of the navy men who became supreme commanders, Admiral Chester W Nimitz was of the Eisenhower type, imposing his wisdom through courtesy, tact, and optimism.

The Germans and Japanese were less successful with supreme commanders. Indeed, the nature of their regimes precluded such a success. There is some irony in the fact that one result of the Japanese attack on Pearl Harbor, was the replacement of the incumbent US Commander in Chief, Pacific, by Nimitz, who proved to be an outstanding choice and who in several ways hastened the defeat of Japan.

A Texan, Nimitz graduated from the Naval Academy in 1905. Court-martialled in 1912 for running a ship aground, he nevertheless did well in his early career and, having specialized in submarines, rose by 1917 to become Chief of Staff to the admiral commanding submarines in the Atlantic. Later, he was a battleship executive officer, then commander of a submarine squadron, as well as training for higher staff duties. His submarine experience later proved very useful, for his deployment of submarines in the Pacific War was masterly and provided much of the intelligence on which he based his operations. In the 1930s he commanded a heavy cruiser of the Asiatic Fleet, and later, as rear admiral, he commanded a cruiser division and then a battleship division. In 1939 he gave up his last seagoing command and immediately after Pearl Harbor became Commander in Chief, Pacific.

His experience of aircraft carriers was limited, but this did not prevent him seeing their purpose and how they should be deployed. His immediate task was to resore confidence after the Pearl Harbor disaster, and to develop a fleet, and a general plan, to hold the Japanese offensive. At this period his calm optimism, the trust he obviously placed in his subordinates, and his refusal to make risky attempts at a quick restoration of the naval balance, were precisely what the situation required. One of his strengths was officer selection. He made a point of knowing his subordinates well, and carefully allocated them to the tasks most suited to their competence and personality. Once they were appointed, they had as much freedom as could be allowed by the overall operational plan, and this included freedom to make mistakes. Nimitz realized that mistakes do accompany initiative and boldness, and his policy was that of 'allowing every dog two bites.' An admiral was not expected to relinquish his command after just one error. An exception, perhaps, was Nimitz's replacement of Ghormley by Halsey during the anxious Guadalcanal campaign, but the written records show that he did have misgivings about the rightness of this decision.

The turning point of the Pacific War was the Battle of Midway. This was the result of a Japanese plan to lure Nimitz's Pacific Fleet into an unequal engagement by an attack on Midway Island accompanied by a real, but diversionary, landing in the Aleutian Islands far to the north. Nimitz had the great advantage of signals intelligence that kept him informed of the Japanese movements. Nevertheless, even with this advantage his deployment was masterly, for he had very few ships. In particular, he had available only three aircraft carriers, of which one was still under repair as she sailed, against the Japanese six. He left the conduct of the operation to the commanding admiral afloat, Fletcher, after advising him that the Aleutians situation could be safely ignored. Fletcher's skill, plus luck, enabled the US carriers to find their targets in good time, resulting in the loss of four Japanese carriers for just one American.

After this overwhelming victory, from which Japanese naval aviation never fully recovered, Nimitz resisted the temptation to exploit it with a naval offensive. Instead, he preferred to wait until the substantial reinforcements promised by Washington reached him. In any case, the Guadalcanal operations, an early example of Nimitz's 'island-hopping' technique, proved costly and absorbed most of the available ships.

As Commander in Chief, Pacific, Nimitz stayed ashore in Hawaii and controlled land, sea, and air forces in his theater. He answered to the Joint Chiefs of Staff in Washington, who both suggested and supervised his plans. Similarly Nimitz suggested and supervised the plans of his subordinate commanders. This line of command had, usually, a strong give-and-take element, which ensured that strategy was evolved with the participation both of those who supplied the means and of those who would be in direct charge of operations. The potential weakness was that the Pacific Theater did not embrace the whole of the Pacific war. There was also the South West Pacific Theater, headed by General MacArthur, and the South East Asia Theater, a British command mainly concerned with holding the Japanese in Burma. Friction between the latter and the US theaters was minimal, partly because the personalities involved got on well together; any fundamental differences of opinion were likely to arise at the London/Washington level and be settled at that level.

On the other hand, the relationship between the Pacific and South West Pacific theaters could have been difficult. They were close enough to need each others' assistance, but also staked rival claims on scarce supplies and equipment. Nor could they see eye-to-eye on strategic priorities. Furthermore, the South West Pacific Theater was commanded by Douglas MacArthur, a general not renowned for tact although capable of swallowing his pride for the general good, and his Chief of Staff was a capable but highly abrasive man. That the relationship between these two theaters did run fairly smoothly most of the time is to the credit of Nimitz, whose patience and courtesy could be relied on to wear down all kinds of sharp objects. Nowhere was this more evident than in the controversy over the best line of advance against Japan.

In Washington, the Chief of Naval Operations was strongly in favor of an attack across the Central Pacific, taking islands en route but culminating in an invasion of Formosa. MacArthur, however, and much of the Army, favored a northern thrust from New Guinea to take the Philippines. Nimitz, like a majority of admirals, favored the first course, but when MacArthur came to Hawaii to present his case to Roosevelt in 1944, Nimitz changed his mind. He did not attempt to deny one argument against MacArthur, that the General was pushed by sentimental motives born of his close relationship with the Filipinos, but he did see that, objectively, the General's plan was the best one. Setbacks in China made his change of mind even more firm, because the original plan for the Formosa operation had presupposed the use of supporting airfields in South Eastern China.

Thus, when the decision to go for the Philippines was

approved by the Joint Chiefs of Staff, Nimitz was willing and ready to offer MacArthur full cooperation. On the other hand, the division of command in this venture was potentially a weakness. The situation was that there were two main and two subsidiary commands, each with their own line of authority which met only in the Joint Chiefs of Staff at Washington. The main commands were MacArthur's and Nimitz's, and the subsidiary commands were the XX Army Air Force with its heavy bombers and, increasingly marginal, General Stilwell's China command, which included long-range bombers. Under Nimitz was the Pacific Fleet, of which Admiral Halsey's Third Fleet was the nucleus, and the VII Army Air Force. Under MacArthur came ground and air forces as well as his own fleet, the Seventh Fleet of Vice Admiral Thomas C Kinkaid.

It was the latter that was responsible for transporting the ground forces to the landing beaches of Leyte, the island that had been chosen as the first objective of the Philippines operation. Kinkaid was also to provide air cover, for it was expected that some weeks would elapse before airfields would be available in the Philippines. However, Nimitz agreed to the use of his Third Fleet in support operations. Halsey would take his fast aircraft carriers to neutralize Japanese airfields within range of Leyte, and especially those of Okinawa, Formosa and the northern Philippines. He would then strike closer to the invasion area and, finally, stand by to deal with any Japanese interference after the landings had been made.

The operations plan supplemented the instruction to cover and support the invasion with an additional duty, that of destroying the Japanese fleet if that should become possible. Not only that, but this last task was to have priority. This was a dangerous priority, especially in the hands of Halsey who, naturally, had favored it. Nimitz included this provision because in a previous amphibious operation the US admiral had given up the pursuit of a Japanese force because it was taking him too far from the beaches he was supposed to protect. For the failure to pursue the enemy this commander had been severely, if unjustly, criticized. Nimitz's orders for the Leyte operation made it clear what an admiral's priority should be, but Nimitz presumably expected that the Third Fleet commander would carefully weigh the situation before availing himself of that provision. In retrospect, this appears to have been one of Nimitz's rare errors of judgement, even though in conversation with Halsey he had impressed upon him the need to protect the transport fleet at all times.

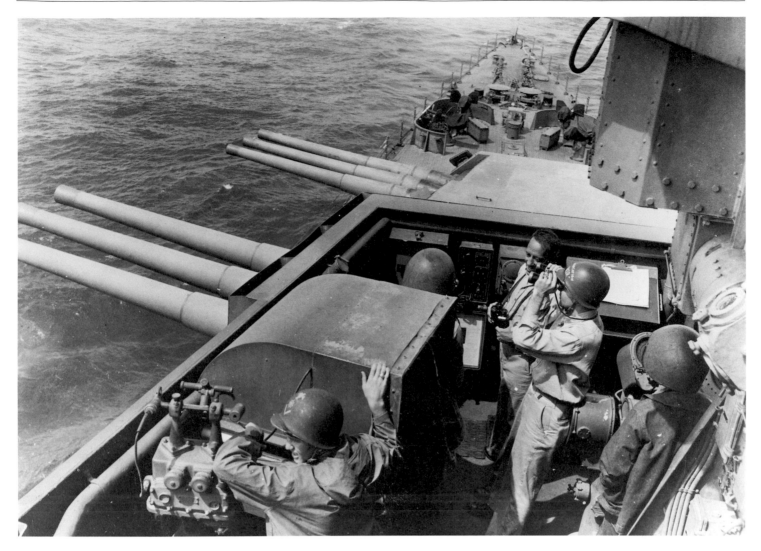

ABOVE LEFT: The Japanese cruiser *Kumano* under air attack after the battle off Samar.

ABOVE: The cruiser USS *Portland* prepares a shore bombardment.

LEFT: US transports come under attack in Leyte Gulf, watched by PT boat crews.

RIGHT: A Japanese sailor is rescued from Surigao Strait by a US PT boat.

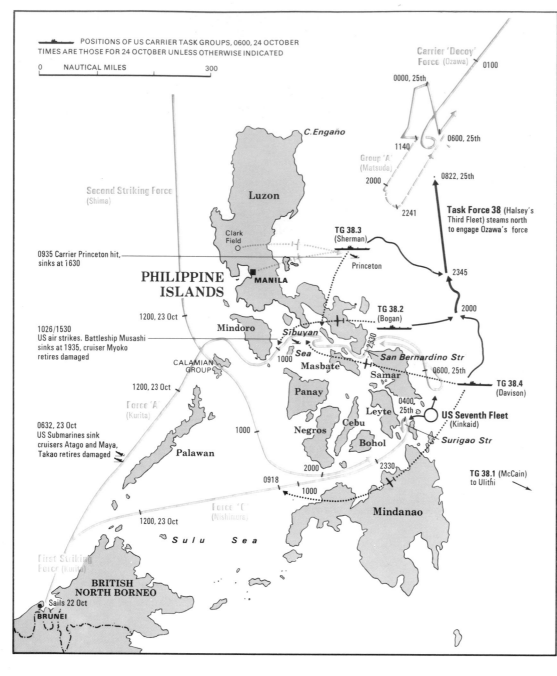

POSITIONS OF US CARRIER TASK GROUPS, 0600, 24 OCTOBER
TIMES ARE THOSE FOR 24 OCTOBER UNLESS OTHERWISE INDICATED

0   NAUTICAL MILES   300

Carrier 'Decoy' Force (Ozawa)

0100
0000, 25th

0600, 25th

1140

Group 'A' (Matsuda)

2000

0822, 25th

2241

Task Force 38 (Halsey's Third Fleet) steams north to engage Ozawa's force

2345

C. Engaño

Second Striking Force (Shima)

Luzon

TG 38.3 (Sherman)

Clark Field

0935 Carrier Princeton hit, sinks at 1630

Princeton

2000

PHILIPPINE ISLANDS

MANILA

TG 38.2 (Bogan)

1200, 23 Oct

Mindoro

1026/1530
US air strikes. Battleship Musashi sinks at 1935, cruiser Myoko retires damaged

Sibuyan

Sea

San Bernardino Str

1000

2330

0600, 25th

Masbate

Samar

TG 38.4 (Davison)

CALAMIAN GROUP

1200, 23 Oct

Panay

Leyte

0400, 25th

US Seventh Fleet (Kinkaid)

Force 'A' (Kurita)

0632, 23 Oct
US Submarines sink cruisers Atago and Maya, Takao retires damaged

1000

Negros

Cebu

Bohol

Surigao Str

Palawan

2000

2330

TG 38.1 (McCain) to Ulithi

0918

1000

Force 'C' (Nishimura)

Mindanao

1200, 23 Oct

S u l u   S e a

First Striking Force (Kurita)

BRITISH NORTH BORNEO

Sails 22 Oct

BRUNEI

LEFT: The Battle of Leyte Gulf, showing the complex Japanese deployment.

RIGHT: A Dauntless dive-bomber, one of the US Navy's most valuable weapons.

RIGHT: The US escort carriers under fire off Samar.

FAR RIGHT: The Japanese monster battleship *Yamato* is struck by a bomb in the Sibuyan Sea.

The Japanese high command still benefited from a good on-the-ground intelligence service, even though in the more sophisticated forms of intelligence gathering it was lagging. This intelligence, together with a sound appreciation of strategic realities, meant that its views coincided very closely with those of MacArthur. It knew only too well that the Philippines would most likely be the next American target, and that the battle for them would be decisive. Once the Japanese lost them, they would be cut off from their raw material supplies in the south. But should they defeat the Americans here, the war would be prolonged and Japan might find a way to avoid total defeat.

With this in mind, the Japanese had for some time been planning on the basis of an American landing in the Philippines. By October they had a good idea of the date and place. By this time the Commander in Chief of the Japanese Combined Fleet was Admiral Toyoda Soemu, who had no doubt of the consequences of a US capture of the Philippines. Realizing that in such an eventuality those of his ships north of the Philippines would be cut off from their oil supplies, and those in the south from their ammunition and equipment supplies, Toyoda saw that he might just as well risk losing his whole fleet as allow the Americans to take a hold on those islands.

Having reached this conclusion, all that remained was to construct a complex operational plan that would take account of all his fleet's strengths and weaknesses, aim at destroying the US convoys on which their troops depended and, if possible, subject the Americans ashore to a devastating bombardment. The strength of Toyoda's fleet would lie in the determination of its men and in the element of surprise, for numerically it was weaker than the American. That weakness was felt especially in the aircraft carrier force. Three carriers had been lost in June in the Battle of the Philippine Sea and, what was worse, hundreds of trained aircrew had perished. This meant that the surviving carriers could put very few aircraft into the air; newly trained (but inexperienced) aircrew would not begin to arrive until the end of the year.

In heavy-gun ships, battleships and heavy cruisers, the Japanese were still quite strong, and in their *Yamato* and *Musashi* they possessed the world's biggest and most heavily-armed battleships. However, the war had shown the primacy of naval aviation, and Toyoda's problem was to bring his ships safely within gunfire range of the Americans. He was not entirely devoid of air support, because he had land-based planes in the Philippines, but the US fleet had numerous carriers by this

stage of the war, the fast fleet carriers being supplemented by light escort carriers that were considerably less formidable but carried a strong fighter complement.

Another problem facing Toyoda was that his fleet was scattered. To reduce the demand for tankers, most of the heavy-gun ships were kept close to their oil supplies at Lingga Roads, near Singapore. Here Vice Admiral Kurita had seven battleships under his command. The aircraft carriers, on the other hand, were stationed in home waters under the command of Vice Admiral Ozawa to receive and train new aircrew. A smaller group of cruisers and destroyers under Vice Admiral Shima was based in the Ryukyu Islands. With good communications this disadvantage might have been turned into a tactical gain, with precisely coordinated squadrons converging from several directions, but Japanese communications were not good. This deficiency was compounded by the chain of command. Toyoda, in Japan, had direct control of Kurita's and Ozawa's forces, but Vice Admiral Mikawa in Manila controlled the land-based naval aircraft and Shima's force. Mikawa was answerable to Toyoda as well, but this merely meant that Toyoda had indirect control of some forces and direct control of others. Strong central coordination by Toyoda would normally have been advantageous, but not when messages took hours to reach their recipient. Moreover, Toyoda had absolutely no control over the Japanese army aircraft in the theater. In this latter respect he had the same problem as MacArthur, who was unable to persuade the XX Army Air Force in China to send its Superfortress bombers to attack Lingga Roads.

Toyoda's plan was probably more complex than it needed to be. He could have deployed three groups, but for some reason he deployed four. Kurita, poised off North Borneo, was to take five battleships and twelve cruisers to form a main striking force that would pass through the San Bernardino Strait to the Leyte Gulf. The other two battleships and four cruisers, under the command of Vice Admiral Nishimura, were to take a more southerly course and would be followed at about 60 miles distance by Vice Admiral Shima's force. Nishimura and Shima were to force their way through Surigao strait (between Leyte and Mindanao) and thereby bring the huge assemblage of American transports within range of their guns. Here, too, off the landing beaches of Leyte, Kurita's strong force would also converge. In effect, a powerful pincer movement would be effected and the striking forces, combined off Leyte, would have an enormous gunfire capacity; in particular, the 18-inch guns of *Musashi* and *Yamato* could outrange any US gun.

The fourth group in Toyoda's plan was Ozawa's aircraft carrier group, consisting of one large and three small carriers, together with two battleships fitted with partial flight decks, and some cruisers and destroyers. Since this force disposed of few serviceable aircraft its role was that of a decoy. Steaming from the north, it was intended to entice Halsey's aircraft carriers away from Leyte, leaving a clear field for the other Japanese groups.

ABOVE: Admiral Mitscher, task force commander and one of the more perceptive US admirals.

ABOVE RIGHT: The destroyer USS *Heermann* lays a smokescreen to protect the escort carriers from Kurita's guns.

LEFT: Deck crews hard at work on a US aircraft carrier. Off Samar the aircraft were put into the air with whatever missiles were immediately to hand.

RIGHT: A Japanese battleship, either *Yamashiro* or *Fuso*, takes evading action in the Sulu Sea.

RIGHT: US carriers and one of their destroyer escorts come under Japanese gunfire off Samar; for the Americans, this was the most perilous phase of the battle.

BELOW: The aircraft carrier USS *Gambier Bay* under Japanese gunfire, from which she later sank.

and refuel but the other three, Nos.38.2, 38.3 and 38.4 were extended north to south to the east of the Philippines, with the likely Japanese routes well within the range of their aircraft.

On 24 October Halsey ordered his carriers to cover the west side of the northern Philippines by reconnaissance flights, but did not send aircraft to the east or north-east, with the result that Ozawa's decoy force, for a few hours more, remained undiscovered. His aircraft did locate the Japanese striking groups heading for the San Bernardino and Surigao straits. He ordered his fourth group, 38.1, to rejoin his force but on that day shore-based aircraft attacked 38.3, sinking the fast carrier *Princeton*. Ozawa, anxious to be discovered, sent in an ineffective air-strike on 38.3, but it was not until late afternoon that US aircraft finally located him, at which time he was too distant for an effective attack before nightfall.

But while Ozawa was craving for US attention, Kurita was getting more attention than he wanted. Hordes of carrier aircraft attacked him, and his *Musashi* was sunk by twenty torpedo hits. One of his cruisers also suffered, but his force was still capable of attaining its objectives. For a time, however, he turned back until he could be sure that the US carriers had turned their attention to Ozawa's decoy force. He had not long to wait. Halsey was only too willing to believe from his pilots' reports that Kurita's force had been rendered ineffective, and ordered his task groups to move north against Ozawa, which he now regarded as the main threat.

In doing this, Halsey left Leyte Gulf and its transports uncovered. He compounded this error by failing to inform Admiral Kinkaid's Seventh Fleet, responsible for the transports, of what he was doing. Moreover, a message from Halsey to his own forces, which Kinkaid picked up, was worded ambiguously. In this signal Halsey spoke of forming a new Task Force 34 that would have been able to cover San Bernardino Strait, but he used the term 'will be formed' which most recipients, including Nimitz, took to be the military imperative (that is, present rather than future tense). Nimitz had additional reason to be confident that Halsey had not left the transports uncovered, for in conversation a few days previously he had emphasized that this was the overriding duty.

As he plunged northward in search of Ozawa, Halsey maintained his bad habit of dealing direct with the task group commanders rather than through Mitscher, his task force commander. Mitscher had considerably better judgement than he had, and suspected that Ozawa could be a lure. Other admirals in Halsey's command had their doubts, too. Some, like Mitscher, believed that the US pilots' reports of damage to Kurita's force were exaggerated. Others, including Lee, the battleship expert, felt that Ozawa's group could be dealt with by just part of Halsey's force. But their advice was ignored and Halsey continued his northward dash, leaving Leyte Gulf uncovered. Kurita, when he led his force out of the San Bernardino Strait, expected a confrontation with at least some US forces, and was agreeably surprised to discover an empty sea. There was not even a picket destroyer to warn the Americans of the Japanese approach.

Meanwhile, Nishimura's group, the second arm of the pincer, had come to a bad end. Advancing through the Surigao Strait during the night, it was attacked first by motor torpedo boats and then, more seriously, by destroyers. The battleship *Fuso* blew up after several torpedo hits while her sister *Yamashiro* received superficial damage. By the time Nishimura came to the exit of the Strait he had only this battleship, a cruiser and a destroyer. He was met by a line of elderly US battleships, part of Kinkaid's fleet, and died when his *Yamashiro* capsized.

It was a good plan that deserved to succeed and almost did succeed. But one of its prerequisites, early American sighting of the decoy group and late sighting of the striking groups, was not forthcoming. On 20 October, only hours after Toyoda had begun his operation, two of Nimitz's submarines not only discovered and tracked Kurita's force but also sunk two of his heavy cruisers, including *Atago*. The latter was Kurita's flagship and was struck by so many torpedoes that it disintegrated and sunk rapidly. Kurita spent some time in the water, and he lost some of his best staff officers.

Later that day Shima's force was also spotted, while a second sighting of Kurita's force located him in the Mindoro Strait. Ozawa's decoy force was not spotted, and Nimitz concluded that the Japanese were intending to pass their striking groups through the Surigao strait in order to wreak havoc in the Leyte Gulf. In response to the threat, Halsey divided his main force, Task Force 38, into four task groups. One of these was to rest

LEFT: A US escort carrier lays a smokescreen while under attack.

RIGHT: The action off Cape Engano; a Japanese battleship, converted to a hybrid aircraft carrier with an after flight-deck, comes under air attack.

LOWER RIGHT: Inside a 16-inch gun turret aboard a US battleship.

The cruiser turned back, and so did Shima, who had been following astern with his group.

Kurita's powerful force, passing down the east coast of Samar Island on its way to Leyte Gulf, sighted a surprised group of Kinkaid's escort carriers, converted merchant ships, unarmored, slow, and with aircraft designed for defense against aircraft and submarines, were taken by Kurita to be fleet aircraft carriers. By this time he was feeling the effects of strain. He had already had to swim from one flagship, had lost many of his staff, including intelligence and signals specialists, and had been shocked to see the enormous *Musashi* succumb to air attack in the Sibuyan Sea the previous day. His first thought on seeing the US carriers was to head them off to prevent them turning into the wind to launch what he wrongly presumed to be their highly dangerous aircraft. He was in so much of a hurry that he ordered a General Attack, thereby converting his advance into a kind of cavalry charge, and losing control of his ships.

The US carriers desperately sought escape in flight, but heavy caliber shells were soon falling among them. Frantic attacks by whatever aircraft could be got into the air, often carrying antisubmarine weapons only, together with heroic torpedo attacks by a handful of US destroyers, enabled the carriers to retire behind smoke screens and into the occasional rain squall. In this fast-moving battle, Kurita's cruisers were hit hard, and his flagship *Yamato*, the most powerful unit, fell behind as it changed course to avoid torpedoes.

Just as the Japanese heavy cruisers were in position to annihilate the carriers, Kurita decided that the engagement should be

broken off. He then reformed his group, hung around for three hours indecisively, and decided to go home. He thereby missed the chance of a certain victory, for he had only to push on to reach the vulnerable US transports, destroying the US carriers on the way. He still had five battleships and several cruisers; if just one of these heavy ships had reached the transports and landing beaches the object of the operation would have been achieved. But Kurita, denied an accurate assessment of the situation, disheartened, discouraged and disturbed by his experiences, had committed a cardinal error. In the tense engagement off Samar, the Americans had lost only one escort carrier and three destroyers, whereas the Japanese lost three heavy cruisers.

Meanwhile, early on 25 October, Halsey far to the north at last formed his Task Force 34, based on six modern battleships under Vice Admiral Lee, and still seemed obsessed with the aim of bringing his battleships into gunfire range of Ozawa's force. Yet it was Halsey's aircraft, in the course of that day, that achieved his main object by sinking three Japanese carriers, even though Ozawa's two aircraft-carrying battleships escaped. Recalling his battleships and sending them back to meet Kurita at the San Bernardino Strait, just as they were about to bring Ozawa's survivors into range, was a difficult decision, so difficult that Halsey delayed too long making it and the battleships arrived back after Kurita had left the scene. That morning, Halsey had been under considerable pressure to send at least part of his force back, to avert castastrophe off Leyte, but he had held fast. It was only an anguished message from Nimitz, asking him

where Task Force 34 really was, that caused him to change his mind. Luckily, because of Kurita's mistakes and the competence and courage shown by the scant US forces off Samar, Halsey's misjudgement and stubborness did not bring the nemesis that might have been expected.

If Nimitz had been closer to the scene of action, those mistakes would probably have been checked in good time. As it was, the penalty was relatively small: the loss of a carrier and three destroyers and the failure to finish off Kurita's striking force as it retreated through the San Bernardino Strait with its four surviving battleships. The series of engagements that made up the Battle of Leyte Gulf constituted by most measures the greatest naval battle in history. It was a battle in which the rival commanders, Nimitz in Hawaii and Toyoda in Japan, never had full control over events. Leaving tactics and local decisions to the admirals afloat could work, but having general responsibility while relying on signals that took hours to arrive, or did not arrive at all, suggested that new ways of allocating command and responsibility were needed.

Reading radio messages as he watched events unfold on his operations chart, unwilling to inhibit his commanders by frequent interventions, Nimitz's role in the battle was more that of a scene-setter than of an operational commander. But it is not wrong to regard him as the architect of this victory, which was the culmination of a long period of preparation in which he had weathered the ravages of the Pearl Harbor attack and created a fleet which, when he put it into position to cover the Leyte operation, did what was expected of it.

CHAPTER SIXTEEN

MACARTHUR
RETURNS TO THE PHILIPPINES

THE TITLE of best general of World War II is inevitably contentious, but there are many who would nominate Douglas MacArthur. Even those who were aware of his less-than-perfect moments conceded that he was an outstanding general who not only conducted his campaigns with great skill but also made contributions to overall strategy that, in retrospect, seem exact and right. The negative events of his life, his theatricality, his antagonism toward some colleagues and toward some allies on purely personal grounds, his oversensitive concern for his reputation and, finally, his dismissal by President Truman during the Korean war, count for less than his contribution to victory in the Pacific and to his sensitive handling of the liberated Philippines and of defeated Japan. His actions in the Philippines probably show him at his best, for his attachment to those islands, while emotional, was also knowledgeable.

The year, 1899, in which MacArthur began his military career at West Point, coincided with his father's leading role in the US Army's campaign in the Philippines, first against the Spanish and then against local nationalists. At West Point he was badly bullied, in a case that was well publicized, but otherwise did very well, his outstanding good looks no doubt contributing to his success. He was commissioned in the engineers, and his first posting was the Philippines. When his father was sent to report on the Far East situation at the time of the Russo-Japanese War, the young MacArthur went with him, and henceforth Asia was the center of his interest. With his natural ability, and the doors opened by the fame of his father, he advanced rapidly, and in 1908 was ADC to President Theodore Roosevelt. Five years later he was the youngest member of the General Staff in Washington. He made a good impression during the 1914 and 1916 clashes with Mexico, and took charge of the Army's public relations in Washington. Here he pleased both the War Secretary and the press. He was only 37, and it was little wonder that he firmly considered himself to be a man of destiny.

In France during World War I he won the Distinguished Service Cross twice. Although a staff officer, he preferred to be at the front during operations and soon learned the value of eccentric clothing to win recognition and then appreciation from his men. If the war had continued a month longer, he would have become a divisional commander. His vanity was flattered by the large number of American and foreign decorations he had been deservedly awarded.

These decorations, or more likely behind-the-scenes influence, meant that, unlike with other US officers, the rank he had obtained in France became permanent, which gave him a seniority jump. He became Superintendent of West Point and introduced long-needed reforms to broaden the academic side and civilize the human side. Then, in 1922, he was posted to command the Manila District of the Philippines, at a time when the islands were taking their first steps toward independence. Then came an interlude spent in the USA, but in 1928 he was back in the Philippines, as commander, before President Hoover chose him as Army Chief of Staff. In this role he did what he could to protect the Army from economies, and also participated in the dispersal by cavalry of a demonstration by army veterans demanding fair treatment. This action led to wide unpopularity, although the evidence suggests that MacArthur was following instructions and did everything possible to minimize violence. However, his subsequent depiction of the demonstration as some kind of communist plot was unworthy, and was an early example of his tendency to shift blame, even undeserved or unexpressed blame, on to others, and to an obsessive anti-communism that could cloud his judgement.

In 1933 he had a violent argument with President Franklin Roosevelt over army economies, and offered his resignation. It was not accepted, and Roosevelt subsequently showed great trust in MacArthur's advice.

The Philippines were due to become completely independent in 1946, and the future rulers of that territory requested MacArthur as military adviser, to prepare for national defense before the US Army departed. So in 1935 he took up his appointment as Military Adviser to the Philippine Commonwealth, with a staff of four, of whom Dwight D. Eisenhower was one. He made friends among Filipino leaders, but also developed the habit of assuming an air of authority and infallibility which, while necessary perhaps to inspire Filipinos to cooperate with him, in the absence of senior officers became unrestrained and virtually part of his character. Eisenhower left as soon as his first term was up.

By 1941, when the Japanese threat had become clear, MacArthur had created a Filipino army which, though promising, was far from in the battleworthy state that he claimed for it. However, the USA was not prepared to strengthen its own forces in the Philippines, even though MacArthur, together with some US, British and Dutch staff officers, thought that the Philippines should be used as a base from which air strikes could be made against Japanese communications.

The US war plan for the Philippines assumed that the Japanese would invade, and that the task of the US and Filipino forces was to hold Manila and the Bataan Peninsula so as to keep Manila Bay open for the eventual arrival of the US Navy with reinforcements. MacArthur disputed this plan, and argued for a defense of the entire archipelago. In November 1941 the US War Department agreed with him, and he was told to make plans accordingly.

Like so many other British and US military leaders, he had a low opinion of Japanese military competence, and from somewhere (probably from an enthusiastic airman) he had drawn a greatly exaggerated confidence in the new Flying Fortress bombers. The idea of holding the Philippines and dominating the surrounding region by bombers seemed very attractive to him. But in reality, when the war started in the Pacific, the US forces in the Philippines were too weak to sustain MacArthur's intentions even though in the final peacetime months Washington had sent him most of what he asked for. He only had 35 Flying Fortresses and about 100 modern fighters. The US Asiatic Fleet consisted of a handful of old ships, and MacArthur's overall command of it was in doubt. Although he was effective Commander in Chief in the Philippines, the rivalry between the US Army and US Navy meant that he could not be certain that the local naval commander would actually follow his orders.

The Japanese probably had a fairer knowledge of the real state of the Philippine defenses than did Washington, or even MacArthur himself, for he had not yet learned to check his wishful thinking. The Philippines stood almost directly on the line of communication between Japan and the East Indian territories which, for economic reasons, were the main object of Japanese expansion. Japan therefore had to capture them, but little more than two divisions were allocated for this task, which was planned to take no longer than 50 days. Evidently the Japanese command had scant respect for the one US and eight Filipino divisions that were defending the Philippines.

The Flying Fortresses were handled badly, despite timely knowledge of Japanese intentions. Half were destroyed by air attack on their airfields, and the remainder were evacuated to Australia. As expected, the Japanese troop landings were at two points on the main island, Luzon, and met little opposition. Filipino troops, not properly trained or led, fled in disorder and

MacArthur decided that, after all, the old plan of withdrawing to the Bataan Peninsula was the best. However, he delayed, for reasons that seem only to have been psychological, the transfer of supplies to the Peninsula. Acting with his commander in the field, General Jonathan M. Wainwright, he achieved a quite successful fighting retreat, very creditable in the circumstances, although events would have taken an even better course if he had not underrated the Japanese. Their tendency to move faster than he anticipated, and to fight better than he expected, merely encouraged him to give credence to intelligence appreciations that ascribed to the Japanese considerably more strength than they in fact had.

Because of the supply situation, the US and Filipino troops in the Peninsula were immediately put on half-rations, but MacArthur might have improved their spirits if he had chosen to use his outstanding presence and undoubted courage by appearing among his troops. But he remained in his new headquarters on the rocky island of Corregidor in Manila Bay, and it was not long before this aroused bitterness among the men who were doing the actual fighting, who found for old tunes new bitter words about 'Dugout Doug' who was 'a-shaking on the rock.' His dislike of Wainwright seems an unlikely reason for his failure to visit the front, but emotional reasons of one kind or another were probably present. He was a man who was influenced by his animosities, and sometimes it seemed excusable. His difficult relations with the US Navy at this time seem understandable; in the days preceding the war the local naval commander received the latest situation reports from Washington hours, even days, before MacArthur received them. Soon after war started the Navy quit the Philippines without even saying goodbye, and then proved unable to send supplies and reinforcements to MacArthur. In this case, however, MacArthur displayed surprising incomprehension of the difficulties facing the US Navy.

ABOVE: Japanese troops land in Lingayen Gulf in January 1942.

ABOVE LEFT: US-trained Filipino Scouts on Bataan in 1942.

ABOVE, FAR LEFT: Japan triumphant.

RIGHT: A US Army dispatch rider takes a careful rest on Bataan.

LEFT: Inside the underground US headquarters on Corregidor Island.

The final stand was made on Corregidor, but by that time MacArthur had left. He went with genuine reluctance, as he would have preferred to stay on the scene. But he had been appointed Commander in Chief of the whole South West Pacific, and the main Allied strength was accumulating in Australia, where he made his headquarters. In the end, with his gift for public relations, the stand of the US troops on Bataan and Corregidor was protrayed as a heroic feat of arms under his leadership that contrasted brightly with the British relinquishment of Singapore, and which delayed the Japanese advance considerably. In reality, he had not done so well as that. The rather slow Japanese advance in Bataan was due to the diversion of part of its strength to operations in Java, and the British in Malaya had faced far more powerful Japanese formations than did MacArthur in the Philippines.

In Australia, MacArthur had to come to terms with the likelihood that his flamboyant promise to the Filipinos, 'I shall return!' was a long-term rather than a short-term undertaking. On Corregidor, he had had to accept that the hoped-for reinforcements would never arrive, and he had also to master his resentment of the fact that while Washington encouraged him to hold out until help came, the War Department and the President had already concluded that the Phillippines would be lost. MacArthur had thereby been deceived into making confident, if not brash, pronouncements to the Filipinos that the real facts could not sustain. Their resultant loss of faith in both the USA and MacArthur meant that the Filipino guerilla movement against the Japanese occupiers would be less enthusiastic than he had hoped.

In Australia MacArthur had the loyal support of the Labour prime minister, which eased his organizational task as American troops and supplies poured in. But his contacts with the Australian forces were sometimes difficult. He was unwilling to listen to the advice of battle-hardened Australian officers, and he was somewhat reluctant to give credit to the ability and the success of Australian troops fighting in New Guinea. On the other hand,

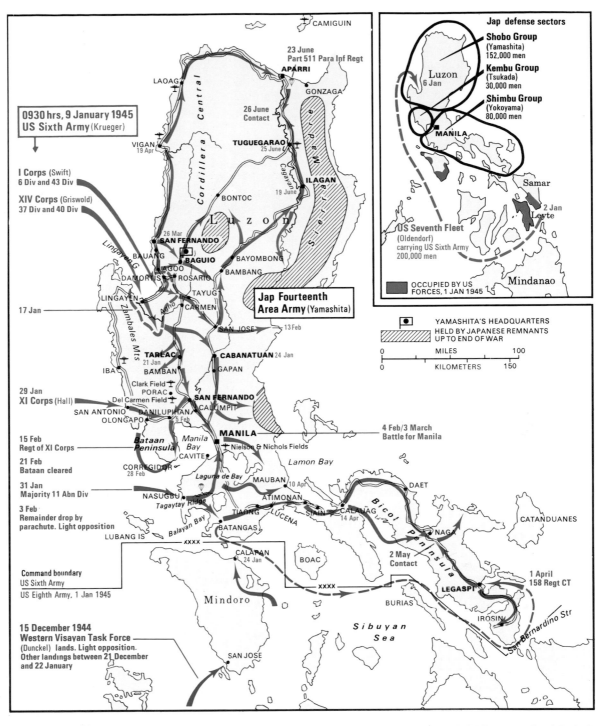

LEFT: Dakota transports bring supplies to an American airbase in New Guinea. Extensive and intelligent use of airpower was one of the hallmarks of MacArthur's return to the Philippines.

CENTRAL LEFT: A Japanese escort vessel comes under air attack off the Philippines.

BOTTOM LEFT: The British Admiral Louis Mountbatten confers with MacArthur in 1945 after the recapture of the Philippines.

RIGHT: MacArthur's campaign to recapture the Philippines.

his strategic grasp was sure, now that he had a true measure of the Japanese.

At this point the task of the Allies was to halt the Japanese. Any further advance would mean that Australia would be at their mercy. Also, the longstanding view that Japan could not long sustain such a distant and wide-flung war was at last coming true. In the South West Pacific theater, the farthest advance of the Japanese and the points at which in due course they were turned back were New Guinea and the Solomon Islands. In the latter, in 1942-43, the Americans turned the tide and in the former, under MacArthur's overall command, the Australians and Americans beat back the enemy.

Thus in 1943 MacArthur was able to contemplate further advances northward, but his plans had to conform with the general overall direction of the Pacific war, which was not to his liking. Ultimately, the chiefs of staff in Washington decided strategic issues, but the local commanders' own opinions and plans were sought. The underlying problem with the American planning was that personal and inter-service differences sur-

faced too often. The US Army and the US Navy, each with their own air forces, usually cooperated well in actual operations, but at the planning level jealousies played a large role.

The agreed aim was to roll back the Japanese advance and then capture bases from which Japan itself could be attacked. There were several ways of doing this, but eventually two main lines of approach were studied. Most of the admirals favored an 'island-hopping' approach westward across the central Pacific, culminating in the capture of Formosa and then an assault on Japan itself. MacArthur and many other generals favored an advance northward, embracing the Philippines first and then continuing to Japan.

To resolve this difference of opinions MacArthur was eventually summoned to Pearl Harbor in summer 1944 to present his case to Roosevelt. Admiral Nimitz, Commander in Chief of the Central Pacific theater was also there, to explain his own preferred strategy of a westward, primarily naval, thrust. Roosevelt, perhaps because he knew and trusted MacArthur, or perhaps because he saw the validity of MacArthur's arguments, accepted the case for an advance via the Philipines.

In retrospect, in this argument MacArthur seems undeniably right, and his personal conduct irreproachable. The conflict between Army and Navy was not of his making, and at this time he seems to have done nothing to have made it worse. But he stuck to his opinion and his arguments, and won the debate, putting an end to a dispute that had begun as soon as he had reached Australia in 1942.

His critics implied, with some justification, that emotional attachment to the Philippines led him to insist that they should be liberated from the Japanese yoke as soon as possible, especially as he had given personal undertakings to them. This is probably true, but it does nothing to weaken the essential validity of his arguments for the northward approach. Moreover, his feeling that the USA had a special responsibility toward the Filipinos, and that to leave them to the mercy of the Japanese until the end of the war would be dishonorable and be bad for the future, might have been emotional but was also perfectly valid.

Those who opposed him urged a main drive on Formosa, with MacArthur's forces reduced to a subsidiary role of liberating the East Indies and then, possibly, some southerly islands of the Philippines. But this would have taken him away from the direct and shortest route to Japan, and would also have left a gap between his theater and that of Admiral Nimitz. With his preferred northward approach, his and Nimitz's forces could cooperate far more easily. In particular, Nimitz's naval strength would be at hand to support and defend the troops.

The essential correctness, MacArthur argued, of a plan involving the capture of the Philippines could be seen from any map. Not only would the acquisition of bases there enable further islands to be captured to the north, but they would also command the sea route between Japan and its oil sources in the East Indies. As soon as the Allies threw back the enemy in New Guinea in early 1943, MacArthur kept his staff busy planning what he considered to be the war-winning thrust northward,

supported by his own land-based bombers rather than naval planes. When it was finally decided in 1944 that the MacArthur strategy should prevail, he was already well-prepared. Three detailed plans were evolved, one for the capture of Mindanao, the southern island of the Philippines, one for Leyte, and a third for the key northern island of Luzon.

However, probing air attacks by Admiral Halsey's carriers suggested that the Japanese defenses were not strong on Mindanao, and the Admiral recommended that Mindanao could be bypassed, with the initial American landing being made on Leyte. Washington agreed, and asked MacArthur if he could plan this change in time for the scheduled invasion. MacArthur's Leyte plan was so well advanced that he was able to impress Washington by a prompt agreement, and the Leyte landing was scheduled for 20 October instead of 20 December.

Already, in September, forward bases had been taken in the Moluccas and Palau islands. A second preliminary step was the neutralization of Japanese bases to the north of the Philippines by Admiral Halsey's aircraft carriers, which made highly destructive raids on airfields in Formosa and Okinawa. The 200,000-man invasion force was then lifted by a fleet of 700 ships from its forward bases to Leyte. Here, because the Japanese army was thinly spread in the Philippines, there was only one defending division, and there was little opposition to the landings. Japanese officers had learned that, because of bombing and naval gunfire, defending the beaches was too costly. Moreover, in the Philippines they had simultaneously to watch the interior with its developing guerilla movement.

MacArthur's plan was to land two divisions each near airfields at Dulag and Tacloban. By midnight of the first day 132,500 Americans had gone ashore and were well supplied. This fast landing enabled them to keep the Japanese off-balance, especially as the Tacloban landing had not been anticipated. MacArthur would later set up his own headquarters at the side of the operational commander's HQ, a most unusual arrangement that

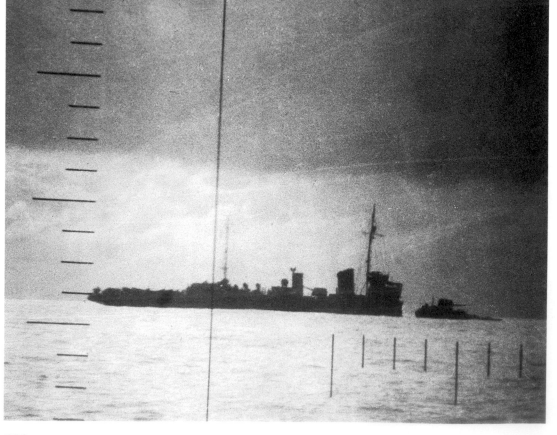

ABOVE RIGHT: US landing ships unload at Leyte.

RIGHT: US landing ships approach the hostile beach at Leyte, supported by naval gunfire.

LEFT: A sinking Japanese patrol boat is photographed through the periscope of the US submarine that torpedoed her.

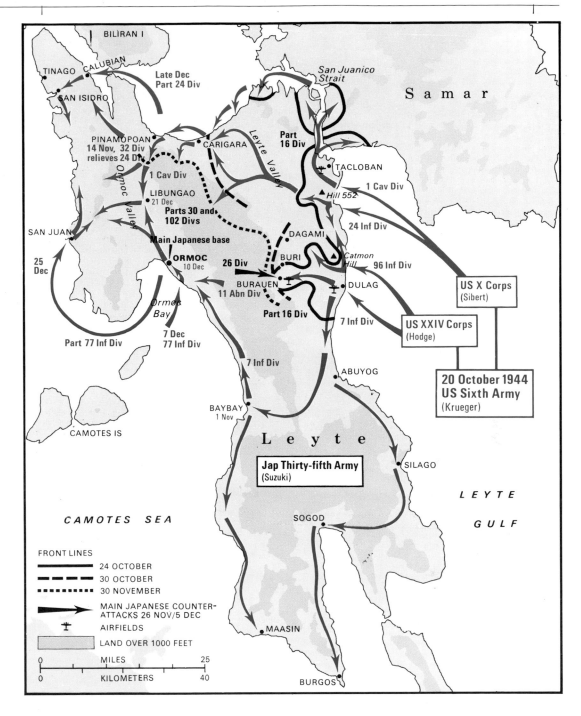

LEFT: MacArthur, accompanied by leading Filipino and US figures, comes ashore on Leyte.

BELOW LEFT: The US invasion fleet off Leyte. The three-funnelled cruiser (lower left) was part of Australia's contribution.

RIGHT: MacArthur's enthusiasm for seaborne assaults was exemplified by his Leyte campaign.

did enable him to respond promptly to requests; because he liked and had confidence in his general, he withstood the temptation to interfere with the latter's operations.

Although by 24 October the Japanese had established beach-heads on both sides of the Juanico Strait, by the end of that month most of the north-east and part of the west were occupied by the Americans. On 22 October MacArthur had come ashore, accompanied by the President of the Philippines and photographers, and had made his celebrated 'I have returned' speech.

But in November, covered by a strong rearguard action, the Japanese managed to bring in to Leyte about 45,000 men. This reinforcement, which almost quadrupled the Japanese strength, together with the mountainous terrain and heavy rainfall, kept the Americans away from the Japanese base at Ormoc. But early in December, with an amphibious landing, MacArthur outflanked the Japanese defenses here. US forces from north and south could link up, and Japanese resistance on Leyte was henceforth desultory and scattered.

The Americans established a beach-head on Samar, and in mid-December landed on Mindoro. The object of this latter landing was the construction of an airfield to assist the imminent operation to capture Luzon. By the end of the year the Americans held Leyte, parts of Samar and Mindoro, and had lost almost 16,000 men. Japanese losses exceeded 70,000.

General Yamashita had a quarter of a million troops to defend Luzon, but no effective air strength. His plan of defense was well thought-out, and based on the premise that the longer he held out the better for Japan. His few aircraft would be used in kamikaze missions against the American landing fleet, while his troops would slowly retreat into the mountains, where they could resist until supplies were exhausted. He divided his men into three groups, with himself commanding the northern group and with a second group to defend the Bataan Peninsula and a third to cover the rest of the island, including Manila.

On 9 January the Americans landed in the Lingayen Gulf. Losses were small, for in keeping with their military tradition the kamikaze pilots aimed themselves not at the vulnerable and all-important transports, but at the defending warships. By nightfall the Americans had established a beachhead four miles deep, and soon they began to press outward in two directions.

ABOVE: A US seaborne landing on one of the Marshall Islands atolls.

ABOVE RIGHT: Heavily-armed US PT boats await their next patrol in Philippine waters.

LEFT: American bombers sink a Japanese escort vessel.

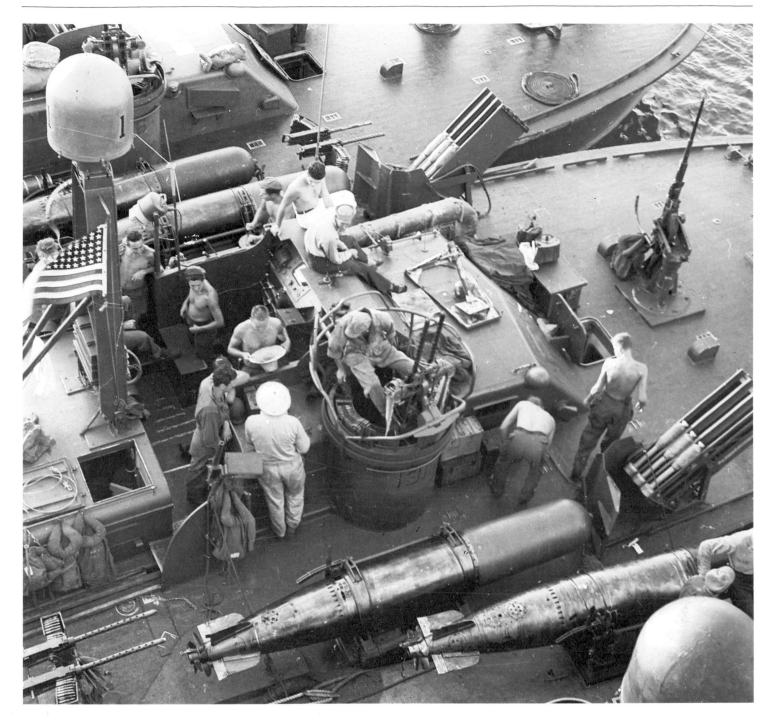

There was some delay because Yamashita had placed troops to threaten the flank of the advance to Manila. But on 23 January the Clark Airfield was reached, and this became the scene of a week of heavy fighting. Meanwhile a US corps that had been left to deal with the southern islands was brought in to help, and captured Olongapo before advancing east. This move cut off the Bataan Peninsula, but Yamashita had foreseen this and moved most of the Bataan troops to the north-east in good time.

Meanwhile US airborne troops were landed south of Manila. MacArthur had stipulated that the battle for the Philipines should be fought with as little physical damage as possible, but when his forces closed in on the capital from north and south they were confronted with a situation that could hardly be resolved without massive destruction. Yamashita, like Mac-Arthur, had not sought a great battle for Manila, but this was a Japanese naval base and there were 18,000 Japanese naval troops there, led by a fanatical rear admiral. The result was a month of street fighting on a scale not seen since Stalingrad. Much of the old city was destroyed, and the local inhabitants suffered grievously. Probably 100,000 civilians were killed, and about a

thousand Americans, before the Japanese sailors were killed. MacArthur's suite in a Manila hotel, preserved undamaged with his furniture and belongings since 1942, went up in flames at this time.

Even after the capture of Manila, Manila Bay was still unusable as a naval base until Corregidor was secured. This took eleven days of fighting, after an amphibious and airborne assault. Fort Drum, another obstacle, was only captured in April, after gasoline and oil had been poured down its ventilators and ignited.

But Yamashita held on in the north-east until the war ended. He was pushed into a part of the mountain area but still had 50,000 men when the war ended. Other islands were still in dispute, the typical sequence being a US amphibious landing, followed by a Japanese withdrawal to the woods and mountains, where flushing them out was a long and costly process. In Mindanao, sizable Japanese formations held out until the end of the war. Meanwhile, MacArthur used his military authority to ensure that the US recapture of the Philippines would not be accompanied by a new colonialism. Remembering that the terri-

CHAPTER SEVENTEEN

ZHUKOV

AND THE BATTLE FOR BERLIN

SOVIET MILITARY leaders during World War II were in a more difficult position than their Western counterparts in so far as the formulation of strategy was concerned, because their warlord, Josef Stalin, insisted on formulating it himself, giving them an even smaller leverage in executing it than Western generals had. It is true that in the case of Marshal Zhukov he was always consulted and much of his advice was accepted by Stalin. However, Zhukov could never be sure of anything. Like Hitler, Stalin insisted on controlling even tactical maneuvers of the various armies under Zhukov's command. The result was that all the strategic planning had to be done through Stalin and the credit for it had to go to him. Much of the tactical execution went to Stalin who not only controlled reserves, but also frequently altered the lines of attack by groups of armies (fronts), armies, corps and even armored units. Thus only within these narrow limits could Soviet generals establish their reputations and claim credit for the battles of Stalingrad, Leningrad, Kiev or Berlin.

Together with Marshal Vasilievsky, Zhukov was in a particularly privileged military situation, for from the very beginning of the war he was Stalin's most intimate adviser on strategy and his personal 'executor' on the spot, at the battles. Thus, for example, Zhukov had to inspect the battleground at Stalingrad long before Stalin finally decided on the strategy of that battle. Zhukov reported his findings to his master and advanced his suggestions. Together with other commanders, who were only allowed to comment on their partial tasks, Zhukov often forced on Stalin his military decisions. However equally often Stalin, who had additional sources of information (the NKVD channel, for example) and his own finger on the strategic reserves button, made his decisions contrary to the military advice proferred. However, Zhukov had an additional privilege; that of commanding the groups of armies – especially toward the end of the war – in the execution of Stalin's strategies which he had helped to formulate. Naturally in the latter capacity Zhukov had a greater scope for initiative and decision making, but even then his powers were limited by Stalin's frequent checks and especially, famous telephone calls, which usually resulted in changes of tactical plans and operations. Thus, with all these reservations in mind, we can now consider Zhukov's role in the Battle for Berlin.

Stalin earmarked his favorite general, Zhukov, for the final Battle of Berlin in October 1944. Zhukov himself says that this was exactly one day after he had persuaded Stalin to halt the Warsaw offensive, whose objectives were unclear to him, and which was draining Soviet military resources quite disproportionately to its significance. Zhukov had only just returned from Bulgaria and was inspecting the Warsaw front: the 1st Belorussian and 1st Ukrainian Fronts came to a halt on the line Praga–Warsaw–Vistula–Jaslo. Stalin therefore began to plan subsequent offensives, the most crucial of which would be the one from the Vistula to the Oder carried out by the 1st Belorussian Front. This would bring this group of armies to the Berlin strategic zone, to be ultimately responsible for the final operation of the war, the taking of the Nazi capital, Berlin. This was Stalin's idea in October 1944, when he appointed Zhukov Commander in Chief of the 1st Belorussian Front, one of the most brilliant staff officers, Colonel General M S Malinin as his

Chief of Staff and Lieutenant General K F Telegin, one of the most experienced political officers, as members of the War Council.

The thrust toward Berlin was to be prepared most thoroughly by Zhukov and Malinin during November 1944. Although Germany still had some 7,500,000 men engaged in the war, Hitler was draining the Eastern Front of its best units in preparation for a counteroffensive in the west, the Battle of the Bulge. Zhukov's strategic planning included a feint thrust in the south toward Vienna in order to draw German reserves from his front, which was approved by Stalin and GHQ (Stavka). However, once again Stalin forced on Zhukov several strategic limitations. First of all, Stalin neglected to reduce East Prussia and in particular Königsberg (Kaliningrad) during the summer of 1944, and though he had now charged General Ivan D Chernyakhovsky and his 3rd Belorussian Front with this task, he still persisted in ignoring the danger to the offensive operations of the 1st Belorussian Front, about to be launched. Next Stalin charged General Konstantin Rokossovsky and his 2nd Belorussian Front to strike in the general Northwest axis, from north of Warsaw, and coordinate this advance with Zhukov's, running along the axis south of Warsaw to Poznan (Posen) and in the general direction of the Oder and Berlin. Even to a politician, Stalin, this joint, coordinated operation, must have appeared as two separate missions to be treated on their own, but once again Stalin insisted on coordination so that he could more easily control the actual operations. Finally, Stalin also ignored the time factor: although the preparations for the offensive were completed early in December 1944 he refused to give it the go ahead, because he thought heavy mud and poor visibility would make it impossible to exploit Soviet armor and mechanized superiority and set the tentative D-Day for 15-20 January 1945. Zhukov and Malinin had therefore unexpectedly more time for the planning and rehearsing of the offensive, which for the first time in the war was taking place on unfamiliar territory. All supply routes were in Poland and the military intelligence seemed unfamiliar coming from the secret service and aerial reconnaissance rather than from guerrilla sources. In addition the Red Army soldiers badly needed political explanations and education, in order, as

LEFT: Zhukov first came to prominence when commanding Soviet forces during a 'border incident' with the Japanese in 1939 and played a leading role in virtually all the major campaigns on the Eastern Front.

RIGHT: An elderly German recruit tries his hand with a Panzerfaust antitank weapon.

Zhukov put it to prevent irresponsible acts by Soviet soldiers in the liberated territory. Thus Zhukov was able to hold staff maneuvers in which he was able to consider logistical support (he had only two comparatively small bridgeheads), and he was able to resolve more or less the problem of cooperation with Rokossovsky's armies by staging maneuvers on the army scale. In a sudden change of direction Stalin launched both armies against Germany on 12 January 1945, apparently in response to Churchill's requests.

For this last but one push forward the combined Soviet forces were staggering: some 164 infantry divisions; 32,143 guns and mortars (7:1 superiority); 6460 tanks and self-propelled guns (5:1); 4772 aircraft (17:1); and 2,200,000 men (5:1). On Zhukov's front there was one infantry division for each 1.3 miles. Artillery barrage on a depth of 2 miles lasted 2½ hours, and after two days of hard fighting Zhukov's forces forced a wedge of over seven miles. After two or three days tank armies were used in support of the infantry and they swiftly developed the offensive pursuing the Germans through breakthroughs up to 62 miles in one day. After six days of the offensive General Guderian had to contend with Soviet penetrations of up to 100 miles on a 310-mile wide front. Cities began to fall – Warsaw was finally liberated – or were besieged and all the objectives were reached ahead of the schedule by 25 January 1945. By this time Stalin wanted to stop Zhukov's offensive to wait for the final defeat of the Germans in East Prussia, but Zhukov objected: instead he asked for one more army to strengthen his right flank and then ordered a forced advance into the fortified Meseritz zone. For he knew that once the line Bydgoszcz-Poznan was reached by his and Rokossovsky's armies, all future operations, which also meant the ultimate one against Berlin, would be decided on the spot.

However, Stalin's telephone calls slowed down Zhukov, especially since Stalin refused to send Zhukov reinforcements

which he needed if he was to reach Küstrin on the Oder river, on the direct line to Berlin. As Rokossovsky's offensive north of Bydgoszcz got stuck, Zhukov's right flank was now in real danger and though the Oder was reached on 3 February Zhukov was obliged to halt, even though he had issued a directive to his armies and staffs to get ready to resume the final offensive on Berlin by 9 February: after all Berlin was only some 50 miles from Küstrin, which his armies had by then reached. Perhaps rather optimistically Zhukov ordered that Berlin be taken seven days later. This was indeed strategy on the spot, but rather different from what Stalin had in mind.

Instead of letting him dash for Berlin he obliged Zhukov to remain on the defensive and wait for the other commanders, Rokossovsky and Konev to complete their tasks. Above all he

TOP LEFT: Old and young were called up for the final defense of Berlin.

LEFT COLUMN, CENTER & BELOW: A 1944 *Volkssturm* parade in Berlin. Goebbels takes the salute.

LEFT: Members of the Hitler Youth visit Hitler at his headquarters during March 1945. At the end of the war these youths were called upon to fight and defend Germany.

ABOVE RIGHT: Russians shell the Reichstag and Reichschancellery on 24 April 1945.

RIGHT: One of the last pictures taken of Hitler in March 1945 at his bunker headquarters in Berlin.

was apparently worried about Zhukov's right flank: Soviet intelligence indicated that the Germans had the Third Panzer Army in Western Pomerania and it could either reinforce the East Pomeranian forces or defend Berlin. In either case it presented a risk to Zhukov's further operations. Although Marshal Chuikov, who was Zhukov's subordinate, claimed subse-quently that the 2nd Belorussian Front could have dealt with any threat along the Berlin axis, Zhukov came to agree with Stalin. On 1 March 1945 assisted by Zhukov's troops Rokossovsky's 2nd Belorussian Front had finally broken through and reached the Baltic Sea by cutting the German armies into two. However, the attacking Russians still had their supply bases on the Vistula and this fact also forced Zhukov to slow down. Marshal Konev in the south reached Breslau with his 1st Ukrainian Front, but failed to cross the river Neisse as envisaged. Delays were caused on this front by the erratic supplies of ammunition, by the slowness of aviation to afford him cover, and above all by the lagging of the pontoon bridge units. Still by the end of March 1945 all these tasks were accomplished and Stalin summoned Zhukov and Konev to Moscow to discuss the final phase of the war and let them into a few political secrets.

It must have been an unpleasant surprise for Zhukov to find on arrival at the Stavka in Moscow his chief rival, Marshal Konev (who had been exclusively a field commander) was in on the final operation. He probably suspected that his warlord might trick him of the final war trophy, Berlin, or make him divide the laurels with that 'simple' Konev. Indeed Stalin was already engaged trying to outmaneuver the Allies. Before the generals arrived he had received a telegram about an Allied attack on Berlin under Field Marshal Montgomery, so Stalin now decided to give the operation top priority. However, fooling the Allies was child's play compared to tricking his own generals. General Eisenhower, with his straightforward naivety, informed Stalin, against Churchill's advice, that his main thrust in Germany would aim at Erfurt, Leipzig and Dresden and not at Berlin as the British had desired. Stalin in turn told Eisenhower that Soviet main effort would also aim at Dresden and would be launched in the second half of May. After misleading Eisenhower he immediately turned round to his generals and urged them to take Berlin before the Western Allies. Thus Stalin trusted neither his Allies nor his generals: now he played one general against another as he had previously done with the American and British allies.

In Moscow both Zhukov and Konev wanted to take Berlin now that they had been given the green light. With his tough soldier mentality, Zhukov wanted a frontal attack by his 1st Belorussian Front while the 'politician' Konev favored a coordinated attack. Other general staff leaders proposed pincer movements. Stalin had made up his mind long before and was just playing games with his generals. After all he had approved Zhukov's front proposal on 27 January 1945 and two days later Konev's coordinated drive; the latter was a thrust from Silesia and the river Neisse toward the river Elbe with the right flank of the 1st Ukrainian Front helping the 1st Belorussians cut the German Army Group Center to ribbons, south of Berlin. However, both these proposals consider the reduction of the capital to be the business of the 1st Belorussian Front, that is Marshal Zhukov. This would have been the climax of the Marshal's war career and might in a political sense overshadow even the real achievement of the Generalissimo. Cleverly Stalin pretended to consider all the proposals anew and rather predictably approved the Zhukov-Konev plans making them dependent on the demarcation line between the two army groups: the line ended at Lubben on the Spree river and Stalin added rather explicitly 'Whoever gets there first, will also take Berlin.' Thus he not only usurped all the prestige from the overall success of the operation, but made sure that he would control it throughout its stages up to the final point at Lubben, when he could decide which of the competing generals would be allotted the final trophy. As was usual with Stalin, once he had defined and safeguarded his own interests, he gave a completely free hand to Zhukov and Konev to prepare and execute the operation.

As always Zhukov took the coming battle of Berlin most seriously. Immediately after his return from Moscow he invited all the commanders to his HQ and the conference lasted two days (5 to 7 April 1945). Commanders of support services also took part in these staff conferences and all the command aspects of the offensive were thoroughly thrashed out. Between 8 and 14 April Zhukov ordered more detailed war games to be conducted by the lower commanders. To Zhukov's mind the taking of

Berlin whose defenses were well prepared and covered some 350 square miles was a formidable task and he ordered six aerial surveys by Soviet reconnaissance aircraft. Above all he was worried by the overextended lines of communications which made supplies difficult to move into operational zones. After all the 1st Ukrainian Front also had its supply problems, but it was the supplies of Rokossovssky's 2nd Belorussian Front (which was to launch its offensive five days later) which complicated Zhukov's supply situation. Up to the last moment Zhukov could not be sure that his supply requirements would be met in time.

Since 'never before in the experience of warfare had (Zhukov) been called upon to capture a city as large and as heavily fortified' he had his engineers construct an exact model of the city and its suburbs in planning the final assault: every street, square, alley, building, canal, bridge and the underground network were taken into consideration. Detailed assault maps compiled from aerial surveys, captured documents and interrogation reports of POWs, were supplied to all commands down to company level. Zhukov's next consideration was how his offensive would make the maximum impact on the enemy and he decided to launch it during the two hours before dawn. In order to avoid confusion among his own troops powerful searchlights were to be used to illuminate the German positions. Thus Zhukov personally took care of every detail of the operation even allowing his politruks [political commissars] to take care of his men's morale, which they did without unduly disturbing the general, who was completely absorbed in military matters.

BELOW LEFT: Soviet troops in the heart of Berlin. Thousands of civilians died in the intense house-to-house fighting.

BELOW: Soviet sharpshooters pick off snipers in the streets of Berlin. The fighting for the inner city was bitter and lasted for five days.

When Zhukov began to plan the Berlin operation, following his great victories between the Vistula and Oder rivers in January–March 1945, he knew practically nothing of Allied military plans. Stalin must have let him know that General Bradley had turned down the operation against Berlin on account of heavy casualties. However he did not add Bradley's rider 'that after all that the Americans would have to hand over Berlin to the Russians because of the zonal agreement.' Still Zhukov never cared much about casualties and this time he was prepared for any sacrifice, since Stalin himself urged the final operation for political reasons. In March 1945 Zhukov had to face new factors on the German side as soon as he had finished his own regrouping in his zone of operations between Schwedt and Gross Gastroze and particularly in the Küstrin sector, where he had a beachhead on the other side of the Oder river. These new factors would make the Berlin operation even more costly. After the February breakthrough the German High Command reorganized its Berlin defenses into three zones: the first, main defense line and two other, rear ones. The first line ran along the left banks of the rivers Oder and Neisse and consisted of three fortified networks protected by minefields, in the depth of three to six miles. The second defense line was some 10-14 miles from the first defense line and was connected by means of strongpoints, up to the depth of two miles. The third line was seven to 14 miles from the second one, but was unfinished when Zhukov launched his attack.

On paper Zhukov, who had detailed intelligence reports, had to face a formidable enemy: for the defense of his capital Hitler concentrated round and in Berlin Third Panzer Army and Ninth Field Army from the Army Group Vistula and Fourth Panzer Army and Seventeenth Field Army from the Army Group Center. Thus only in regular troops Hitler, who assumed the defense of the capital himself, had some 48 infantry divisions, four Panzer divisions and 10 motorized divisions. In addi-

tion Berlin contained a garrison of some 200,000 men, of whom, however, 200 battalions were Volkssturm formations. Youths of 16-17 years of age were specially trained in Panzerfaust handling and were to perform miracles in the defense of the capital against the Russian tanks. Hitler also concentrated some 72 percent of his Luftwaffe in Berlin. Altogether Hitler amassed some 1 million men, 10,400 guns and mine-throwers, 1500 tanks and self-propelled guns, more than 3,000,000 antitank rockets (Panzerfaust) and 3300 aircraft. Thus he had one division per nine kilometers of the front; 17.3 guns per kilometer of the front; and in the Küstrin sector, where a frontal attack was rightly expected, he had one division per three kilometers and 66 guns and 17 tanks per kilometer of the front. (A greater density was achieved only at Kursk in 1943, where the Russians deployed 105 guns per kilometer in the expected sector of attack.) In addition Hitler put in charge of the Küstrin defenses General Heinrici, an acknowledged Wehrmacht expert on defense fighting: once again Heinrici succeeded in withdrawing from the first line of defense under cover of darkness, so that the Russian artillery barrage hit empty trenches. While the German High Command was a little disorganized, because of Hitler's interference, German soldiers were in a desperate mood, ready to defend the capital to the last shot, largely because of the barbaric behavior already shown by the Red Army in East Prussia.

To bring this impressive edifice of Hitler's power crashing down Zhukov was given a free hand in the actual offensive planning and execution and Zhukov could also alter the deployment of the Stavka's strategic reserves. Stalin, nevertheless, sent another of his watchdogs to check on his tough general in the shape of General Vasiliy Sokolovsky, whom he appointed as 1st deputy commander. In fact Sokolovsky, who was a finer soldier than Zhukov himself, strengthened Zhukov's forces rather than restricting him and Stalin never forgave him, giving him no appointment of distinction while alive.

Zhukov's front was narrowed from some 200 to 120 miles and for his frontal assault it was in fact some 28 miles. In this narrow zone Zhukov concentrated a group of shock armies consisting of Forty-seventh Army, Third and Fifth Shock Armies, Eighth Guards Army, Third Army and First and Second Tank Guards Armies. His artillery had some 250 guns and minethrowers per kilometer of the assault sector and some 1000 rocket guns (Katyushas) which were mobile. From the air Zhukov was supported by Colonel General S Rudenko's 16th Air Fleet and the Polish Air Corps. With the support from the 2nd Belorussian front (Marshal Rokossovsky) and 1st Ukrainian front (Marshal Konev) Zhukov had overall control over some 2,500,000 men, 41,600 guns, 6250 tanks and 7500 aircraft.

According to Zhukov's plans, approved previously by Stalin, this formidable force was to be launched on 16 April 1945 to annihilate frontally the opponent in the Küstrin sector, break through toward Berlin which at first would be bypassed from the northwest and southeast and then stormed. The tank armies were made responsible for the exploitation of the breakthroughs: on the second day the Second Tank Guards Army would fight its way in the northwesterly direction while the First Tank Guards Army would do the same in the southeasterly. As a result the Fifth Shock, Eighth Guards and Sixty-ninth Armies would take the city on the sixth day of the operation. Zhukov was to achieve this straightforward success provided that Konev's Twenty-eighth Army and Third Tank Guards Army succeeded in breaking through into Berlin from the south and Rokossovsky's armies covered his right flank, for they were not intended to launch their offensive until two days later.

It was only on 15 April 1945 that Stalin informed the Supreme Allied Command of the Berlin operation; up to then he maintained that the Russian main thrust would be in the direction of Leipzig. Then at 0300 hours on 16 April Zhukov's barrage was started, but Heinrici had anticipated it and evacuated the first line at 2000 hours the previous evening. During the murky dawn, before 0500 hours, the barrage was shifted farther on, and the four armies (Third and Fifth Shock, Eighth Guards and Sixty-ninth) pulled out of their positions to attack the empty German line in the artificial light of massed batteries of search lights. However, the terrain was extremely difficult for tracked vehicles and the German Flak and antitank guns were hitting Russian tank formations with alarming accuracy. Men on both sides exhibited incredible heroism and in many sectors Russian attackers were beaten back. By 1430 hours, after some nine hours of fighting, Zhukov's armies had hardly dented the German lines, advancing only some four miles, without achieving a breakthrough. Zhukov, suitably depressed, telephoned Stalin, who after listening to him quietly, just told him that Konev's armies had already crossed the Neisse river. However, Zhukov was given permission to react to the circumstances of the battle as he deemed necessary.

Zhukov immediately changed his tactics ordering the 16th Air Fleet to make massive air strikes: enemy gun positions were to be blasted to smithereens; Soviet artillery was ordered to pulverize German strongpoints on the heights and tank armies were thrown into combat even before the important Seelow Heights had been reduced. Tough fighting continued – in the sector of the Third Shock Army the German 309th Infantry Division lost 60 percent of its men – and the Russians only succeeded in destroying the first line of German defense. That night Zhukov once again telephoned Stalin who excitedly reprimanded him for throwing in the tanks prematurely, altering their axis of attack to a sector (Seelow Heights) where defenses were too strong. Zhukov defended himself with ability by pointing out that he was annihilating the enemy and drawing to his sector Berlin reinforcements. Stalin, however, ended the conversation on a sour note: If Zhukov got stuck, Rokossovsky would take Berlin from the north and Konev from the south. Still Zhukov's progress on the 17th would decide the issue.

On the following day, albeit the Seelow Heights were taken, the Germans did manage to bring up reinforcements, especially antiaircraft artillery from Berlin, and their stubborn resistance slowed down the advance of Zhukov's armies. Zhukov personally inspected his armies before they lurched forward and used all sorts of gimmicks to boost up Soviet morale. Thus fighter pilots covering and supporting the Eighth Guards Army, threw down on the advancing guards, four parachutes with copies of the keys to Berlin captured by the Russian armies in the Seven Years' War, together with an unhelpful exhortation: 'Forward to Victory – here are the keys to the city.' However, the three reserve divisions and 50 tanks which the enemy threw into the battle slowed down the attacking Russians considerably. On this decisive day of the 17th Zhukov's armies failed to annihilate the second enemy line and Stalin told Konev in the evening to direct his tanks to Berlin from the south and gave him a free hand to take it.

Zhukov later claimed that he had asked Stalin to shorten his

RIGHT: How Berlin fell to encircling attacks from Zhukov's and Konev's army groups.

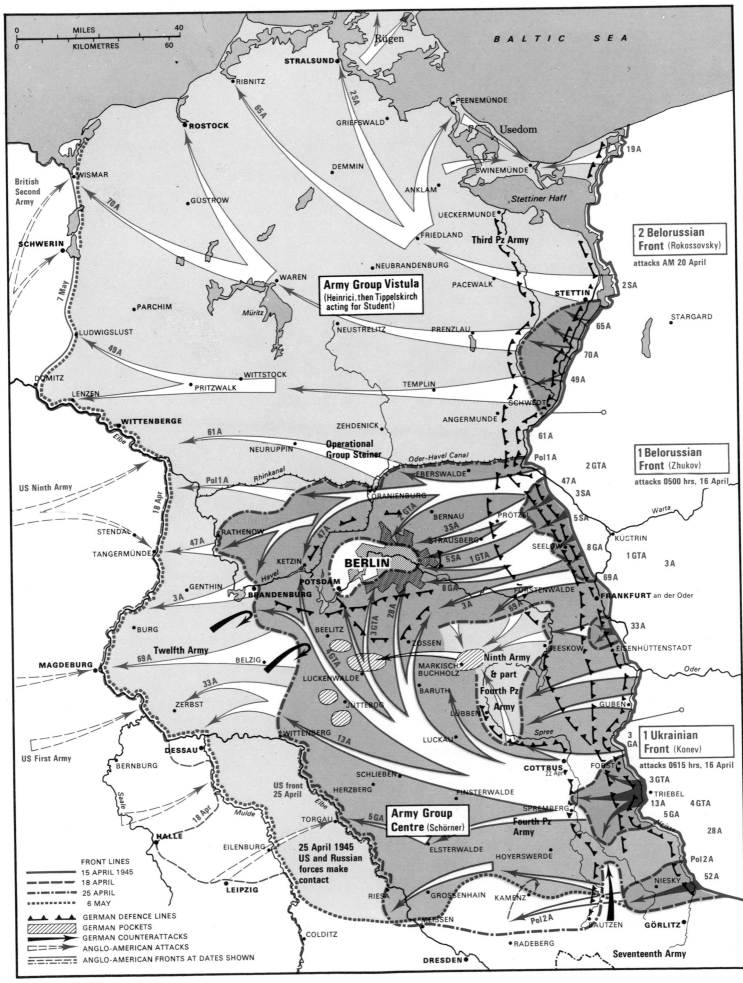

MILES
0   40
KILOMETRES
0   60

BALTIC SEA

Rügen

STRALSUND
• RIBNITZ
2SA
GRIEFSWALD
PEENEMÜNDE
• ROSTOCK
Usedom
DEMMIN
65A
SWINEMÜNDE
19A
WISMAR
ANKLAM
Stettiner Haff
British Second Army
Third Pz Army
70A
FRIEDLAND
SCHWERIN
NEUBRANDENBURG
2 Belorussian Front (Rokossovsky)
attacks AM 20 April
7 May
WAREN
Army Group Vistula
(Heinrici, then Tippelskirch acting for Student)
PACEWALK
STETTIN
2SA
PARCHIM
Müritz
NEUSTRELITZ
PRENZLAU
65A
LUDWIGSLUST
STARGARD
49A
70A
DÖMITZ
WITTSTOCK
TEMPLIN
49A
LENZEN
PRITZWALK
SCHWEDT
WITTENBERGE
Elbe
ZEHDENICK
ANGERMUNDE
61A
NEURUPPIN
Operational Group Steiner
Oder-Havel Canal
1 Belorussian Front (Zhukov)
attacks 0500 hrs, 16 April
US Ninth Army
Pol 1A
Rhinkanal
EBERSWALDE
61A
Pol1A
Warta
ORANIENBURG
2GTA
18 Apr
47A
2 GTA
BERNAU
PRÖTZEL
47A
3SA
STENDAL
RATHENOW
3SA
5SA
KÜSTRIN
TANGERMÜNDE
KETZIN
STRAUSBERG
SEELOW
8GA
1GTA
3A
BERLIN
5SA 1GTA
69A
Havel
POTSDAM
8GA
FÜRSTENWALDE
FRANKFURT an der Oder
GENTHIN
BRANDENBURG
3A
69A
3A
BURG
BEELITZ
3GTA
28A
ZOSSEN
33A
Twelfth Army
69A
BELZIG
1GTA
MARKISCH-BUCHHOLZ
BEESKOW
EISENHÜTTENSTADT
MAGDEBURG
LUCKENWALDE
Ninth Army & part Fourth Pz Army
Oder
33A
BARUTH
JÜTERBOG
ZERBST
LÜBBEN
GUBEN
WITTENBERG
13A
LUCKAU
Spree
1 Ukrainian Front (Konev)
attacks 0615 hrs, 16 April
US First Army
BERNBURG
DESSAU
COTTBUS
22 Apr
3 GA
US front 25 April
SCHLIEBEN
FORST
3GTA
HERZBERG
FINSTERWALDE
TRIEBEL
13A
4GTA
18 Apr
Mulde
Elbe
SPREMBERG
5 GA
Saale
TORGAU
5 GA
Fourth Pz Army
Neisse
28A
25 April 1945 US and Russian forces make contact
ELSTERWALDE
Army Group Centre (Schörner)
HOYERSWERDE
Pol 2A
HALLE
EILENBURG
Pol2A
NIESKY
52A
LEIPZIG
RIESA
GROSSENHAIN
KAMENZ
GÖRLITZ
COLDITZ
MEISSEN
BAUTZEN
RADEBERG
Seventeenth Army
DRESDEN

FRONT LINES
—— 15 APRIL 1945
— — 18 APRIL
· · · · 25 APRIL
· · · · · 6 MAY
▲▲▲ GERMAN DEFENCE LINES
/// GERMAN POCKETS
➤ GERMAN COUNTERATTACKS
⇢ ANGLO-AMERICAN ATTACKS
≈≈≈ ANGLO-AMERICAN FRONTS AT DATES SHOWN

attacking front even further concentrating thus the most formidable firing power to blot out the enemy, but Stalin refused. As it was Zhukov acted feverishly and in despair, as he saw his competitor, the dullard Konev, taking from him the final prize. He ordered night raids on enemy strongpoints by the 18th Air Fleet. At 1030 hours the Eighth Guards and First Tank Guards, went forward after an artillery barrage lasting half an hour. Colonel General V I Kazakov, one of the greatest artillerymen, personally directed fire and even he had to acknowledge defeat, when the two attacking armies were brought to a standstill. General M Y Katukov's First Tank Guards performed all sorts of miracles with their armor, while Chuikov's Eighth Guards pressed on despite their losses. However, this was all a crawl reducing plans to nought and upsetting time schedules. Only early in the morning of the 18th did the right flank of the attacking armies (Forty-seventh and Third Shock Armies) break through the second line of defense: Zhukov's armies were two days behind the schedule. Stalin had to issue new directives to the supporting armies: on the 17th Konev was ordered to advance on Berlin from the south; a day later Rokossovsky was ordered to drive in the southwestern direction instead of northwest. Thus during the operation itself the offensive was transformed into a tripartite one, instead of the envisaged frontal attack with subsidiary attacks on the right and left flanks.

Zhukov continued his inspections to resolve the problem of non-advancement. He realized that the Russians did not have a full picture of German defenses and above all failed to take into account the water obstacles which the Germans skillfully exploited against the advancing tanks. He also noticed that his armies wasted a lot of artillery fire and the air forces failed to penetrate enemy defenses and annihilate them. Thus on the 19th Zhukov decided on new tactical changes. He considered that his right flank, consisting of the Forty-seventh and Third Shock armies, managed a great enough break to continue its drive in northerly and northwesterly directions in order to take Berlin

from the western side. Colonel General P Belov's Sixty-first Army also changed the direction of its advance along the Hohenzollern canal, while the First Polish Army, Forty-seventh Army and Third and Fifth Shock Armies were ordered to strike in a southwesterly direction instead of westerly. Orders went out to continue the offensive night and day until modified objectives were achieved. Although this concentric attack did drive the Germans from their second defense line they swiftly reorganized and dug in in the unfinished third line. The Ninth German Army took the overall command in this sector, and was reinforced with three infantry divisions and the 11th motorized division, SS Nordland, withdrawn from the northern sector.

Thus on the 18th, when the Third Shock Army advanced to Bazlow where the SS reinforcements were concentrated, they were halted. Both Shock Armies waited until the night and then, after an artillery barrage, they fought all night in close hand-to-hand fighting to overcome this strongpoint. However further advance was checked by increased German air activity: in groups of 30 the Luftwaffe attacked Russian ground formation and kept them pinned down in this sector all day long. However, the right flank once again achieved a breakthrough of some 14 kilometers in the third line and Zhukov poured his tanks into this breach. This was taking his armies further away from Berlin rather than into the city. It was only on the 20th that the Forty-seventh and Third Shock Armies finally broke through the third line and Colonel General S Bogdanov's Second Tank Guards wheeled through to reach Ladeburg–Zepernik pass north of Berlin. The guns of the Third Shock

things was GHQ Wehrmacht-Heer. On the approaches to Zossen at Barut the Third Tank Guards had to fight hard and once in the defense perimeter it took them two full days to reduce the strongpoint. The terrain was not ideal for tank maneuvers and when at night on the 22nd the strongpoint was taken the Germans blew up and flooded the underground GHQ. However, the Fourth Tank Guards commanded by Colonel General V Gordov, succeeded even better, for after their breakthrough at Kottbus, they drove on toward Potsdam, on the western side of Berlin, ripped a hole in the German defense round Zossen, forcing the German Ninth Army to give up its stand to avoid outflanking. On 21 April Konev's tanks crossed the outer belt road, but further progress was slowed down by tough resistance especially round the Teltow Canal. It was only on 25 April that Konev's forces finally made contact with Zhukov's and Berlin was encircled. Even before Lelyushenko's tanks made contact with Perkhorovich's soldiers their respective supporting air forces were strafing and bombing each other. On that day Stalin ruled that the city be divided between Konev's and Zhukov's fronts along a line running 150 meters west of the Reichstag building. Also on that day Konev's soldiers reached the river Elbe near Torgau and met for the first time American troops advancing from the West.

Zhukov was however completely absorbed in directing the fighting. It became clear that Hitler had ordered General Steiner's Army Group and General Wenck's regrouped Twelfth Army to counterattack and relieve the city. While the former's attack never really got off the ground, the latter was joined by a hastily assembled group isolated in the south of the city, consisting of one motorized, three infantry and a tank division, and they managed to break through between Konev's Twenty-eighth and Third Guards. Once again there was some tough fighting around the town Barut, but within a day the Third Tank Guards were let loose on these improvised and desperate formations and they broke them up. This was the final masterstroke that Hitler conjured up and sent Keitel to implement. Afterward the Germans acknowledged that they were surrounded in the capital, but rather than surrendering they were willing to go through the *Götterdammerung* while Hitler was alive and even after. Although their situation was hopeless they continued to form Volkssturm battalions and at the time that the capital was encircled they had some 200 battalions in position. Apart from the Volkssturm they had some 80,000 infantry in the city from the various armies defeated on the approaches. Hitler and the Nazis could feel quite safe from the security point of view, for there were some 32,000 police troops. Throughout Berlin at strategic crossroads, squares and parks the defenders had built block houses and pillboxes, tanks were dug in and mobility was assured by the underground railroad network. However, there was also the population to feed and no anti-aircraft cover: the Russians now concentrated the 16th and 18th Air Fleets on heavy bombing. Thus in the night of 26 April 563 aircraft of the 18th Air Fleet dropped on Berlin some 569 tons of bombs.

Despite all this Zhukov found it quite a task to reduce and take the city fiercely defended by some 300,000 fanatical soldiers under the leadership of General Weidling. However, once the breakout efforts by the Germans had been contained, both Zhukov and Konev, after Stalin had altered still further the respective front boundaries on the 29th, threw themselves onto the hapless city with great gusto. According to Stalin's ruling Zhukov's troops would take the central sector of Berlin and in compensation Konev's armies were permitted to divert to Prague, which had risen against the Germans at this time, and

Army closed on Berlin sufficiently to fire two symbolic shots at the city. However, it was only a day later that the Russian armies reached the northern fortifications of the city and the northern ring of the *autobahnen* and began systematic shelling. On that same day the Fifth Shock Army and XII Tank Guard Corps pushed their way into north eastern suburbs achieving the original objective of the whole 1st Belorussian Front after considerable delay.

The toughest fighting had to be undertaken by the Eighth Tank Guards and First Tank Guards; even as late as 19 and 20 April both armies were bogged down on the third line of defense. Although their superiority was threefold the fanatical resistance of the 23rd Motorized Division, SS Niederland together with five Volkssturm battalions and a special antitank brigade, was able to halt these two elite tank armies. In the sector Fürstenwalde the Germans counterattacked several times; only on 21 April did the units of these two Russian armies reach the outer defense of Berlin at Petershagen and Erckner, while they were supposed to storm the inner city next day.

By 20 April Zhukov more or less acknowledged the failure of his frontal attack on Berlin and decided to wheel round the city and by joining with Konev's and Rokossovsky's forces cut the capital off, encircle it and storm it afterward. Although Konev's Third and Fourth Tank Guards were three times as distant from the city as Zhukov's tanks, they reached the outer defenses of the city, after some tough fighting, on the 19th. In this drive to northwest, far from their original objective, the hardest nut to crack was the Zossen defense strongpoint, which among other liberate that capital. Zhukov ordered the Third Shock, Forty-seventh Armies and two tanks armies, First and Second Guards, to storm the inner city from the north. Zhukov said that he had thrown in the two tank armies, because they had no other operational tasks and their impact would further destroy the morale of the enemy. It seems, however, that the employment of the tank armies in storming a city was the result of political pressure. Stalin had been worried by the lack of progress and by delays, and was once again suspicious of his allies. He thought they just might make a dash for Berlin from Torgau, despite an agreement with him. He therefore ordered Zhukov to engage in this costly way of taking a city. The tanks undoubtedly demoralized the German defenders, but at a cost: in the street fighting they could not maneuver and were sitting ducks for the youthful defenders with their Panzerfausts. In all parts of the city hand-to-hand fighting continued from house to house, block to block, street to street.

The central sector of the city (9th district) was particularly well prepared for the defense. The river Spree formed a natural defense in the north, while in the south the Tiergarten and other parks and boulevards were transformed into fortresses. The Reichstag building in the very center, at which the two Russian armies were both aiming, was a veritable fortress, with reinforced walls, railings all round, and windows covered with cement plates. All the streets leading to the Reichstag were barred with barricades and fierce fighting continued from one to another. The Third Shock Army forced its way into Moabit and reached the Spree and was poised near the Moltke bridge to fight its way to the Reichstag. The Fifth Shock Army and the Eighth Guards with the First Tank Guards were making their way into the center from the east and southeast. Konev's Third Tank Guards and Twenty-eighth Armies were making their way through the southern defenses. The Second Tank Guards, after taking Charlottenburg, began to make their way into the center from the northwest. In the west the Forty-seventh and Thirteenth Armies together with Fourth Tank Guards were protecting the rear of the storming armies.

To demonstrate how fierce the fighting was we must realize that on 29 April, when units of the Thirteenth Army stormed and captured the Moltke bridge they were some 300 meters from the Reichstag, which Stalin, for his own reasons, singled out as the ultimate objective. Still it took the Russians three days before they could hoist their flag over the ruined building. In the night of 1 May the Third Army command ordered Colonel Zinchenko with his 756th Regiment to get the flag on the building for symbolic reasons, even though the Reichstag block was still largely in German hands. Sergeants Yegorov and Kantariya, under heavy fire, scaled the ruins, and the Russian generals and soldiers in the center could see their flag flying. The Russians give enemy casualties in that sector (2500 dead and wounded, 2604 captured; 28 guns destroyed, 59 captured together with 15 tanks), but not theirs, for their symbolic gesture must have cost Zhukov and Stalin heaps of casualties.

Even after the Soviet flag had been unfurled on the Reichstag fierce fighting continued. The Russians had no idea what was happening in Hitler's bunker under the Reich Chancellery and on 1 May they thought the Germans would surrender, when at 1500 hours General Krebs, then Chief of Staff, appeared on the line of the Eighth Guards and asked for parley with the Soviet command. Zhukov refused to see him, but he sent his first deputy, General Sokolovsky to assist General Chuikov in negotiations. They all had Stalin's order to accept unconditional surrender only. Krebs, who was the last military attaché in Moscow before the war, told Chuikov that Hitler had committed suicide

and handed over power to Admiral Karl Dönitz and Dr Josef Goebbels. The latter was interested in an armistice, but the Russians told Krebs that it would have to be unconditional surrender: if the garrison surrendered Chuikov guaranteed them their lives, personal belongings to the soldiers and small arms to the officers. At 1800 hours Krebs brought back a message from Goebbels that Russian conditions were unacceptable and the fighting was resumed.

Immediately after artillery barrages the Russians went on with street fighting; it was only now, 1 May, that the Third Shock Army effected junction with the Eighth Guards south of the Reichstag. Only early next day did the Second Tank Guards finally meet Eighth Guards and First Tank Guards in the area of the Tiergarten. Although they had met, not all Berlin was under their control; in fact counterattacks continued in all areas, even in the Tiergarten, where the Russians overran General Weidling's command post. Now the hapless general decided to throw the sponge in and sent Colonel von Duwing to negotiate surrender. For the German command it was all over at 0630 hours when they all trudged into Russian captivity; in the afternoon, at 1500 hours, the rest of the garrison, some 70,000 men, gave up, it was only now, on 2 May 1945, five days before the general surrender, that Zhukov could report to Stalin that he had successfully completed his mission and that the Nazi capital was in his power. At this stage Zhukov had no idea at what cost this had been accomplished. Only in 1963 were we given details: the Berlin operation was described as one of the biggest of the war. Some 3,500,000 men fought in it equipped with 50,000 guns, 8000 tanks, and over 9000 aircraft. The Russians captured 480,000 Germans, 1500 tanks, 4500 aircraft and 10,917 guns. They lost 304,887 dead, 2156 tanks, 1220 guns and 527 aircraft. We can quickly see General Bradley's point: overall Allied casualties for the whole of 1945 operations were 260,000 men.

Immediately after the unconditional surrender, 8 May 1945, Marshal Georgy Zhukov held a press conference at which he briefed the world about his part in the surrender of the German Reich. He emphasized that the German armies were smashed on the river Oder and that the Berlin operation was really a mopping up. He did not mention any other generals who might have helped him with Berlin and generally seemed to play down 'this crowning achievement of World War II.' Still in 1965 when he finally published his memories of this battle, he acknowledged that the Berlin battle was his greatest. It is true that he had planned and executed the three decisive battles in Russia, at Moscow, Stalingrad and Kursk, but in all these battles his participation was overshadowed by that of his warlord, Stalin. It was only at this last battle that the warlord singled Zhukov out for the 'crowning glory,' very much against the opposition of the other generals. Stalin not only accepted Zhukov's strategic plans, but gave him a completely free hand in tactical matters. Thus he foisted Zhukov on the 1st Belorussian Front (and transferred Zhukov's rare friend, Rokossovsky, to command the 2nd Belorussian Front), and then determined, by means of demarcation lines that the 1st Belorussian Front and not the 1st Ukrainian Front take the capital.

However, he also revised the time schedules and demarcation lines to suit his personal and political purposes. It is thought that he delayed Zhukov's dash for Berlin in February 1945 for political purposes – he had the Yalta conference to attend and Allied political pressures to consider. In the final phases of the operation he changed the demarcation lines between Zhukov's and Konev's armies several times, probably not to give any of his generals total credit. So apart from these two basic considerations Zhukov, for the first time in the war, acted not as a representative of the Stavka, or coordinator, or 'Spasitel' (Savior) as in the Battle of Moscow, but on his own with control over strategic reserves, changing both strategic and tactical plans as he went, with the Stavka (and Stalin) approving them subsequently.

Thus the battle of Berlin had all the characteristics of Zhukov's past battles. Each time he amassed and commanded huge armies; millions of men were involved on both sides; meticulous staff work, preparations and rehearsals were conducted before each battle; each time he expended artillery and air power lavishly; each time armor was massively deployed and used; each time infantry did the actual fighting on a gigantic scale inflicting irreplaceable losses on the enemy; each time his own casualties were enormous. The series of Zhukov's battles was started in 1939 against the Japanese Kwantung armies and even then it was described by the British expert, Professor John Erickson, as brilliant but costly. This was a characteristic Zhukov had in common with Stalin and may be the key to their wartime close friendship: both believed military aims can only be achieved by sacrificing life on a massive scale.

In addition Zhukov's personal characteristics contributed to this 'crowning victory' of his military career. he was not a popular figure; he never put a human touch to his orders; he had no friends, only subordinates and one superior. He had a will of iron, tempestuous temper and almost supernatural determination, all of which characteristics were those of his principal opponent, Hitler. While Hitler could let loose these terrible traits on the German nation and the Wehrmacht to a certain extent, Zhukov let them loose liberally. He spoke rough, acted rough: his terrible threats – obey orders or face the firing squad – were invariably backed up. By means of these unattractive qualities he achieved success everywhere, and though he was a lonely figure, he was respected even by his rough fellow soldiers. The Berlin battle reflected both his character and military genius, and Stalin recognized it by sharing the podium with him at the victory parade in Moscow in June 1945. In Berlin Zhukov proved to the world that he was the master of twentieth-century mass warfare and had no equal either at home or abroad. However, in strictly military terms he cannot be ranked highly. All the strategic decisions concerning his battle were taken by a committee whose chairman was Stalin. Even his tactical decisions were controlled by the committee, and above all Stalin, who rectified some of the costly errors: the initial frontal assault was a failure, and the line of the armor attack had to be changed several times to achieve success. In the battle for the city Zhukov also made many costly tactical mistakes, which undoubtedly overshadowed the overall achievement. One judgment that can safely be made about his generalship was that he was infinitely ruthless about his men in order to achieve overall success: however, such generals of World War I, were termed butchers of their men, not great generals.

ABOVE LEFT: The Soviet flag flies over the Reichstag, 2 May 1945.

RIGHT: Roosevelt and Stalin at the Yalta conference in February 1945.

ACKNOWLEDGMENTS

Bildarchiv Preussischer Kulturbesitz: 7, 15(below), 173(middle 2), 183(below)
Bison Archive: 6, 10(both), 11, 12(right), 14(middle), 15(top & middle), 18(top 2), 19, 20, 22(both), 23, 24(below), 26(top), 27(below), 31, 36, 39(below), 40, 41(both), 42(both), 51, 54(both), 55, 56, 62, 66(both), 67(both), 71(below), 76(top), 78, 79(top), 81, 82, 84(below left & right), 85(top), 88(both), 89(both), 92(top), 115(top), 121, 124, 126(top), 128(below), 130(all 3), 131(both), 137(top), 138, 139(both), 142, 143(both), 144(below), 145(both), 153(below), 189(top & below left), 190(top), 192(below), 195(below), 198(all 3), 199(both), 200(middle), 209(top), 221
Bundesarchiv: 9, 12(top, middle & below left), 13(both), 14(top & below), 43, 45(below), 46(top), 47, 48(middle), 49, 52, 53, 84(both), 85(below), 86(both), 87(both), 90, 91, 92(below), 94(both), 101, 103(both), 107(both), 126(below), 128(top), 129, 132, 135, 141, 154(below), 172, 173(top), 174(top left, middle & below left), 178-179(both), 181, 182, 183(top), 211, 212(bottom 3 left & right), 213(below)
Fleet Air Arm Museum: 29, 30(top)
Imperial War Museum: 8, 16, 17, 18(below), 21, 24(top), 26(middle & below), 28, 30(below), 32, 33(both), 34, 39(top), 44, 45(top), 46(below), 48(top & below), 50(both), 70(top), 74, 75(both), 76(below), 77(both), 80(both), 93, 96, 97, 98, 102, 105, 107(top), 122, 123(both), 127(below), 133(top), 137(below), 144(top), 150(below), 151(below), 152(below), 154(middle), 156(top), 157(top right), 160, 163(all 3), 165(all 3), 166(both), 167(all 3), 168(both), 169(both), 194, 210
Library of Congress: 69(below)
Museum of London: 153(top)
National Archives: 59, 65(both), 68(both), 71(top), 109, 110, 111(both), 114(both), 115(middle), 116(top & below), 119(both), 134, 155, 156(middle), 186(both), 187(below), 189(right), 191(both), 195(top), 196, 202, 203(both), 204(below), 207, 208(top)
National Army Museum: 152(top)
National Maritime Museum: 37, 38
Novosti Press Agency: 120, 133(below), 140(both), 220
Robert Hunt Library: 107(middle), 108, 177(top)
Signal Corps: 204(top)
The Research House: 190(below)
Ullstein: 212(top), 213(top), 214, 215, 216, 218(both)
US Airforce: 154(top), 161, 200(top), 206(below)
US Army: 79(top), 146, 147, 150(top), 157(top left & below), 158, 159, 170, 171, 172, 173(below), 174(below right), 175, 177(below), 180, 200(below), 209(below),
US Marine Corps: 113(both), 115(below), 118, 206(top), 208(below)
US Naval Historical Center: 57, 63(both), 64, 65(below), 69(top), 71(below), 116(middle), 156(below), 184, 187(top), 192(top)